On Philosophy,
Politics, and Economics

On Philosophy, Politics, and Economics

Gerald F. Gaus
University of Arizona

WADSWORTH
CENGAGE Learning™

Australia • Brazil • Japan • Korea • Mexico • Singapore • Spain • United Kingdom • United States

On Philosophy, Politics, and Economics
Gerald F. Gaus

Executive Publisher:
Marcus Boggs

Acquisitions Editor:
Worth Hawes

Assistant Editor:
Patrick Stockstill

Editorial Assistant: Kamilah Lee

Marketing Manager:
Christina Shea

Marketing Assistant:
Mary Anne Payumo

Marketing Communications Manager:
Darlene Amidon-Brent

Project Manager, Editorial Production: Samen Iqbal

Creative Director: Rob Hugel

Art Director: Maria Epes

Print Buyer: Linda Hsu

Permissions Editor: Bob Kauser

Production Service:
Tintu Thomas, Integra

Copy Editor: Linda Ireland

Compositor: Integra

Library of Congress Control Number: 2007936260

ISBN-13: 978-0-495-00898-9

ISBN-10: 0-495-00898-2

Wadsworth Cengage Learning
20 Davis Drive
Belmont, CA 94002-3098, USA

Cengage Learning is a leading provider of customized learning solutions with office locations around the globe, including Singapore, the United Kingdom, Australia, Mexico, Brazil, and Japan. Locate your local office at **www.cengage.com/global**

Cengage Learning products are represented in Canada by Nelson Education, Ltd.

To learn more about Wadsworth, visit
www.cengage.com/wadsworth

Purchase any of our products at your local college store or at our preferred online store **www.cengagebrain.com**

Printed in the United States of America
2 3 4 5 6   22 21 20 19 18

Contents

About the Author

Gerald F. Gaus is James E. Rogers Professor of Philosophy at the University of Arizona. He was previously Professor of Philosophy and Political Economy at Tulane University; in 2005–2006 he was Distinguished Visiting Professor in the University of North Carolina/ Chapel Hill-Duke PPE program. Among his books are *Contemporary Theories of Liberalism* (2003), *Justificatory Liberalism* (1996), and *Value and Justification* (1990). He and Chandran Kukathas edited the *Handbook of Political Theory* (2004). Along with Jonathan Riley, he is a founding editor of *Politics, Philosophy and Economics*.

List of Figures and Tables

FIGURES

TABLES

Acknowledgments

The roots of this little book go back to my days at the University of Queensland, when my good friend David Gow insisted that I read William Riker's *Liberalism Against Populism*. I had worked through A. K. Sen's great *Collective Choice and Social Welfare* as an undergraduate, but it was David and Riker who impressed on me the importance of this line of inquiry for politics and philosophy. Since then I have taught versions of this material to my students at the University of Queensland, the University of Minnesota–Duluth, Tulane University, the joint UNC–Chapel Hill/ Duke Philosophy, Politics and Economics program, and at the Di Tella University Law School in Buenos Aires. Thanks to all those students for putting up with me thinking things through on my feet, and for so often helping me get things right. Fred Miller of Bowling Green State University used a draft of this book in one of his Philosophy classes; I appreciate him doing so, and I have greatly benefited from the suggestions he provided after the course. My deep thanks also to Julian Lamont of the University of Queensland, who, as he always does, provided important and insightful comments. I also found very useful the suggestions and comments of Fred D'Agostino, Chandran Kukathas, Peter Vanderschraaf, and an anonymous reader. The book would not have been written without the encouragement of Bob Talisse, the editor of this series: I hope he is not disappointed. Special thanks are due to the Murphy Institute of Political Economy, and especially its director, Richard Teichgraeber III, who generously supported my work in this area for more than five years.

Gerald F. Gaus
Philosophy
University of Arizona

Introduction: The Economic Approach and Politics and Philosophy

Social scientists and political philosophers are both concerned with how people act, and how they interact. One way to go about studying how people act and interact is to appeal to psychological or social laws that allow us to predict what they will do in certain situations. But we almost always want more than to merely predict the behavior of others—we want to make sense of what they do, to see it as an intelligible way of acting. Making others intelligible to us is closely bound to seeing them as rational. True, sometimes it is intelligible to us why people are not rational, as we can understand all too well why someone who is drunk accepts a dangerous and silly dare. But usually, when we are confronted by simply irrational behavior, we don't understand what it is really all about. The persuasiveness of Sigmund Freud's work was in taking totally unintelligible behavior and making it more intelligible by showing it to be based on some sort of reasoning—so that in the end the behavior was not as bizarre as it first appeared. Consider one of his cases—a 19-year-old girl with obsessional sleep ceremonies:

> The pillow at the top end of the bed must not touch the wooden back of the bedstead.... The eiderdown...had to be shaken before being laid on the bed so that its bottom became very thick; afterwards, however, she never failed to even out this accumulation of feathers by pressing them apart.[1]

At this point the behavior is simply incomprehensible. Freud appeals to reasoning—albeit still odd reasoning—to make some sense of it. In the course of her therapy

> [s]he found out the central meaning of her ceremonial one day when she suddenly understood the meaning of the rule that the pillow must not touch the back of the bedstead. The pillow, she said, had always been a woman to her and the upright wooden back a man. Thus she wanted—by magic, we must interpolate—to keep man and woman apart—that is, to separate her parents from each other, and not allow them to have sexual intercourse....
>
> If a pillow was a women, then the shaking of the eiderdown till all the feathers were at the bottom and caused a swelling there had a sense as well. It meant making the woman pregnant; but she never failed to smooth away the pregnancy again, for she had been for years afraid that her parents' intercourse would result in another child....[2]

As Freud notes, these are "wild thoughts." Admittedly, if "wooden bedstead = father," and "pillow = mother," then we can see a crazy sort of reasoning in keeping bedstead and pillow apart. *If* she was correct in thinking that what she does to the bedstead and pillow affects what her parents do at night, *then* keeping the bedstead and pillow apart has a certain sort of rationality to it. We have made progress: what was simply incomprehensible now is becoming intelligible as it is becoming a bit more rational—but we still need to know why she believes these things. As we will see in Chapter 1, our puzzles about the rationality of behavior often lead to puzzles about the rationality of the underlying belief.

If our aim as political scientists and social philosophers is to understand social interaction as rational, we cannot ignore the contribution of economics, which has developed by far the most sophisticated social theory based on the assumption that humans are rational. Students of society outside of economics are often hostile—or at least skeptical—of "economic" analyses of humans-in-society.

Often it is said that economic analysis is based on a narrow conception of humans as selfish, or even worse "greedy," and such assumptions, even if appropriate to economics, are inappropriate to politics and social philosophy. Economists, in turn, wonder why a model that has been so enlightening for some human interactions should suddenly be inappropriate when applied to others. James Buchanan—a Noble Prize winning economist—has long insisted that *Homo Economicus* ("economic man") is a general model of rational action, applying to politics as well as economics. He challenges those who would restrict the application of *Homo Economicus* to economics with the argument from symmetry. Along with Geoffrey Brennan, he writes:

> The symmetry argument suggests only that whatever model of behavior is used, this model should be applied across all institutions. The argument insists that it is illegitimate to restrict *Homo Economicus* to the domain of market behavior while employing widely different models of behavior in nonmarket settings, without any explanation how such a behavioral shift comes about.[3]

Whether one accepts or rejects the general applicability of *Homo Economicus*, one must understand *Homo Economicus*—either to apply it or to reply to Buchanan and Brennan's challenge. I aim to show in this book that once we do try to understand *Homo Economicus* we shall see that it is far more sophisticated than many critics—and indeed supporters—of economic analysis believe. The theory of rational agents at the heart of economics does not inherently imply a "selfish" or "greedy" acquisitive consumer; the model is quite general and encompasses a wide diversity of concerns and goals. And that is why, I think, all students of social interaction must know the basics of the economic approach to society.

Buchanan, then, argues that economics and politics share a unified approach: the theory of rational agency that underlies economics ought to underlie politics too. But "ppe" is the study of *philosophy*, politics, and economics: how does philosophy come in? In two ways. First, reflecting on the nature of rational agency and its explanatory power is essentially a philosophical enterprise—the philosophy of economics. But secondly, and I think far more importantly, moral and political philosophy are themselves concerned with questions about how rational people will interact, whether such people will act cooperatively or competitively, and whether they need sort of "social contract" if they are to live together in peace. Thomas Hobbes

3

(1588–1679) constructed his political philosophy on an analysis of rational agents in strategic interaction which, as we will see in Chapter 4, many believe can be understood in terms of the famous "Prisoner's Dilemma" analyzed by economists. But though Hobbes is the most obvious example, all moral and political philosophers must be concerned with understanding what is involved in being a rational agent, and what is required for such agents to live together cooperatively and according to common rules. I do not believe that one can be a good moral or political philosopher without understanding the economist's approach to social interaction. One of the things that made John Rawls (1921–2002) the greatest political philosopher of our time was his deep knowledge of economic approaches to studying society. Often Rawls drew on this knowledge in his own work, but even when he declined to do so, his decision was informed by a thorough appreciation of economic analysis and its shortcomings.

My aims in this book, then, are first to provide an introduction to those areas of the economic approach to society that are of most interest to students of political science and political philosophy, and secondly to analyze the economic approach, so that we can better understand its presuppositions and commitments. This second task, I think, should be of special interest to students in economics. In my years of teaching these topics, I have found that economics students are familiar with basic concepts and theorems, especially in their formal presentations, but often have not reflected on just what they mean. When I have asked students who have completed intermediate micro economics to explain what they mean by "efficiency" or "utility," frequently they respond by saying they have not really thought about it. Hopefully this book will spur them to do so.

In writing this introductory text to philosophy, politics, and economics, I have tried to avoid two extremes. Rather than simply reporting the standard results, I have endeavored to explore the reasoning behind various claims, to show where I think mistakes have been made, and to take positions on some controversial issues. When doing so I have tried to be clear where there is difference of opinion and why I take the position I do. Because of this, much of what I say should be of interest to students in economics, and to graduate students in philosophy and political science. On the other hand, I have also sought to make this book accessible to undergraduates outside economics. This means, firstly, that I have tried to survey the main issues and report what I see as the standard results. And, secondly, it means that no mathematics is employed. Where there are formal points to be made, I have made them graphically or via simple notation that is explained in the text. This book assumes no prior knowledge of economics, though students who have had several courses in economics will, no doubt, bring away more from reading the book.

So, what, specifically, do I talk about? I begin in the first chapter by exploring the concept of rationality that lies at the core of economic analysis. This chapter is the most "philosophical": my aim here is to explore the notion of "instrumental" rationality (i.e., the rational thing to do is what best achieves one's goals) and to see how it relates to "economic rationality." The second chapter continues the analysis of rationality by considering the relation of instrumental rationality to "utility theory." Utility theory is the foundation for the rest of the book, so it is important to understand just what it means to say that "rational individuals are utility maximizers." I shall argue that there is a great deal of confusion about the meaning of this claim. Many people who reject the "economic approach"—and, alas, even many who accept it—do so on the basis of misconceptions about what it means to say that rational agents always maximize their utility. After clarifying the formal characteristics of utility maximization, I close Chapter 2 by briefly looking at the work of social psychologists who have investigated whether actual people act in the ways predicted by utility theory.

Chapter 3 introduces the idea of efficiency, another idea about which noneconomists tend to have misconceptions. A basic claim of Chapter 3 is that efficiency is very closely tied to rationality: rational individuals will seek efficient exchanges. This leads to the important notion of Pareto efficiency. The chapter concludes with a brief discussion of basic failures of efficiency in relation to externalities and public goods.

Chapter 3 also introduces the idea of social interaction between rational individuals in the form of market exchanges; Chapter 4 continues this focus on rational interactions as analyzed in the theory of games. Just about every student in the social sciences or political philosophy will at some point encounter game theory, if only in the form of the ubiquitous Prisoner's Dilemma. This chapter gives an overview of some of the main ideas in game theory, while arguing that a deeper knowledge of game theory can help us avoid many of the pitfalls and mistakes that are common; I am especially critical of the long-standing quest to "solve" the Prisoner's Dilemma. I try to show in this chapter how focusing on the decision trees underlying games makes the nature of the games clearer.

Chapter 5 turns to the application of economic analysis to large-scale political interaction: democracy. The chapter commences by examining the contrast between two views of politics—as a sort of market or a "forum" in which economic analyses is somehow inappropriate. Although the contrast captures an insight, I suggest that rather too much has been made of it, and even the "forum" view in the end has to see democracy as having a crucial "economic" component. The chapter then examines democracy in light of "axiomatic social choice theory" which investigates how the preferences of many people might be aggregated into a social decision. The core topic of this chapter is Arrow's impossibility theorem.

The last chapter brings us back to where we began: Buchanan's challenge that just as *Homo Economicus* is the best model to explain economics, it is also the best way to explain politics. Buchanan and others have developed "public choice theory" (not to be confused with axiomatic social choice theory, the subject of the previous chapter), which seeks to explain politics by depicting political actors as simply economic actors transferred to a new arena in which the rules of the game are different, leading to different (and often socially inefficient) outcomes. The lesson that Buchanan and his colleagues have drawn from public choice analysis is that if we are going to achieve a politics that avoids these regrettable outcomes, we must fix the rules of the game so that interest of "economic actors" in the political arena will converge with the public good.

By the close, I hope, the reader will have a better grasp why I think economics, politics, and philosophy are closely related disciplines. But even those who disagree—who respond to Buchanan's challenge by showing that *Homo Economicus* is not relevant to politics or philosophy—should have a much better idea of just what it is they find inappropriate about the economic approach.

NOTES

1. Sigmund Freud, *Introductory Lectures on Psychoanalysis*, translated by James Strachey, Lecture 17.
2. Ibid.
3. Geoffrey Brennan and James M. Buchanan, *The Reason of Rules: Constitutional Political Economy*, p. 50.

1

Instrumental and Economic Rationality

OVERVIEW

This chapter considers basic questions concerning the nature of instrumental rationality, and how "economic" rationality relates to our general conception of instrumental rationality. I begin in Section 1.1 by analyzing instrumental rationality: I argue that we cannot understand an *action* as rational without reference to the beliefs on which it is based. Section 1.1 thus constitutes an argument for a specific way of understanding instrumental rationality. Sections 1.2 and 1.3 examine "economic rationality," arguing that *Homo Economicus* adds a number of additional specific features to the general idea of an instrumentally rational action.

1.1 INSTRUMENTAL RATIONALITY

What Is Instrumental Rationality?

In a sense all of economics is about rationality. Economic analysis is based on a certain conception—or, we shall see, conceptions—of rational choice. The (very) short answer to the question "what is economics?" is "the theory of rational choice, and its consequences, under constraints." It is because this basic idea is so powerful, and economists have developed it in such sophisticated ways, that economic approaches have come to dominate other social sciences such as political science, as well much of political philosophy. The core of the economic model—and indeed, all our thinking about rational action—is the instrumental theory of rationality.[1] This theory was developed by Thomas Hobbes and later British empiricists and became, through them, basic to the emerging science of political economy in the nineteenth century. The model has given rise to a variety of specifications. Some follow David Hume (1711–1776) and argue that all rational action is intended to satisfy desires. Others put the point in terms of satisfying preferences (which, we shall see, leads to confusions; Section 2.1), while yet others, more prevalent in political science, tend to talk of advancing one's goals or interests. To call an economic agent a "utility maximizer" is often taken to be much the same as saying that she has "purposes that her action is designed to promote."[2]

The most obvious interpretation of instrumental rationality might be called Rationality as Effectiveness (RE):[3]

> RE: Alf's action is instrumentally rational if and only if ϕ-ing is an effective way for Alf to achieve his desire, goal, end, or taste, G.

However, RE is both too narrow and too broad. To see how it is too narrow, suppose that Alf is a loyal viewer of the Weather Channel, which forecasts a clear day today. Alf, though, is very cautious, so he compares this with the forecasts of the National Weather Service and with the local meteorologist, Sam the Smiling Weatherman. They concur; it is going to be a gorgeous day. On the basis of all this information, Alf goes out without an umbrella, gets soaked in a freak thunderstorm, ruins his Converse high-tops, and comes down with pneumonia. According to RE, Alf's decision not to carry an umbrella was not rational: it was anything but an effective way to achieve his goals. More generally, RE deems "not rational" any action that sets back one's goals, no matter how diligent the agent was in getting information and hedging against risks. So any risky action—such as an investment—that turns out badly runs counter to rationality: it is irrational.

That can't be right. Whether a risky action that turns out badly is irrational depends on, say, whether the agent took care to inform himself about the risk, whether he sought to minimize the risks, and so on. Rationality, including instrumental rationality, is a concept that concerns a person's cognitive processes and her choices about what to do, and so cannot be reduced to simple effectiveness of action. This becomes even clearer when we consider the way in which RE is too broad. Suppose that Betty never bothers with weather forecasts of any sort, but consults her Ouiji board. On the day that Alf gets soaked, Betty's Ouiji board instructed her to carry an umbrella, so she kept dry. RE deems her action rational: after all, carrying the umbrella was an effective way to achieve her goal (of staying dry). But this really seems a case of dumb luck, not instrumental rationality. As Amartya Sen reminds us, the concept of rationality focuses on the relation between goals and choices between options: it asks, given your goals, what is the rational course of action *to choose*.[4] Our concern is the quality of the choice about what to do, not simply the effectiveness of what is done. Of course to choose an option is still to *do something*: it is to buy the Honda rather than the Ford, or to go out to dinner rather than order a pizza to be delivered. But when we evaluate the rationality of what is done, our focus is not on the actual consequences of what is done (whether, in the end, the action secured the person's goals), but whether, when she chose that action over the alternatives, it was the one that, given her beliefs, *had the best prospects for satisfying her goals*. To say that Betty's decision to φ was instrumentally rational is not to say that in the end she achieved her goals, but at the time of choice, given what Betty believed, it was her expectation that it would satisfy them best.

The inadequacies of Rationality as Effectiveness have led some to adopt a purely subjective test of rational choice, as in Subjective Rationality (SR):

SR: Betty's action φ is instrumentally rational if and only if when she chose φ:

(i) her choice was based on her beliefs (*B*),

(ii) *if B* were true beliefs, φ-ing would have best satisfied her desire, goal, end, purpose, or taste (*G*).

Alf believed that it would not rain, so SR deems Alf's action instrumentally rational even though he was soaked despite all his precautions: *if* he was right that it was not going to rain, *then* his action would have achieved his goals. So SR absolves Alf from irrationality, and that seems correct. But SR also implies that Betty was rational when she consulted her Ouiji board; indeed, according to SR Betty would be instrumentally rational even on those days when she consults her Ouiji board, it tells her *not* to carry an umbrella, and she gets thoroughly soaked. After all, *if* her beliefs about the accuracy of Ouiji boards were true, then doing what they say *would be* an effective way to pursue her goals. Despite this rather odd implication, subjectivist theories of rationality have appealed to many, and we can see why. If we take Betty's beliefs as given, then we can see her *reasons* for carrying an umbrella, even though they are not *good* reasons for doing so. Insofar as our only concern is to make Betty's choice to carry her umbrella intelligible,[5] we can understand her action as displaying a sort of "instrumental rationality." Recall here the case from Sigmund Freud that I mentioned in the Introduction. Freud renders more intelligible a patient's apparently totally unintelligible sleep ceremonies by showing that, given the girl's rather odd beliefs, she chose her sleep ceremonies because, *on her view*, it helped keep her parents apart, which was her goal.

Although thoroughly subjective theories of instrumental reasoning have their attractions in social scientific explanation, almost all attempts to develop the idea of rational action have sought to justify some constraints on what constitutes reasonable beliefs that underlie an instrumental choice.[6] An account of instrumental rationality must build in some reference to the well-groundedness of the beliefs on which the agent acts.[7] Consider another case of Freud's, that of "Little Hans." Little Hans "refused to go out into the street because he was afraid of horses."[8] He believed that if he went out into the street, horses would bite him. Now *if* Little Hans's beliefs were correct, then his choice not to go on to the street would seem instrumentally rational—it makes sense to avoid getting bitten by horses. But Little Hans strikes us, as he did Freud, as not being rational, since Little Hans had no good reason to believe that horses *would* bite him if he went on to the street. Thus Freud set out to uncover why Little Hans believed such an odd thing. (Freud's conjecture was that Little Hans, desiring his mother, feared retribution from his father; Little Hans transferred his fear that his father would castrate him onto horses: they would, thought Little Hans, "bite" him.) If you think there is something irrational about Little Hans's choice not to go on to the street, you do not accept a purely subjective theory of instrumental rationality.

In our rather more mundane cases, Alf seems instrumentally rational when he does not wear a raincoat, even though he fails to achieve his goals, because his beliefs about the weather (on which he acted) were well-grounded; Betty, even though she succeeds in achieving her goals, is not instrumentally rational because her beliefs about the weather are, from an epistemic point of view, terrible. And

Little Hans is irrational because the horses will not bite him; also, if he is afraid that his father will castrate him, avoiding horses will not help much. An adequate characterization of Instrumental Rationality (IR), then, must go something like this:

> IR: Alf's action ϕ is instrumentally rational only if Alf chooses ϕ because he soundly believes it is the best prospect for achieving his goals, values, ends, etc.

An agent who is instrumentally rational acts in light of his goals; his decision must be based on at least minimally sound beliefs (ones that are not grossly defective from an epistemic viewpoint), and the deliberation leading to action must not be grossly defective. I shall employ the admittedly vague ideas of a "good reason" and a "sound choice" to cover these minimal epistemic requirements.

The very idea of an instrumentally rational action leads us to questions of justified belief—"epistemology." Some resist this: they would like the theory of rational action to be independent from an account of rational belief (or at least they would like the account of rational action not to depend on an independent theory of what constitutes rational belief), and so they advance "pragmatic" justifications for constraints on what constitutes a rational belief. For example, some might agree that Little Hans is instrumentally irrational because avoiding horses is a singularly ineffective way to avoid being castrated by his father. Or think about the case of the sleep ceremonies discussed in the introduction: the girl's obsession with keeping her bedstead and the quilt apart is not apt to keep her parents from having more children. *So, it might be said, holding a belief is rational only if holding that belief is an effective way to achieve your goals.* Note that this proposal simply revives Rationality as Effectiveness (RE) by applying it to belief: the act ϕ of adopting a belief B is rational if and only if it effectively achieves one's goals. Sometimes these effective beliefs will be true beliefs, and other times not. Sometimes the best way to achieve your goals may be to have false beliefs (if you want to lose weight, it is better to believe that food which is really scrumptious tastes like dirt—then you won't be tempted to eat it). This proposal, however, seems unappealing. First, it still is apt to identify the rational with dumb luck: suppose Little Hans's refusal to go out on the street so upset his father that his father left town, and left Little Hans alone with his mother. His beliefs about horses would turn out to be rational after all. Second, we seem to confront a troublesome regress. Remember, we have concluded that an instrumental reason to perform act ϕ presupposes a notion of sound (or rational, or justified) belief (B). Now, as a way of explaining rational belief, we simply are treating "believing B" as another rational action. But then, to evaluate the rationality of *this* "action" ("believing B") we still require some notion of a rational belief—we need to know whether it is rational to believe that believing B would advance one's goals. So suppose we accept B', the belief that believing B advances one's goals. Then, however, we must consider the rationality of embracing B'—does believing *it* effectively advance one's goals? Further appeals to the general criterion of effectively advancing one's goals will merely lead to new levels of regress of rational justification. And this because— according to Instrumental Rationality—the rationality of accepting ϕ cannot be explicated simply in terms of whether adopting it would advance one's goals (as RE suggests); we must consider whether one soundly believes adopting it would do so.

Can Goals Be Irrational?

Instrumental rationality, though, is not only about beliefs, but goals: we choose the best prospects to achieve our goals. Beliefs can be irrational—can goals be? Here most follow the spirit of David Hume:

> 'Tis not contrary to reason to prefer the destruction of the whole world to the scratching of my finger. 'Tis not contrary to reason for me to chuse my total ruin, to prevent the least uneasiness of an Indian or person wholly unknown to me. 'Tis as little contrary to reason to prefer even my own acknowledg'd lesser good to my greater, and have a more ardent affection for the former than the latter.[9]

For Hume, our reason cannot tell us what to desire, so *no desire* can ever be against reason. Contemporary philosophers, however, often hedge Hume's thesis. Although Robert Nozick acknowledges that "we have no adequate theory of the substantive rationality of goals and desires, to put to rest Hume's statement, 'It is not contrary to reason to prefer the destruction of the whole world to the scratching of my finger'," he still seeks to take "a tiny step beyond Hume"[10] by identifying some rational limits on desires, goals, etc. We can identify three "tiny" steps that philosophers try to take to go beyond Hume.

1. Consistency Requirements Nozick advocates a consistency requirement between desires or goals.[11] According to Nozick, a person shows herself to lack "rational integration" if she has some desire for x, yet also desires not to desire x. When such a "second-order" desire (a desire directed at another desire) conflicts with a "first-order" desire (the desire for x), Nozick argues, "it is an open question" which should be given up, but it is clear that "they do not hang together well, and a rational person would prefer that this not (continue to) be the case."[12] Perhaps. Take a standard case where this story appears to make sense: a desire to get drunk. We can imagine a person with a desire to get drunk, and also with a desire to get rid of his desire to get drunk. There appears to be the sort of conflict of desires that Nozick has in mind, a conflict between a desire and a desire directed at that desire. And this, he believes, is an irrational inconsistency. Yet this is not really so clear. Take a parallel case: suppose I desire fame but I also think I would be wiser if I didn't care about popular opinion of my work, so I desire not to want fame. But I do want fame, and yet I wish I didn't. I cannot see that this alone in any way makes me irrational. To be sure, I cannot satisfy both desires, but that occurs between all sorts of desires—say, between a woman's desire to be a stay-at-home mother and to be a CEO. She wants both— she can see the attractions of both—but she cannot have both. So long as she can order these desires for purposes of choice—so long as she consistently chooses, say, to be a CEO rather than a stay-at-home mother—she is a rational chooser, even though she wants both (she always is attracted to being a stay-at-home mother, even after she achieves her dream of being a CEO). Is it any different if the conflict is not, as in this case, between two "first-order" desires (to be a CEO and to be a stay-at-home mom), but between a first-order desire (to be famous) and a "second-order" desire (to want not to desire fame)? I am, indeed, *ambivalent* about my desire for fame, but am I irrational? If, like the woman having to choose between being a CEO and staying home with her children, I can rank my two desires for choice purposes (in the end, I choose fame), I can consistently choose, though there will always be a desire that I won't satisfy. Some say this is irrational: it is like believing that the world is a sphere and that it is flat. To others it shows that we are often ambivalent creatures who, perhaps typically, are not fully satisfied with our choices, because we have a hankering after the opposite.

2. The Master Goal According to Nassau William Senior, a leading political economist of the nineteenth century, economics could assume that everyone seeks wealth because "wealth and happiness are very seldom opposed."[13] The ultimate goal is happiness: no matter what one desires, this is a manifestation of the pursuit of happiness or pleasure. Our goals, then, have a rational structure to them: they all serve the end of the achieving the master goal. So basic was this idea to early political economy that "utility" generally meant "pleasure." This "hedonistic" view of our ends, long discredited, has been making something of a comeback: a number of works have been published recently about how we measure happiness, and whether market economies really make people happy.[14] The old criticisms, though, remain. If hedonism is intended as an account of rationality, it follows that those who aim at goals that do not serve their own happiness are *ipso facto* irrational. That seems a very restrictive notion of rational action: the action "Alf sacrificed his own happiness to help others" would be, by definition, irrational. In response to the oddness of defining such actions as intrinsically irrational, many hedonists switch ground, arguing, as did the early utilitarian Jeremy Bentham, that:

> Nature has placed mankind under the governance of two sovereign masters, pain and pleasure. It is for them alone to point out what we *ought to do*, as well as *to determine what we shall do*. . . . They govern us in all we do, in all we say, in all we think: every effort we can make to throw off our subjection, will serve but to demonstrate and confirm it.[15]

We ought to pursue pleasure *and* we must do so. If it is impossible not to pursue one's own pleasure, then we clearly can't have cases of rational action that don't aim at pleasure, since it is impossible not to aim at pleasure. This psychological claim is extremely dubious: people aim at a variety of goals, and it hard to see how they all are ways to gain pleasure. Consider helping the poor: is that a way to give you pleasure? It is said that Thomas Hobbes argued it was. Hobbes, who was famous for arguing that people only cared about themselves, was once seen giving money to a beggar. When pressed why he did so, Hobbes replied that it gave him pleasure to see the poor man happy. But was that what Hobbes really cared about? Is helping the poor, just like drinking beer, a way to gain pleasure? (Unless one gets a lot of pleasure from it, there seem to be cheaper ways to get pleasure than giving money away!) Supposing that we can and do act for other goals besides our own pleasure, then surely it is not irrational to do so. If Hobbes thought that his reply was necessary to show that he wasn't being irrational, I think it is safe to say that he was mistaken.

3. Procedural Requirements   A more common way of taking a small step beyond Hume's thesis is to provide a test that distinguishes our rational from our irrational desires. Two sorts of tests are widely supported. According to the *Autonomous Formation Test,* only desires that were formed free of undue pressure or force, free of manipulation by others, or were formed under conditions of adequate formation, are rational desires. For example, it might be argued that if a desire to smoke cigarettes has been induced by advertising and peer pressure, and so was formed in a procedurally objectionable way, it is not rational. Alternatively, according to the *Critical Reflection Test,* only desires that *could* survive a process of critical reflection are truly rational. An adherent of the Critical Reflection Test might hold that the desire to smoke is not rational because it cannot withstand critical reflection: if people reflected on smoking and the risks, it is said, they would not continue to desire to smoke.[16] On this view people who smoke only maintain their desire by refusing to look at the evidence, or engaging in wishful thinking, and so on.

Such proposals are interesting, and I do not wish to dismiss them out of hand. Their weakness, though, is that while they eliminate the obvious "bad" desires, they are also effective against "good" ones. Consider the Autonomous Formation Test. The procedure by which people come to develop a desire to be moral, for example, seems to have a lot to do with a desire to please one's parents and conform to their commands—not a desire formation process that would seem to pass muster. Even the Critical Reflection Test can have counter-intuitive consequences. As many physicians know, giving patients too much information, or asking them to vividly picture the recommended procedure, may lead them to not desire things that are clearly good for them, and which they realize are good for them. Suppose a patient has a desire to have a colonoscopy, but if he really reflected on what this involved, he would no longer desire the procedure. Would this render the desire irrational? Or is that just a good reason not to think too much about some things?

1.2 "CONSUMPTION RATIONALITY" AS DIRECT SATISFACTION OF GOALS

Action That Directly Achieves Goals

It is tempting to characterize *Homo Economicus*—"economic man"—simply in terms of instrumental rationality; indeed, I shall argue later that instrumental explanations are the preferred mode for *Homo*

Economicus. However, we cannot restrict *Homo Economicus* to instrumental reasons to act, for if we do so we cannot adequately explain consumption behavior. Say, for example, that Betty is eating ice cream and she explains her behavior by proclaiming "I like ice cream." Now a hedonist (Section 1.1) might explain Betty's action by saying that it was an instrumentally effective way of achieving pleasure. If pleasure is the sole end, and if we are constructed in ways such that we always pursue pleasure and avoid pain, then indeed all action is instrumental to experiencing this mental state. However, if we reject hedonism, this interpretation of Betty's ice cream eating is strained. In general, consumption activity is noninstrumental; if φ is a consumption activity, it is not usefully understood as a way to achieve some goal that is distinct from φ. This is an important, but often ignored, point. Suppose a person has a desire for an ice cream cone; she ate one. We do not want to say that her decision to eat the ice cream cone aimed at "satisfying her desire for an ice cream cone" as if there was a distinct thing called a "desire to eat the ice cream cone" that her eating somehow assuaged—as if it were an itch that she sought to get rid of. On this "itch" theory of desires, we perform acts that satisfy desires because we actually have the aim of getting rid of the desire. But the itch theory seems wrong. Betty does not eat the ice cream cone to get rid of her "itch" to eat the ice cream cone: she eats the ice cream cone because she likes ice cream cones. The "aim" of her eating the ice cream cone is, well, to eat an ice cream cone.

This, however, raises the specter of entirely vacuous explanations of people's actions. We see Betty φ-ing (eating the ice cream cone) and we "explain" it by saying that "Betty's goal is to φ (eat the ice cream cone), so φ-ing (eating the ice cream cone) satisfies her goal." But now that which is doing the explaining (Betty has a goal to φ) and that which is to be explained (Betty φ-ed) look as if they are the same thing. The worry is that the only way we can really know that Betty has a goal of φ-ing is by observing her φ-ing. Our explanation would then be of the form:

Explanandum: (1) Betty φs.
Explanans: (2) Betty's reason for φ-ing is that she has a goal to φ.

which looks too much like:

(3) Betty φs because she is observed to φ.

This does not seem very promising as a way to explain her action; the *explanans* is essentially a restatement of the *explanandum*.

16

Although it is tempting to revert back to a thoroughly instrumentalist account of *Homo Economicus* and say that the "aim" of our action is to "satisfy" our desire to perform that very action, we can solve the problem without resorting to the itch theory. Betty's specific act, φ, can be genuinely *explained* (as opposed to merely restated) if it is an instance of a general disposition to Φ, or engage in Φ-type acts—i.e., a disposition to engage in actions of a certain *type*. Thus, for instance, when Betty explains eating ice cream cones by saying "I like them," this counts as an explanation if Betty is generally disposed to eat ice cream cones. The explanation here is one of token and type, or specific instance and general kind. Now this sort of explanation is not altogether empty. Consider:

Explanandum: (1) Betty φs.
Explanans: (2) Betty's reason for φ-ing (in this instance) is that she likes Φ-type.

which might be translated:

(3) Betty's reason for φ-ing (in this instance) is that she is observed to Φ-type.

In this case what is doing the explaining is not a restatement of the thing to be explained; the specific act is explained by showing it to be an instance of a general type. Again, one may be tempted to reduce this to an instrumental explanation: Betty φs as a way to bring about her goal of Φ-typing. But this really is to get the relation of the specific act and the general type wrong: φ-ing is not a means to Φ-typing, it is an instance of it.

We can, then, complement the idea of instrumental rationality with what I shall call "Consumption Rationality" (CR):

CR: Betty's action φ is "consumptively rational" only if it is an instance of Φ-type—a general desire, value, or end of hers.

Let us, then, combine IR and CR for a preliminary account of Economic Rationality (ER):

ER: Charlie's action φ is economically rational only if it is (a) instrumentally rational or (b) consumptively rational.

Note that ER provides necessary but not sufficient conditions for economic rationality. It does not, for example, determine what is economically rational for Charlie to do if he must choose, say, between two consumptively rational acts—ϕ and ψ. We shall turn to that problem in Section 1.3.

Instrumentalism as the Preferred Explanation

Although the full explication of *Homo Economicus* must allow for both instrumental and consumptive rationality, its power and persuasiveness stems from instrumental explanations. *Homo Economicus* rests much of its claim to our allegiance on the "almost unbelievable delicacy and subtlety"[17] of its analysis of the market. And this analysis shows that individuals with diverse goals engage in certain sorts of economic activity because they believe that such activity is instrumentally effective in achieving their different goals. Thus, for instance, the economic model can explain the choice of medicine as a career by citing relative costs of training, opportunity costs, etc., and showing how occupational choices are instrumentally rational in achieving an agent's ends. For some economists the crux of the economic model is to explain how different actions in different situations are instrumentally rational to satisfying a stable set of goals.[18] Choices, such as the choice of an occupation, are ways of achieving the satisfaction of stable goals in different circumstances. Such economists, then, would not explain occupational choice by appeal to the goal to be a doctor but, rather, as a way to satisfy one's stable goals for income and prestige.

However, it is important to note that citing the brute desires or goals of people to be doctors does not abandon the notion of economic rationality: after all, people must have desires or goals if the economic model is to work. And market research, which sometimes seeks to uncover things people noninstrumentally value, is not opposed to *Homo Economicus*. But direct appeal to a desire to Φ-type as a way to explain ϕ-ing is not the preferred mode of economic explanation. We might say that it is an explanation of the last resort, for while it is not empty, neither does it explain much. The preferred explanation is to show that action ϕ is instrumentally rational for agents with a wide variety of goals, which are not directly about the merits of engaging in the general type of activity, Φ. Thus, the tendency I cited earlier to identify *Homo Economicus* with instrumental rationality is not entirely off the mark: although economically rational agents have access to other reasons besides instrumental ones, *Homo Economicus*, as a model of rational action, prefers explanations in terms of instrumental rationality.

2. Decreasing Marginal Value   We have seen that *Homo Econom-icus*, other things equal, will always prefer a greater over a lesser degree of goal satisfaction. However, although we always prefer the greater amount over the lesser, the increase in value diminishes from the nth to the $n + 1$ unit of a goal. This idea of diminishing marginal utility was one of the revolutionary developments in modern economics. In the words of Carl Menger, one of the economists usually credited with its discovery:

> The satisfaction of every man's need for food up to the point where his life is thereby assured has the full importance of the maintenance of his life. Consumption exceeding this amount, again up to a certain point, has the importance of preserving his health (that is, his continuing well-being). Consumption extending beyond even this point has merely the importance—as observation shows—of a progressively weaker pleasure, until it finally reaches a certain limit at which the satisfaction of the need for food is so complete that every further intake of food contributes neither to the maintenance of life nor the preservation of health—nor does it give pleasure to the consumer, becoming first a matter of indifference to him, eventually a cause of pain, a danger to his health, and finally a danger to life itself.[20]

Menger's basic insight was that the amount of extra value we place on additional increments of a good decreases as we gain more of the good. As we see from the last lines of this quote, Menger himself thought that at some point we reach satiation and beyond that we *dis*value increments; so not only does the extra value of an increment become smaller, but at some point there is no increment at all (this then conflicts with "more is better than less," at least when applied to the good of food). If, though, we accept that "more is better then less," then we suppose that we never quite reach the point at which a person is entirely indifferent, though the extra value he achieves from the increment might be miniscule.

Somewhat surprisingly, although decreasing marginal utility is fundamental to economic analysis, its grounding is not obvious. Some treat it simply as an empirical generalization about how people do in fact typically choose rather than a basic feature of rationality itself or a deep psychological law.[21] Hedonists can provide a more secure foundation for it, claiming that since everything we do aims at pleasure, it is a deep psychological law that the more we have of something, the less extra pleasure we get from each additional unit: the first slice of pizza gives a lot of pleasure, the second less, the third even less. While this makes sense of decreasing marginal utility, it does so only if we accept hedonism, something we have already questioned (Section 1.1).

Another possibility is to see decreasing marginal utility as fundamental to the concept of an instrumentally rational agent with multiple goals. Thus far we have been treating instrumentally rational agents as if they had only one goal, desire, etc. Instrumentally rational agents, though, must act on a variety of goals. Now suppose one had a variety of goals but the satisfaction of each goal had no diminishing marginal effect: achieving the $n + 1000$ unit was just as important as achieving the nth. Suppose further, that goal G was the most important goal for you, and you could always do something to achieve G; suppose G is watching 24-hour Australian Rules Football. If so, you would do nothing but watch Australian Rules Football. Agents whose goals are not characterized by decreasing marginal utility would tend to be monomaniacs: they would be apt to seek the same the thing over and over and over again.[22] We can, then, see decreasing marginal utility as crucial to the idea of a *rational multiple-goal pursuer* who seeks to satisfy different goals at different times. As one goal is achieved its importance tends to go down so that other goals rise to attention. To say that a goal's "utility" decreases, then, is simply to say that its relative importance decreases as it is increasingly satisfied and so at some point the agent will choose an action that secures a basic satisfaction of a less important goal over an act that yields ever more satisfaction of a more important goal. Insofar as we think an instrumentally rational agent is not a monomaniac who pursues just one thing all the time, we will have to include in our model some version of decreasing marginal utility.

Consider another example: suppose a person is deeply conservative, and she performs the same religious ritual over and over again. One might think this means that the value of performing the ritual does not decrease at the margins for her. Am I saying that she is *economically irrational*, because her choices do not reflect decreasing marginal utility of rituals? I would tend to think that her choices *do* reflect decreasing marginal utility: after all, she does not perform the ritual all day every day. Having performed her religious ritual, she then chooses to eat, work, or read. That we do something repeatedly is not a counterexample to decreasing marginal utility. I watch old movies every day, and sometimes two in a day. I put great value on

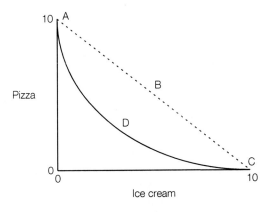

FIGURE 1-1 An Indifference Curve

them, but the point is that despite the great value I put on them, I do other things that apparently I "value less." Why would I *ever do anything but watch old movies?* Why does our traditionalist *ever do anything other than perform her valued ritual?* Decreasing marginal utility explains why.

Much the same idea can be put in terms of *decreasing rates of substitution.* Suppose we have two goods, pizza and ice cream. And suppose Betty has $X total to spend on some combination of pizza and ice cream. We then get Figure 1-1.

At point A, Betty spends all her money on 10 pizzas; at point C, all is spent on 10 quarts of ice cream; at B, she divides her expenditure. Given decreasing marginal utility, Betty prefers B to either A or C. This can be put in terms of decreasing rates of substitution between pizza and ice cream: when you have all pizza, you will give up quite a bit to get some ice cream; but as you get more and more ice cream, you will give up less pizza to get the same increment of additional ice cream.[23]

This leads to the important idea of an *indifference curve*: Betty is *indifferent* between all bundles of ice cream and pizza on the curved line (A-D-C). Betty is, of course, not indifferent between B and A since she prefers B to A; she is, though, indifferent between A, D, and C (and this even though D is a smaller bundle of goods than A or C—because of decreasing marginal utility, D, as it were, manages to squeeze more utility out of the goods). Vilfredo Pareto (1848–1923), who is often

23

credited with the modern development of indifference curve analysis, described them as contours on the "hill of pleasure." Like the contours on a map, each line connects points of equal elevation, or in our case equal value; as we go up the hill, we go up in value.[24]

3. Downward Sloping Demand Curves   I have suggested that an important ground for accepting the assumption of decreasing marginal utility is that we are pursuers of multiple goals. In many ways the heart of economic thinking is that we always choose between goals (or goods). The crucial contribution of economic analysis is the idea of *opportunity costs*: the cost of getting one good thing is that we forego the opportunity to have something else that is good. This is not a lesson easily learned. When my daughter was around five years old, she would sometimes get money from a relative on a special occasion, and she would promptly go to the toy store. But it was always a tragedy for her: although she desperately wanted the toy, she desperately wanted to keep the money too. She could not bear to pay the cost of the toy, but could not bear to forego the toy either. Typically the trip ended with her breaking into tears (and me buying the toy!). The tragedy resulted because she sought an action without opportunity costs.

Given that choice always involves opportunity costs, as the cost of a choice increases it becomes less attractive to *Homo Economicus*. We can say that *Homo Economicus's* willingness to act to satisfy goal G_1 decreases as the costs of achieving G_1 (in terms of lost opportunity to achieve G_2) increases. This is a gloss on the notion that the demand curve for any good is "downward sloping": the more a good costs, the less of it is demanded. Unlike our simple model of an instrumentally rational agent with which we began, we now see that *Homo Economicus* is a much more complicated fellow: he must be able to choose between competing actions promoting different ends through a system of trade-off rates according to which the "demand" for a goal/end decreases as its cost relative to other goals/ends increases. This is the crux of what we mean by an efficient pursuit of goals.

4. Selfishness/Wealth Maximization/ Non-Tuism   *Homo Economicus* is generally understood as an egoist or, even more narrowly, a wealth maximizer.[25] And it is surely right that at the core of the "economic approach" to society has been the explanatory power of self-interest.[26] It is, of course, precisely this aspect of *Homo Economicus* that has attracted so much criticism from social scientists resisting the economic approach.[27] It remains, though, a matter of dispute whether narrow motivations such as egoism or wealth maximization are really basic to the economic conception of rationality or whether they are best understood as simplifying assumptions that allow for more determinate applications of the model. The latter, I think, is more plausible. This is especially clear regarding wealth maximization: it surely is not part and parcel of being a rational agent that one maximizes wealth. However, to *assume* that people are, generally, devoted to maximizing wealth allows for determinate applications of some (not, actually, very many) economic models by allowing us to specify what the agents' goals are, and so see what actions are indeed instrumentally rational given those goals. And in many contexts it does well enough to suppose that what people are really interested in is wealth and income. However, the usefulness of this assumption is surely context-dependent. It makes sense in a few areas of economics, but most of economics does not suppose that people are wealth maximizers. Indeed, much economics does not even suppose that people are necessarily self-interested; certainly such a supposition is questionable when applied generally to political science or analysis of the law (see Chapter 6). I have tried to show here that the real crux of *Homo Economicus* can be explicated without any reference to wealth maximization or even self-interest: more is better than less, decreasing marginal value, and downward sloping demand curves all can be explained without any reference to self-interest. They simply assume that people have goals they wish to pursue, and are devoted to pursuing their own goals in the most efficient manner. Just what those goals are is another question.

Not even economics, much less all social science, must suppose that *Homo Economicus* is self-interested. According to Philip Wicksteed, "the specific character of an economic relation is not its 'egoism,' but its non-tuism."[28] By this Wicksteed meant that each party to an economic relation is seeking to advance her own goals, desires, and ends and not those of the other party; economics is not a study of transactions among altruists, but of non-tuists. These goals, though, may not be at all self-interested. Parents engage in economic transactions with universities: they pay large tuitions to educate their children and the universities use this money to support their own academic and social goals. Neither party need be concerned with its own self-interest. To be sure, we can save the characterization of *Homo Economicus* as inherently self-interested by describing all goal pursuit as self-interested: if it is your goal, then it is in your interest to pursue it. This, though, is to expand the meaning of "self-interest" so that it includes anything the self is interested in. If my values lead me to give to charity, educate my children, and help my neighbors, then on this view I am being just as "self-interested" as one who keeps all her money, ignores her children, and dumps her garbage in her neighbor's yard. The idea of being "self-interested" loses its typical meaning and simply becomes just another name for non-tuism.

Even Wicksteed's "non-tuism" is merely a simplifying assumption: it allows us to calculate your "utility" as, in principle, independent of my "utility" (see Chapter 2 on the idea of "utility"). If my aim is to promote your aim, and your aim is to promote my aim, calculating what actions further our aims becomes exceedingly complicated. In such cases our utility functions are not independent, and the mathematics of modeling such interdependent functions is quite complicated. If we accept Wicksteed's "non-tuism" things are much simpler—but that is the point, it is a simplifying supposition, not something inherent to the economic understanding of rational agents.

5. Constrained Maximization   The picture of *Homo Economicus* that emerges is of an instrumentally rational agent, who seeks more rather than less, who is responsive to the costs of her choices, and who does not pursue one goal again and again, but acts on a variety of goals. In this way she maximizes the achievement of her goals or ends. Economists, though, understand this maximization to occur against a background of constraints. Individuals maximize given budget constraints: in Figure 1-1, the line A-B-C is the budget constraint, showing possible combinations of goods for a fixed budget. More broadly, economic agents operate within a set of rules and institutions that constrain what they can do. That a person may maximize by attacking others is not included in most economic models, as non-coercion is usually understood as a constraint.

Need *Homo Economicus* maximize? Given her goals, must she always seek the greatest possible amount of goal satisfaction? Herbert Simon, a Nobel prize winning economist, has famously argued for an alternative to *Homo Economicus* the Maximizer—a "satisficing" agent.[29] Instead of seeking the best outcome—maximizing the achievement of her goals—an agent who "satisfices" seeks an outcome that is satisfactory or "good enough." Many insist that rational agents often satisfice rather than maximize. However, it is not always clear whether satisficing is really an alternative to maximizing. On one view, satisficing is simply a strategy that a maximizer might follow. People who *try* to maximize—who always seek the best—

are apt to waste a lot of time; they incur search and information costs seeing if they can do a little bit better than the "good enough" choice, and in so doing may not achieve as many of their goals as a satisficing agent, who finds a good enough option and then moves on to something else. Conceived thus, satisficing is not an alternative to maximizing, but a way to maximize (you can do best by settling for good enough and then moving on to a different goal). More radically, though, some see satisficing as an inherently rational way of acting that does not turn on a claim to ultimately maximize.[30] It is rational to settle for good enough even if one could, all things considered, do better. Understood in this way satisficing requires a fundamental revision of *Homo Economicus*: "more is better than less" must be abandoned, since sometimes, on this satisficing view, "good enough is as good as more."

SUMMARY

This chapter explored the foundation of all economic analysis—the notion of a rational agent. The main aims of this chapter were:

- *To provide a defense of one conception of instrumental rationality.* Although some tend to equate "instrumental rationality" with any behavior that satisfies one's aims, I have argued that such a view of instrumental rationality is inadequate. Instrumental rationality, I have argued, is concerned with whether, on the basis of sound beliefs, one chooses an action that has good prospects of successfully achieving one's aims.

- *To consider whether there are good grounds for modifying Hume's claim that reason cannot tell us what our goals should be, but can only tell us how to best achieve the goals we have.* We considered three proposals that "go beyond" Hume's view: (1) that desires can be inconsistent, and so a rational agent only has consistent desires or aims; (2) that happiness or pleasure is the true master goal, and all other goals are only valuable insofar as they lead to happiness or pleasure; and (3) that we can identify certain tests that show which desires are rational and which are not.

- *To show that, in addition to "instrumental" rationality, an adequate account of economic rationality must explain the rationality of simple consumption choices—doing something just because you like it.*

- *To sketch the ways in which the standard view of* Homo Economicus *goes beyond the simple idea of an instrumentally rational agent.* I suggested that it is generally agreed that *Homo Economicus*: (1) holds that more is better than less; (2) has goals that are characterized by decreasing marginal value; and (3) has downward sloping demand curves. In Section 1.3 the important idea of an indifference curve was introduced. I also questioned (4) the widespread view that *Homo Economicus* is basically self-interested. Finally, we surveyed a debate as to whether *Homo Economicus* always seeks to maximize the satisfaction of her goals.

NOTES

1. "Instrumental rationality," says Robert Nozick, "is within the intersection of all theories of rationality (and perhaps nothing else is). In this sense it is the default theory, the theory that all can take for granted, whatever else they think. . . . The question is whether it is the whole of rationality." *The Nature of Rationality*, p. 133.

2. Geoffrey Brennan and Loren Lomasky, *Democracy and Decision: The Pure Theory of Electoral Preference*, p. 9. Note omitted.

3. For another treatment of the issues I discuss here see G.W. Mortimore, "Rational Action," pp. 96ff.

4. Amartya Sen, "Choice, Orderings and Morality," p. 55.

5. On the importance of intelligibility to economic explanations, see Alexander Rosenberg, *Philosophy of Social Science*.

6. This is true even regarding those decision theorists who describe themselves as "subjectivists." As one of the most eminent subjectivists insists, "your 'subjective' probability is not something fetched out of the sky on a whim." Richard Jeffrey, *Subjective Probability*, p. 76.

7. See further Jon Elster, "The Nature and Scope of Rational-Choice Explanation," pp. 60–72.

8. Sigmund Freud, "Inhibitions, Symptoms and Anxieties," p. 254.

9. David Hume, *A Treatise of Human Nature*, Book II, Part III, sec. 3.

10. Nozick, *The Nature of Rationality*, pp. 63, 148.

11. Nozick talks of "preferences" or goals. We shall see in Section 2.1 that "preference" is used in ambiguous ways; for now I put off employing it.

12. Nozick, *The Nature of Rationality*, p. 141.

13. Nassau William Senior, *An Outline of the Science of Political Economy*, 5th edition, pp. 187–188.

14. See, for example, Bernard van Praag and Ada Ferrer-i-Carbonell, *Happiness Quantified: A Satisfaction Calculus Approach*.

15. Jeremy Bentham, *Introduction to the Principles of Morals*, p. 65. Emphasis added.

16. There are many such views. For an example, see Cass Sunstein, *Free Markets and Social Justice*, pp. 18ff.

17. George J. Stigler, *The Economist as Preacher*, p. 21.

18. See Gary Becker, *The Economic Approach to Human Behavior*.

19. Russell Hardin, *Indeterminacy and Society*, p. 16.

20. Carl Menger, *Principles of Economics*, p. 124.

21. See Daniel M. Hausman, *The Inexact and Separate Science of Economics*, p. 32. Cf. Ludwig von Mises's claim that "there is no question of any such thing as a law of increasing marginal utility" (i.e., marginal utility never increases over the range of possible quantities). *Human Action: A Treatise on Economics*, 3rd edition, p. 125.

22. See Sigmund Freud, "The Disposition to Obsessional Neurosis" pp. 134–144.

23. Decreasing marginal utility and decreasing rates of substitution are closely related but not the same idea: whereas the idea of decreasing marginal utility requires a cardinal measure of utility, decreasing rates of substitution can be expressed in purely ordinal terms. See Sections 2.2 and 2.3.

24. Those already familiar with indifference curves may find this odd: indifference curves are an ordinalist notion, but Pareto seemed to have in mind here cardinal utility qua amounts of pleasure. I explore these distinctions in Chapter 2. On Pareto's attraction to cardinal utility, see Luigino Bruni and Francesco Guala, "Vilfredo Pareto and the Epistemological Foundations of Choice Theory."

25. Brennan and Lomasky, *Democracy and Decision*, pp. 9–10.

26. See Stigler, *The Economist as Preacher*, p. 21. Cf. Gary Becker, "Altruism, Egoism and Genetic Fitness," in his *The Economic Approach to Human Behavior*, chap. 13.

27. See, for example, *Beyond Self-Interest*, edited by Jane J. Mansfield.

28. Philip H. Wicksteed, *The Common Sense of Political Economy*, vol. 1, p. 180.

29. See, for example, Herbert Simon, "Theories of Decision Making in Economics and Behavioral Science."

30. See Michael Slote, "Two Views of Satisficing," pp. 14–29.

2

Utility Theory

OVERVIEW

The analysis of economic rationality in Chapter 1 was somewhat unorthodox. Typically discussions of economic rationality commence with the idea of *preferences*, the axioms of *ordinal utility* theory, and then, finally, *cardinal utility* theory. Instead, I have tried to determine the relation of *Homo Economicus* to instrumental—goal-based—rationality. I have two reasons for adopting this slightly unorthodox approach. *First*, it is important to see how economic rationality relates to our broader, nontechnical conceptions of practical rationality. *Second*, as I will try to show in this chapter, the relation of formal utility to instrumental rationality, and so to *Homo Economicus*, is usually misunderstood. Now that we have a reasonably firm grasp of instrumental rationality, we are well-positioned to avoid some common errors.

Utility theory is about satisfying preferences. I begin by considering an often overlooked question: just what is a "preference"? The next two sections explain ordinal and cardinal utility theory. After explaining the basics of utility theory, I consider whether utility theory is, as many think, a formalization of the idea of instrumental rationality. I argue that it is not: it can model both instrumental and noninstrumental reasoning. The chapter concludes by discussing the experiments of social psychologists as to whether utility theory really explains human behavior.

2.1 PREFERENCES: WHAT ARE THEY?

The idea of a "preference"—and, especially, of "satisfying a preference"—is fundamental to utility theory. Economists explain rational
action as that which aims at preference satisfaction: a rational agent is
typically held to maximize the satisfaction of her preferences
(see Section 1.3). Unfortunately, "preference" is an especially ambiguous term. We can identify at least three interpretations of preference:
as (1) a noncomparative "taste" for something; (2) "choice behavior"
itself; and (3) the agent's deliberative rankings of her outcomes and
options.

Nonrelational Tastes or Desires

Philosophers, lawyers, and even some economists tend to equate the
idea of a preference with a liking. To have a "preference for pizza" is
to like pizza, or to have a taste for pizza.[1] "I prefer it" means "I like
it" or "I have a taste for it." Thus, for Louis Kaplow and Steven
Shavell, to say a person has a preference for a fair outcome is simply to
say that she has a "taste" for fairness: "if individuals in fact have tastes
for notions of fairness—that is, if they feel better off when laws or
events that they observe are in accord with what they consider to be
fair—then analysis under welfare economics will take such tastes into
account...."[2] Notice the echo of hedonism (Section 1.1): a person's
sole aim seems to be to "*feel* better off."

Now although we sometimes talk this way, there are two reasons
why this notion of preference cannot enter into utility theory. (1)
Consider a famous story presented by Michael Walzer:

> a politician who has seized upon a national crisis—a pro-
> longed colonial war—to reach for power. He and his friends
> win office pledged to decolonization and peace; they are
> honestly committed to both, though not without some sense
> of the advantages of the commitment. In any case, they have
> no responsibility for the war; they have steadfastly opposed
> it. Immediately, the politician goes off to the colonial capital
> to open negotiations with the rebels. But the capital is in the
> grip of a terrorist campaign and the first decision the new
> leader faces is this: he is asked to authorize the torture of a
> captured rebel who knows or probably knows the location of
> a number of bombs hidden in apartment buildings around

the city, set to go off in the next twenty four hours. He orders the man tortured, convinced that he must do so for the sake of the people who might otherwise die in the explosions—even though he believes that torture is wrong, indeed abominable, not just sometimes, but always.[3]

If we think of a "preference" as something akin to "liking" or "having a taste for," we can interpret this case in two ways: we can say (a) that the politician has a preference (taste) for torture or (b) that he does *not have a preference* to torture the terrorist rather than to let the buildings blow up, though *he does choose* to torture the terrorist. The first interpretation is obviously wrong. As Walzer tells the story the politician despises torture; he certainly does not have a taste for it. So perhaps we should adopt the second interpretation, and say that the politician chooses to torture but does not have a preference for it (since he certainly does not like it). But this is inconsistent with utility theory. Under utility theory, if our politician ranks option x as more choice-worthy than y, then he prefers x, even if he detests both (though he detests x a little less than y).[4] If he is rational and he chooses x then he *must* prefer x to y, even though he doesn't like either. We need, then, to make sure that we do not confuse the technical notion of a preference with the ordinary language conception of a "liking."

(2) More importantly, understanding preferences as tastes is to understand preferences as noncomparative: I like x, or have a taste for x, or desire x, where x is one thing or option. But in utility theory preferences are always understood as comparative: one always prefers one thing (or option) to another. A preference always and necessarily relates two options and compares them in terms of choice-worthiness. In utility theory one simply cannot have a preference for one option. In this way "preference" is more like "bigger" than "big." One thing can be "big," but "bigger" relates two things: it is inherently comparative. We now see why it is a confusion to take "preference" as synonymous with "goals," "desires," or "values" (Section 1.1). The latter ideas are all non-comparative: my goal can be just x, I can desire just x, or I can simply value x. But in utility theory I cannot simply have a preference for x—it must be a preference for x over y, some second option. We must, then, *define* preference as the " $>$ " relation, such that $x > y$ means x is preferred to y—it is more choice-worthy.

Revealed Preferences

Economists often insist—at least in their more official pronounce-ments—on a purely behavioral conception of preference: Alf is said to have a preference for x over y if and only if Alf chooses x over y, where choice is conceived of as overt behavior. On this view to prefer x to y is simply to choose it over y; if one has never made the choice then one does not have the preference. Preference so understood is, then, equivalent to actual choice. When pressed, economists are apt to say that a preference is simply choice behavior, and if one has consistent preferences this means simply that one chooses consistently. Thus, it is said, one's actual choices "reveal" one's preferences.

The very term "revealed" preference is somewhat misleading. If preferences just *are* choices, what sense can be made of saying that a choice *reveals* a preference? To use this sort of language is to suggest that the choice is "revealing" something else, something hidden and mental, as when a person makes a "revealing state-ment," showing something previously hidden about her character. However, avoiding any appeal to such mental entities was the explicit aim of the behavioristically inclined economists who stressed "revealed preference" theory.[5] Leaving aside the confusion about what is supposed to be "revealed," we have powerful reasons to question the plausibility of the behavioristic project; the attempt to rid the mental from social science looks doomed to failure. Choice is an intentional concept: any effort to describe Alf's choice of x over y will necessarily involve a reference to his understanding of what he is doing, and the nature of the choices confronting him (see further Section 2.3). "Voting for candidate x over y" for example, is not a piece of behavior qua movement of a body. A description of an act as "a vote for x" necessarily turns on the intentions—mental states—of actors involved. The behavior of "raising an arm" may be the act of asking a question or casting a vote (or innumerable other acts); only reference to the intentions of the agent can distinguish the two. And very different pieces of behavior (raising a hand, marking a piece of paper, or shouting "yea!") all may constitute the same act of "voting for x." This is not to say that an intention is sufficient (I cannot vote for the President of Russia even if I intend to), but it seems quite impossible to rid the intentional from our conception of choice. If so, we can hardly purge the mental from our explanation of choices.

Deliberative Preferences

We cannot do without appeal to the mental in accounting for what is involved in choosing on the basis of one's preferences. Although in their official pronouncements economists are apt to adopt a behavioristic notion of revealed preference, most economic writing, and almost all accounts of rational action, suppose that actual choice is taken to *reveal* (or advance) preference qua a deliberative ranking of the options by the agent. A person deliberates and, ideally, can rank all the possible "outcomes"—the ways in which things may go or, as philosophers sometimes say, "states of affairs." Of course it is impossible to actually do this: you would have to identify every possible event that might result from your action. The number of states of affairs that could result from your action looks indefinitely large, if not infinite. I shall return in Section 2.4 to this fundamental problem of how to specify the options; for now I follow the common practice of assuming away the problem by stipulating some finite feasible set of mutually exclusive options that the agent orders in terms of choice-worthiness. The agent is assumed to order the options in the feasible set—her actual choice from the feasible set would then *reveal* her deliberative preference over the feasible set of options.

This leads us to a fundamental issue in utility theory: what ultimately do our preferences range over—states of affairs (outcomes) or possible actions that we might undertake? Say you prefer to live in New Orleans rather than New York (states of affairs), but now you have to consider how this preference over outcomes relates to what action you are to choose. Perhaps the actions open to you are to accept an offer of going to chef school in New Orleans and accepting an offer of law school in New York: if your deliberative preference over outcomes is to live in New Orleans, perhaps the action you should choose is to accept the chef school offer because that action-option will better satisfy your deliberative preference over outcomes. It looks like we must, then, consider both a person's ranking of *outcomes* (roughly, how much one values the various states of affairs that one can bring about) and a person's ranking of *action-options* in terms of which action is most choice-worthy.[6] Let us say that the *consequence domain* of a choice involves everything relevant to a person's ranking of states of the world that might obtain (the world in which you earn a million dollars a year through your legal practice, the world in which you earn half a million by being a successful chef, the world in which you eat great food, the world in which you eat

**Deliberative rankings
of consequences**

**Deliberative
rankings
of action-options**

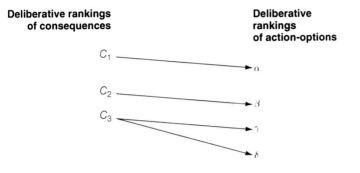

FIGURE 2-1 Mapping Actions to Outcomes

yogurt).[7] Suppose you can rank all these states of the world in terms of which best satisfies your goals and desires, etc. However, the important point for utility theory is not *why* you rank states of the world the way you do, but that you are *able* rank them. Now suppose that you confront a variety of action-options (a choice to be a lawyer or a chef); you will rank the actions highest that are correlated with the highest-ranked outcomes.[8] *Thus, your preferences over outcomes determine your preferences over options.*[9] We can think, then, of a *mapping* of an ordering of outcome-consequences on to the action-options, producing an ordering of action-options as in Figure 2-1.

Although the ordering of action-options (α, β...) will be correlated with the ordering of outcome-consequences ($C_1 \ldots C_n$), there need not be a unique one-to-one relation. As we see in Figure 2-1, two actions (γ, δ) may be correlated with the same consequence C_3: in this case a rational agent will be indifferent between γ and δ since they are associated with the same consequence. If, on the other hand, α is correlated with C_1 and β is correlated with C_2, where C_1 is a higher ranked consequence than C_2, then a rational agent will prefer α over β. We suppose that a person's preferences over outcomes are simply given;[10] one's preferences over action-options, however, change as one gets new information about the relation of the acts to one's rankings of outcomes. The distinction between preferences over outcomes and over actions is especially important when we get to utility theory under risk and strategic situations such as games, where one cannot be certain what action-options produce certain outcomes (see Section 2.3; Chapter 4).

2.2 ORDINAL UTILITY THEORY

The Axioms

Let us focus on the core idea of preferences over outcomes: they are clearly at the heart of the story (we will reintroduce the distinction between such preferences and preferences over options in the next section). We can generate an *ordinal utility function* for any person in terms of his preference rankings for the different outcomes if his rankings satisfy the following standard conditions for a *weak* ordering:

1. The ordering is *complete*. If Alf has a complete ordering, he can always rank options in his feasible set—he can always decide whether one possible outcome is better than another, worse than the other, or equally choice-worthy. Note that in this sense Alf "orders" a pizza and a taco if either (a) he strictly prefers one to the other or (b) he is indifferent between them: a pizza and a taco are equally worthy of being chosen. More formally, we can say that for every pair of outcomes (x,y) it must be the case that in Alf's ordering: (a) x is strictly preferred to y; or (b) y is strictly preferred to x; or (c) y and x are indifferent. Let us use "$x \succ y$" for "x is strictly preferred to y"; "$x \sim y$" for "x is indifferent to y"; and "$x \succeq y$" for "x is either preferred to y or x is indifferent to y." So for all (x,y): $x \succeq y \lor$ [i.e., or] $y \succeq x$.[11] I shall call "$x \succeq y$" the general preference relation, and "$x \succ y$" the strict preference relation.

2. If Alf strictly prefers a pizza to a taco, it must be the case that he does *not* strictly prefer a taco to a pizza. The strict preference relation is, then, *asymmetric*: $\neg$ [i.e., not] $(x \succ y \ \& \ y \succ x)$. In contrast, if Alf is indifferent between a pizza and a taco, he is also indifferent between a taco and a pizza; indifference, therefore, is *symmetric*: $(x \sim y)$ if and only if $(y \sim x)$.

3. We also need a rather obvious but uninteresting axiom: Alf must hold that a pizza is at least as good as a . . . pizza! The general preference relation is *reflexive*: $x \succeq x$.

4. More interestingly, Alf's preferences must be transitive. If Alf prefers a pizza (x) to a taco (y), and a taco (y) to a cup of yogurt (z), then Alf must prefer a pizza (x) to a cup of yogurt (z). Also, if Alf is indifferent between a pizza (x) and a taco (y), and indifferent between a taco (y) and a cup of

TABLE 2-1 **Three Equivalent Ordinal Utility Functions**

Preference	μ function A	μ function B	μ function C
x	3	10	1000
y	2	5	99
z	1	0	1

yogurt (z) (!), then Alf must be indifferent between a pizza (x) and a cup of yogurt (z). So, more formally, $(x \succeq y)$ & $(y \succeq z) \rightarrow x \succeq z$. (Both strict preference and indifference are transitive.)

We can now define *utility* in terms of preference. Letting μ stand for utility, we can say that $x \succ y \equiv \mu(x) > \mu(y)$ (i.e., "x is strictly preferred to y" is equivalent to "the utility of x is greater than the utility of y"). It is, then, an error to say (as is all-too-often said) that a person prefers x to y *because* x gives him more utility. Utility does not explain the preference: *utility is simply a representation of the preference.* Utility is not something apart from, or additional to, preference satisfaction: it is a numerical function that represents the degree to which a person's preferences are satisfied. Ordinal utility functions map preferences over outcomes on to numbers. If we assume that the most preferred outcome is mapped on to the highest number, then the next preferred is mapped onto a smaller number, the next on to a yet smaller number, and so on. The sizes of the differences, or ratios between the numbers, provide no additional information. A person's preference ranking can generate an infinite number of ordinal utility measures: the strict preferences $x \succ y \succ z$ might be represented by any of the three utility functions in Table 2-1.

It should be clear that it makes no sense to add together different people's ordinal utilities (or even to add a single person's ordinal utilities for different outcomes). All the ordinal utility function tells us is that, for a specific person, a higher-numbered outcome is preferred to a lower-numbered one.

Why Accept the Axioms?

Can we show people that they *should* order outcomes according to the ordinal axioms? Suppose someone challenges the transitivity axiom:

Yes, I can understand what transitivity is. According to transitivity, if I prefer x to y, and I prefer y to z, I must prefer x to z. But in fact that isn't the way my preferences go. I prefer a pizza (x) to a taco (y), and a taco (y) to a cup of yogurt (z), but I just do prefer a cup of yogurt (z) to a pizza (x)! Given any pair of options I can always make a choice. So what's wrong with that?[12]

Before we proceed, I want to point out that this is an extreme case: we assume that the person *simultaneously* asserts all three strict preferences ($x \succ y$, $y \succ z$, $z \succ x$). With actual agents, we would expect them to choose x over y at one point in time, y over z at another, and finally z over x at yet another. In these sorts of sequential choices we can only infer that the person's preferences violate transitivity if we assume that her preferences are *stable*. One possible explanation of her third choice (of z over x) is she has now tired of pizza; in that case she has undergone preference change and we cannot say that her preferences violate transitivity. If her preferences shift back and forth from moment to moment, we could never infer that her ordering violates transitivity. Thus we need either to suppose stable preferences over outcomes or a nice case in which at one moment the person entertains all three preferences.

Many respond to the above challenge by invoking once again the idea of instrumental rationality (Section 1.1), providing an *instrumental* justification for the transitivity axiom. Hence the "money pump" argument. Suppose Betty has the preferences just described. If she prefers a taco to a cup of yogurt, there must be a trade of the following type that she will agree to. Alf tells her that he will give her a taco in return for her cup of yogurt and some quantity of money (say one cent). Since she strictly prefers the taco to the yogurt, there must be some amount of money she will hand over to Alf (along with her yogurt) in exchange for a taco. So she makes the trade. Alf then proposes another trade: in return for another one cent and the taco, he will give her a pizza. Since she strictly prefers the pizza to the taco, there must be some amount of money she will hand over to Alf (along with her taco) in exchange for a pizza. So she makes the trade. So at this point she has traded her cup of yogurt, her taco, and two cents for a pizza. This makes sense, since she prefers pizza. But now Alf makes another offer: in exchange for her pizza and one more cent *he will give her yogurt back*. Since her preferences are not transitive, and so $z \succ x$ (she strictly prefers yogurt to pizza), she will make the trade. Now she is back where she began, with the yogurt, but she has spent three cents—all to get back to her original yogurt. And of course if Alf again offers to trade her a taco for her yogurt plus one more cent, again she will take the trade, and around and around she will go, serving as a money pump, making Alf richer and richer while she ends up where she started. So, it is said, we can see an instrumental or pragmatic justification for the transitivity axiom: agents who reject it could not possibly achieve their goals.

The money pump argument depends on the "more is better than less" axiom of *Homo Economicus* (Section 1.2): more money is better than less. That Betty ends up with less money is, other things equal, a bad outcome. Putting aside any worries that "more is better than less" may not hold for goods without qualification, the main worry is that the "more is better than less" axiom is itself an application of transitivity to amounts of goods. If quantity $2q$ of a good is better than quantity q, and if quantity $3q$ is better than $2q$, "more is better than less" requires that $3q$ is better than q. This, though, is just transitivity applied to quantities of goods. If one *really* questioned transitivity, one would also question whether more is better than less; and if so, then one would not be convinced by the money pump argument. If Betty holds that $q\$ > 3q\$$ the money pump argument won't move her.

This is not to deny that there is something deeply irrational about Betty; agents like her probably would have died out a long time ago. The money pump argument is persuasive in demonstrating to *us* how important transitivity is, but we should not expect it to move Betty. What it really shows is that *we* are deeply committed to transitivity.[13] It does not, though, provide an instrumental justification for transitivity if by that we mean a route to *accepting* transitivity, because only someone already committed to transitivity has access to the instrumental justification.

Rather than trying to provide instrumental or pragmatic justifications for the axioms of ordinal utility, it is better, I think, to see them as constitutive of our conception of a fully rational agent. Failure to recognize relations of transitivity is characteristic of schizophrenics;[14] those disposed to blatantly ignore transitivity are unintelligible to us: we can't understand their pattern of actions as sensible. This is even more obviously the case with the *asymmetry* of strict preference. If someone prefers a pizza to a taco *and* a taco to a pizza, we just do not know what to make of his choices. To say that he would fail to satisfy his preferences, or be unsuccessful in practice, misses the point: we can't even understand what his preferences are. We cannot even make sense of ascribing a preference to an agent who does not conform to the *asymmetry* of strict preference.[15]

Some claim that the axioms of ordinal utility are more demanding than our understanding of a practically rational agent. Completeness seems especially strong and controversial. Completeness requires that for every possible pair of outcomes (x,y), $x \succeq y \succeq y \succeq x$. But suppose the agent never has to choose between x and y; perhaps x and y only occur in the presence of z, and the agent always prefers z to both x and y. Say that x is a pizza with pepperoni, y a pizza with salami, and z a plain cheese pizza; perhaps our plain-cheese-loving pizza eater just has no preference relation between pepperoni and salami pizzas, but this doesn't matter, since she never has to make a choice between them. If we are impressed by such cases we may insist that a rational agent simply be able to have a *choice function* over *options* such that for any set of options (x,y,z), the agent can select the *best* option—that which is preferred to all others (see further Section 5.3). It looks as if our plain-cheese-loving pizza eater has such a choice function even though for her $\neg\,(x \succeq y \vee y \succeq x)$. But unless the agent is able to relate all options, even her ability to choose may break down. If she goes to the Philosophy Department's Christmas party and finds only pepperoni and salami pizzas she will not be able to choose. Because she does not have a complete ordering she cannot say that pepperoni is worse than salami, better than salami, or even that she is indifferent between them. She just cannot relate them at all. For her, the choice between pepperoni and salami pizza is *incommensurable*: should she be confronted with those options she simply has no way to choose between them.[16] It is this that makes her look potentially irrational as a chooser. If we require that a person *always* has a choice function open to her (over all possible sets of options there is always a best choice), then she must conform to completeness.[17]

2.3 CARDINAL UTILITY THEORY

The Axioms

We have seen that an ordinal utility function for a person can be generated if her rankings satisfy completeness, asymmetry of strict preference/symmetry of indifference, reflexivity, and transitivity. But recall Table 2-1: ordinal utility function A, which numerically represents the options $(x, y, z,)$ as $(3, 2, 1)$ is equivalent to ordinal utility function C, which represents them as $(1000, 999, 1)$. We cannot say whether option y is "closer" to x or z: the numbers only represent the ordering of the options. We can get some idea of the *relative preference distances* between the options (roughly, *how much* one thing is preferred to another) by developing *cardinal utilities*, using some version (there are several) of additional axioms. On one accessible view, four further axioms are required. The key to this approach—pioneered by John von Neumann and Oskar Morgenstern—is to assume certain preferences over lotteries (risky outcomes), and then confront an agent with lotteries involving her ordinal outcomes.[18] Her ordinal preferences *over the lotteries* allow us to infer a cardinal scale (or, rather, as we shall see, a set of such scales). This is an incredibly powerful idea: it generates a cardinal utility measure from a series of ordinal preferences.[19]

One version of the axioms goes like this. In addition to the four axioms of ordinal utility we have just examined, we also need:

5. *Continuity.* Alf's preferences must be *continuous*. Suppose Alf has ranked three possibilities: having a pizza, having a taco, and having a cup of yogurt. Now suppose we give Alf a taco (his middle choice). He has the taco, but now we offer him a gamble: he can give up his taco and take a lottery ticket, in which the good prize is his first choice and the booby prize is his third choice (a cup of yogurt). Now we can easily imagine him rejecting many possible lotteries and keeping his taco. For example, suppose I offer him a lottery that gives him a .01 chance of getting a pizza and a .99 chance of getting a cup of yogurt. He probably will say, "thanks, but no thanks; I'll keep my taco." But suppose I offer him the opposite: a lottery that gives him a .99 chance of getting the pizza and only a .01 chance of getting the yogurt. Now we wouldn't be surprised if he gave up his taco for the lottery ticket: after all, he does prefer a pizza to a taco. For Alf's preferences to be continuous, it has to be the case that there is always some lottery in which the chances of getting his first choice and ending up with his third choice are such that he is indifferent between keeping his taco and accepting the lottery ticket. A little more formally, we can say that for all options (x,y,z) where $x \succeq y$ & $y \succeq z$ there must exist some lottery L that gives Alf a probability p of getting x (and so a $1-p$ of getting z) such that he is indifferent between having y and playing L.

41

6. *Better prizes.* Imagine that Alf is now confronted with two lotteries. In each lottery he is certain to end up with one of two prizes. The first lottery, say, is between a pizza and a cup of yogurt. The second lottery is between a taco and a cup of yogurt. Suppose the lotteries have the same probabilities of prizes: in Lottery 1 there is a .6 chance of a pizza and a .4 chance of a cup of the yogurt; in Lottery 2 there is a .6 chance of a taco a .4 chance of the yogurt. To conform to better prizes, Alf must prefer Lottery 1: when we compare the lotteries we see that they offer equal chances of winning the good prize (.6) and they offer equal chances of ending up with the bad prize (.4). Now in these lotteries the bad prize is the same, but in Lottery 1 the first prize is better, since Alf prefers a pizza to a taco. According to this axiom, Alf prefers to play the first lottery. Let us say (again, a little more formally) that if (i) Alf is confronted with lotteries L_1 over (w,x) and L_2 over (y,z); (ii) L_1 and L_2 have the same probability of prizes; (iii) the lotteries each have an equal prize in one position; (iv) they have unequal prizes in the other position; then (v) if L_1 is the lottery with the better prize, then for Alf $L_1 \succ L_2$; if neither lottery has a better prize, then for Alf $L_1 \sim L_2$.[20]

7. *Better chances.* Imagine that Alf is again confronted with two lotteries. In each lottery he is certain to end up with one of two prizes. Both lotteries are between a pizza and a cup of yogurt. In Lottery 1 there is a .7 chance of a pizza and a .3 chance of a cup of the yogurt; in Lottery 2 there is a .6 chance of a pizza and a .4 chance of the yogurt. To conform to better chances, Alf must prefer Lottery 1: the prizes are the same, but Lottery 1 gives him a better chance of his more preferred prize. So (i) if Alf is confronted with a choice between L_1 and L_2, and they have the same prizes, (ii) if L_1 has a better chance of the better prize, then for Alf $L_1 \succ L_2$.

8. *Reduction of compound lotteries.* If the prize of a lottery is another lottery, this can always be reduced to a simple lottery between prizes. This eliminates utility from the thrill of gambling: the only ultimate concern is the prizes.

If Alf meets these conditions, we can convert his ordinal utilities into cardinal utilities, which not only give the ordering of the payoffs but the size of the differences in the payoffs for each (or, more strictly, the ratios of the differences) where the higher the number, the better the outcome.

To grasp the crux of this method of generating cardinal utilities, assume that we have our three options: a pizza (x), a taco (y), and a cup of yogurt (z), where $x > y > z$ and we define the best option (x) as having a utility of 1, and the worst, (z), as 0. The question, then, is where on the scale of $1-0$ we should place y, the taco. If we were dealing simply with ordinal utilities, any number less than 1 and greater than 0 would suffice: but the idea is to get some notion of the amount of "preference distance" between, on the one hand, the taco, and on the other, the pizza and the cup of yogurt. Suppose that Alf is confronted with a lottery which gives him a p chance of getting the pizza and a $1-p$ chance of getting the yogurt. If he wins, he gets his pizza and if he loses he gets the cup of yogurt. Now we give him a binary choice: he can either have y, the taco (for certain), or he can play the lottery. It seems that Alf is very likely to prefer playing the lottery, when it gives a near 1 (perfect) chance of getting the pizza and a minute chance of getting the yogurt, to the certainty of the taco. In that case, he is essentially trading his second choice for the near certainty of his first choice. As p (the probability of winning the lottery) decreases toward zero, we would expect Alf to prefer to keep his taco (the certainty of getting his second choice) to a lottery that gives a tiny chance of a pizza and a very large chance of the booby prize—the cup of yogurt. At some point in between, as I have said, the continuity axiom says there is a value of p for which Alf is indifferent between the lottery $[L(x,z)]$ and y.

Suppose it turns out that he is indifferent between keeping y (his second choice) and playing a lottery that gives him a p of .9 of getting x and .1 chance of getting z. What we infer from this is that it takes a very large chance of getting his first option (.9) to induce Alf give up his second. He must, then, see y (the taco) as pretty good, if he will only play the lottery when he has a very great probability of winning. So we can say that on our scale of 1 (x, the pizza) to 0 (z, the yogurt), y, the taco, is at .9. In contrast, suppose that Alf was indifferent between having the taco for certain and playing a lottery than gave him a small chance (say .1) of getting the pizza and a .9 chance of ending up with the yogurt. From this we can infer that the taco must not be much better than the cup of yogurt, but the pizza must be a lot better: so we now give the taco a score of .1. We thus can generate a measurement in which the ratios between the numbers are significant from purely binary (ordinal) preferences involving lotteries.

I have said that the new cardinal measures tell us something about the "preference distance" between the options, but this interpretation is resisted by some. If we wish to be *extremely* careful, we will restrict ourselves to saying that all these "von Neumann–Morgenstern" utilities tell us are a person's preferences between lotteries or gambles, and so what he will do in certain situations that involve *risk*. That is, situations in which the chooser does not know for certain what outcome-consequences are associated with his action-options, but can assign a specific probability p that a certain action-option α will produce a certain consequence C_1.[21]

Questioning the Axioms

The von Neumann–Morgenstern axioms are especially controversial: there are well-known paradoxes associated with them and they are the object of continued debate. Consider first a simple objection. According to the continuity axiom there always must be some lottery L in which a rational agent is indifferent between certainty of keeping y and playing L, which has x and z as prizes. As R. Duncan Luce and Howard Raiffa acknowledged in their classic book on decision theory, some choices may not be continuous. To use their example: even if we all agree that \$1 > 1¢ > death, not too many people are indifferent between 1¢ and a lottery with chance p of \$1 and a $1 - p$ chance of death.[22]

A more complex objection, in this case to the better prizes axiom, is discussed by James Drier:

> Suppose you have a kitten, which you plan to give away to either Talia or Horace. Taila and Horace both want the kitten very much. Both are deserving, and both would care for the kitten. You are sure that giving the kitten to Taila [x] is at least as good as giving it to Horace [y, so $x \succeq y$]. But you think that would be unfair to Horace. You decide to flip a fair coin: if the coin lands heads, you will give the kitten to Horace, and if it lands tails, you will give the kitten to Talia.[23]

The problem is that you seem to have violated the better prizes axiom, according to which, it will be recalled, if (i) you are confronted with lotteries L_1 and L_2; (ii) L_1 and L_2 have the same probability of prizes; (iii) the lotteries each have an equal prize in one position; (iv) they have unequal prizes in the other position; then

(v) if L_1 is the lottery with the better prize, then $L_1 \succ L_2$ (in the story, $x \succeq y$.) To see the problem, suppose that L_1 has the prizes (x,z) and L_2 has the prizes (y,z), where z is simply a variable for the same outcome. Suppose further that L_1 and L_2 both give a .5 probability of winning z, and so there must be a .5 probability of winning the other prize (either x or y). L_1 and L_2 have equal prizes in the second position, so one's concern is just the first position. Since $x \succeq y$ (it is at least as good to give the kitten to Taila as to Horace), then according the better prizes axiom, $L_1 \succeq L_2$. Now let us substitute for the variable z a particular prize: x (Talia gets the kitten). So now L_1 is a .5 chance of (x,x) [that is, x—that Taila gets the kitten—for certain, since it is the prize in both positions] and L_2 a .5 chance of (y,x) [that is, a .5 chance that Horace will get the kitten and a .5 chance that Talia will]. In the first lottery (heads it's Talia's kitten, tails it's Taila's kitten); in the second lottery (heads it's Horace's kitten, tails it's Talia's). By better prizes, one prefers the first lottery. But this violates one's commitment to justice through a fair lottery; the person concerned with fairness holds that $L_2 \succeq L_1$, so better prizes is violated.

We again confront the deep issue of how to identify the correct description of the outcomes and options (see Section 2.4). Still, I think, however we characterize the outcomes, it looks like a rational person should conform to better prizes in this case. Suppose first that the only relevant differences between the outcomes concern who gets the kitten: all preferences are "who-gets-the-kitten" preferences. Now it looks as if the chooser ought not to violate better prizes by employing the fair lottery. To use the fair lottery to give away the kitten seems irrational if we suppose that *all you care about is who gets the kitten*. Why would you select a mechanism that sometimes gives the kitten to your preferred person and sometimes to the other *if the only thing you had preferences over was who ended up with the kitten?* So here violating better prizes seems objectionable. Assume, though, that you do not simply have preferences over "who-gets-the-kitten" but over "the process by which kittens are distributed." Here you opt for the fair lottery which can distribute to either Talia or Horace. Now the options may be better described as [a] "giving the kitten to the person who would be a better owner" and [b] "giving the kitten in a fair way," and you might hold that $b \succ a$.[24] If we understand the options in that way—that one of the things you have preferences over is the fairness of the process of distribution—the outcomes, and so the value of the action-options (your preferences over them), change and

T A B L E 2-2 The Allais Paradox

	Options	Red Ball (1)	White Ball (89)	Blue Ball (10)
			Payoffs	
Lottery 1	A	1 million dollars	1 million dollars	1 million dollars
	B	zero	1 million dollars	5 million dollars
Lottery 2	C	1 million dollars	zero	1 million dollars
	D	zero	zero	5 million dollars

there is no violation of better prizes. So here, though it is rational to employ the fair lottery, employing it is consistent with better prizes.

The most famous challenge to the axioms of cardinal utility theory was presented by Maurice Allais.[25] Suppose that one is to draw a ball from an urn that has one red ball, eighty-nine white balls, and ten blue ones. Table 2-2 gives two pairs of lotteries.

Intuitively, we can see that according to better prizes and better chances, one's preferences over lotteries are to be determined only by differences in the size of the prize and the chance of getting it; if two lotteries have the same prize configurations and the same chances of winning the prize, then one will have the same preferences in the lotteries. Now in Lottery 1, your preference for option A could not be determined by the white ball, since both options give you the same chance of getting the same prize (an 89% chance of getting one million dollars). Better prizes and better chances tell us, when choosing between lotteries, to ignore in each the equal prizes with equal chances, and make our choice on the basis of better prizes and better chances. So if you do choose option A, then it must be the case that, in your estimate, the 10% chance of gaining an extra four million dollars in option B should the blue ball come up does not make up for the 1% chance of getting one million less in option B if the red ball comes up. So (roughly) if you choose A, you essentially prefer a gamble that, out of every eleven times, you get one million each time to a gamble that, out of every eleven times, you get five million ten times and nothing once.

If this is your reasoning, then you must also prefer option C in Lottery 2. Again, your choice cannot be made on the basis of what happens if the white ball comes up, since there are equal prizes with equal chances in both lotteries. Everything turns on the prizes and chances if the red or blue balls come up, but these are exactly the same prizes and chances as they are in Lottery 1. So the axioms commit you to option C. But many people who take option A in Lottery 1 take option D in Lottery 2. In Lottery 2, the idea of getting five million dollars ten out of eleven times and nothing one in eleven times seems like a reasonable bet, but it doesn't seem like a reasonable bet in Lottery A. And that seems to be because in Lottery 1, if one chooses A one is certain of getting a million dollars *no matter what happens*, and people have a hard time turning down the certainty of a million dollars. In contrast, in Lottery 2, there is no certain outcome and one is forced to gamble, and then people do seem to prefer a good chance of getting five million dollars, at the cost of a small chance of getting nothing.

This, though, means that what makes people choose differently in Lotteries 1 and 2 are the prizes concerning the white balls, but we have seen that since in both lotteries the white ball has equal chances of equal prizes, it should not affect one's choice between A and B, or between C and D. The issue, then, is whether people's tendencies to select A and D show that the axioms of cardinal utility are flawed insofar as rational people make choices that violate them, or whether we are often irrational in the way we judge probabilities. A crucial question here is whether rational people only seek to determine how well they might do, or whether rational people also seek to avoid regret.[26] In Lottery 1, if we select B and lose we might have deep regrets—"I had a million for sure and now I have nothing!"; but in Lottery 2 everything is a matter of chance, so we have little cause to regret our choice (we made a good bet and just had bad luck). As I see it, from the Allais Paradox we should not conclude either (a) that the axioms of cardinal utility fail to adequately capture our understanding of rational choice or (b) that those who choose A in Lottery 1 and D in Lottery 2 are irrational. Rather, it looks like people's utility functions—their rankings over outcomes—are often far more complicated than the monetary bets would indicate: one lottery leaves a person with the possibility of regrets and the other does not. As I will argue later in this chapter (Section 2.4), one's utility function can depend on the menu of options one faced, not just on the option one chose.

Clearly there are good questions that can be raised about cardinal utility theory. We can safely conclude that its axioms are far more controversial than the ordinal axioms: it is by no means hard to imagine rational agents who have noncontinuous preferences or who simply prefer to gamble (and therefore violate the reduction of compound lotteries). In general, however, I think philosophers have been rather too skeptical of the axioms: while some are rationally rejectable, they are not implausibly strong. The much-attacked better prizes and better chances axioms are not as vulnerable as is often thought. We also must not lose sight of the fact that the axioms are ways to generate cardinal measures out of ordinal preferences: ordinal *preferences* (meeting the axioms, of course) over outcomes and lotteries are all that are required. This is an especially elegant idea, but the very idea of cardinal utility does not depend on it. We should expect that doing something as neat as deriving the cardinal from the ordinal may invoke some contestable axioms. Although it is sometimes claimed that all uses of cardinal utility measures implicitly rely on the existence of the von Neumann–Morgenstern axioms,[27] in practice economists and game theorists are quite happy to appeal directly to the idea of a cardinal scale on which outcomes can be placed. Indeed, John Pollock has recently developed a computationally realistic model of rational decision making according to which cardinal, not ordinal, utility is fundamental. Pollock argues that a cognitive system that stored its basic values in an ordinal ranking would have to relate so many possible pairs of options that it would be unable to function—essentially such an agent would require an infinite data structure. (Pollock shows that a person who used pairwise comparisons to relate every possible state of the world over which she might choose would have more comparisons than the number of elementary particles in the universe!) Thus, rather than taking ordinal data as basic and trying to show how we might derive cardinal data from it, Pollock argues that real agents store their utility information in cardinal form.[28]

Why Cardinal Measures Are Enticing

Why, a reader might ask, if there is so much dispute about cardinal utility functions, don't we content ourselves with ordinal utility? One reason, of course, is that some of us are not as skeptical about cardinal utility as are others: I have suggested that the criticisms are not as serious challenges as they are often thought to be. But another way to answer the question is to show why—if it could be achieved—cardinal utility is such an appealing idea. That would show us why, at least in the eyes of many, the worries and objections are not enough to make us run back to pure ordinalism! Suppose, then, that we did develop a cardinal measure of a person's utility. What could we do with it that we could not do with simple ordinal utility?

One of the problems we saw with simple ordinal utility was that we could not sensibly add the utility of different people into an overall, aggregate measure of utility. Think back again to Table 2-1: given the very different sets of numbers that represent the same preference structure, it was clear that ordinal utility functions do not lend themselves to addition. To add we need a cardinal measure. Now suppose that in Alf's utility function option y gives him .7 utility and y gives Betty .5: can we now proceed to add these nice cardinal numbers together, and say that the total utility of y is 1.2? Can we say that Alf gets more utility than Betty from y? Not without a *lot* more argument. We have assumed arbitrary highs (1) and lows (0) for each person: there is nothing to say that Alf's score of 1 for his best option identifies the "same utility" as Betty gets from her best option, to which she gives a score of 1. Given that the end points cannot be equated as the same, none of the ratios of distances that we identify in between can be automatically identified. More formally, cardinal utility functions derived through our axioms are only unique up to a linear transformation. If our function is U then any function U', where $U' = aU+b$ (where a is a positive real number and b is any real number), gives exactly the same information about ratios of differences between the options, and so serves equally well to describe a person's preferences.[29] Because of this, summing the utilities identified by one of the functions is not meaningful without an independent account providing a rationale of how they should be combined and at what ratios. There is no reason to suppose that Alf's .5 = Betty's .5; one might have an interpersonal measure that equates Alf's .5 with Betty's .75. Ken Binmore insists that "the problem isn't at all that making interpersonal comparisons is impossible. On the contrary, there are an infinite number of ways this can be done."[30] This is too strong, for there may be an infinite number of mathematical formulas for doing it but yet none might be justified. Certainly, though, the mere derivation of cardinal utility functions for each person does not tell us whether there is such a plausible function.

So, while cardinal utility might be inviting because some wish to add and compare different people's cardinal utilities, that looks more like a temptation to be avoided than a reason to embrace cardinal utility. What is genuinely inviting about cardinal utility is that it can be employed to perform expected utility calculations. Cardinal utilities have the *expected utility property*. Let us assume that Betty has a cardinal utility scale according to which the following outcomes are scaled: $w = 9$, $x = 8$, $y = 5$, $z = 3$. Suppose further that she is confronted with two action-options (α,β). Option α has two possible consequences (x,y); β has two possible consequences (w,z). We also need to suppose that Betty can assign probabilities to each outcome that would result from her performing the relevant act. Say that the probability of α producing x is .7; so the probability of α producing y must be $(1-.7)$, or .3 (since there is a probability of 1 that if she performs the act either x or y will occur, the probabilities must always sum to 1); similarly, if we assume that the probability of β producing outcome w is .5, the probability of producing z must also be .5. We can now calculate the expected utility of α and β using the formula that the expected utility $(E\mu)$ of an action-option is the expected utility of its outcome multiplied by the probability that the outcome will be produced. Hence $E\mu(\alpha) = .7(8) + .3(5) = 7.1$; $E\mu(\beta) = .5(9) + .5(3) = 6$. Thus because $E\mu(\alpha) > E\mu(\beta)$, then $\alpha > \beta$. Based on her cardinal preferences over outcomes, Betty has been able to generate a preference over action-options even in cases where she is not certain what outcomes will be produced by her action-options. Notice that we can only make sense of expected utility theory by distinguishing a person's preferences over outcomes from her preferences over action-options (Section 2.1).

2.4 IS UTILITY THEORY A FORMALIZATION OF INSTRUMENTAL RATIONALITY?

No, It Isn't

Most see decision theory as an account of instrumental or a goal-oriented reasoning. Those who believe that all reasons are instrumental typically embrace decision theory because they think it is essentially a formalization of their view. Just as an instrumentally rational agent aims to maximize the satisfaction of her goals, it is thought, an agent who corresponds to the axioms of ordinal and cardinal utility theory seeks to maximize the satisfaction of her preferences. And if "goals" and "preferences" are the same thing, decision theory is simply a formal version of instrumental rationality. To be sure, the axioms add constraints on the structure of the preferences, but the core of the model is still seen as instrumental rationality. This, I think, is a serious mistake, albeit a common one.[31] Decision theory allows us to model choice based on one's notion of the overall ordering of outcomes by *whatever criteria one thinks appropriate*. What is required to generate a utility function is that one has some way to determine what is the best outcome, what is the next best outcome, and so on—but "best" need not be that which leads to the highest satisfaction of one's goals. There is no reason whatsoever to suppose that Alf's set of evaluative criteria are all about Alf's *goals*, *welfare*, or *goods* that he wishes to pursue.[32] Although decision theory distinguishes acts from outcomes (or consequences), and holds that the ranking of acts is determined by the ranking of outcomes, we should not confuse this sort of decision-theoretic consequentialism implicit in Figure 2-1 with the theory of instrumental action.[33] As Peter Hammond stresses, anything of normative relevance for choice is part of the consequence domain.[34] One of Alf's preferences over outcomes may be that he performs, rather than omits, act α, say "telling the truth when under oath today." If in his current set of options, one action-option is to tell the truth under oath, he will rank that act more highly than failing to tell the truth. Given this, the action of telling the truth under oath has "high utility"—that is, performing that action will "maximize his utility."[35] If, then, one's ranks outcomes on the basis of moral principles, a person acting on her moral principles can be modeled as maximizing a mathematical cardinal function.[36]

To better see how utility theory and instrumental rationality are distinct, consider the "ultimatum game." In this game, there is a good (say, an amount of money) to be divided between two players: in order for either player to get the money, both players have to agree to the division. In ultimatum games, the players make their moves sequentially. One player is selected by the experimenter to go first (call him the "Proposer"): the Proposer gives an ultimatum of the form: "I get x percent; you get y percent—take it or leave it!" No negotiation is allowed ($x + y$ must not exceed 100%). The second player is the "Disposer": she either accepts or rejects the offer. If she accepts, she gets her y percent, and the Proposer gets his x percent; if she rejects, neither gets anything. Now if we suppose that the players meet only once (they do not think they will ever play the game again), it would seem that the Proposer would propose 99% for himself, and 1% for the other. And it seems that Disposer, if she is instrumentally rational, would take the 1%. After all, as an instrumentally rational agent, she sees that 1% will achieve some of her goals, and 0% will not; so once the 99:1 offer has been made, as an instrumentally rational person it looks as if she must take it (more is, after all, better than less). And, as an instrumentally rational person, Proposer should see that it will better advance his ends to insist on 99%. But in experiments this does not happen: if Disposer is offered 1%, or 10%, or even 20%, it is very likely she will reject. And Proposer tends to demand "only" around 60% or so.[37] Does this mean that people act against their preferences, and so do not maximize their utility? I think not. The best explanation is that the players' utility functions are not simply about getting funds to best advance their goals, but about acting according to some norms of fair play. Gary E. Bolton has shown that, by building into a player's utility function (along with the goal of getting money) a concern for fairness to themselves (i.e., that the player is himself treated fairly), the actions of players in such games can be much better predicted.[38] But acting according to norms of fair play does not seem a goal: it is a principle to which a person wishes to conform.

It is true that some sorts of moral principled action cannot be modeled in terms of a cardinal utility function. One who is an "absolutist" about some principle, and so will never contemplate a lottery between acting on it and her second best option, violates continuity, and so we cannot develop a cardinal utility function for her. An absolutist still can have complete, reflexive, and transitive ordinal preferences (at least, so long as she has only one absolute principle).[39] The important point, though, *is that these sorts of worries cannot show that decision theory is about instrumental reasoning (or is instrumental in any interesting sense)*: they are objections to the lottery axioms and the development of *cardinal* utility. The difference between ordinal and cardinal utility regards the information implied about the relation between the ranked outcomes (not that cardinal utility commits us to instrumentalism but ordinal utility does not). Consequently, these problems with modeling some sorts of principled moral choices may be barriers to developing cardinal measures for the utility of such choices, but this by no means shows that moral choices based on principles or rules cannot be modeled in decision theory because it is inherently instrumental.

The power of decision theory is that modest principles of consistency and transitivity of preference allow us to construct a mathematical representation of a person who consistently chooses higher- over lower-ranked options and has a complete ordering of outcomes; for cardinal representations, we have seen, additional and somewhat more contentious principles are required, but they too are pretty intuitive. This mathematical representation allows us to depict consistent choices for higher- over lower-ranked options as maximizing a utility function. Decision theory then formalizes a person's *all-things-considered considerations* in favor of action-options. It is crucial to stress that decision theory simply does not maintain that anyone *seeks* to maximize utility—that idea is a remnant of utility qua hedonism. A utility function is a formal representation of an ordering of outcomes meeting certain conditions. Acting in a way that maximizes utility models choices that are consistent with this ordering; maximization of utility is not itself a goal.

Should We Distinguish Preferences from Duty?

Amartya Sen dissents from my conception of decision theory: he advises us to distinguish actions that follow from "adhering to a deontological principle" from those that are "actually 'preferred.' "[40] The idea is that a moral obligation (say, to tell the truth) may require one to act in a way that sets back one's goals or welfare. Perhaps one's best friend will be convicted if one tells the truth under oath: his conviction is not an outcome "one prefers." Here Sen is pushing decision theory's notion of "preference" closer to its ordinary meaning of "liking" (see Section 2.1), where one can rationally do what one does not prefer ("I had reason to do it, but I sure did not prefer it.").[41]
Sen writes:

> A person's preferences over *comprehensive* outcomes (including the choice process) have to be distinguished from the conditional preferences over *culmination* outcomes *given* the act of choice. The responsibility associated with choice can sway our ranking of our narrowly-defined outcomes (such as commodity vectors), and choice functions and preference relations may be parametrically influenced by specific features of the *act* of choice (including the *identity* of the chooser, the *menu* over which the choice is made, and the relation of the particular *act* to behavioral social norms that constrain particular actions).[42]

Sen distinguishes the "comprehensive" outcome (which can include the utility of the choice process; for example, choosing in a fair way as in our case of Talia, Horace, and the kitten) from the distinct state of affairs that is produced by a choice, the "cumulative" outcome (who gets the kitten). Sen has in mind cases in which the utility of the states of affairs depends on the fact that one passed up what looked to be a more attractive option. Again, Sen:

> You arrive at a garden party, and can readily identify the most comfortable chair. You would be delighted if an imperious host were to assign you to that chair. However, if the matter is left to your own choice, you may refuse to risk it. You select a "less preferred" chair. Are you still a maximizer? Quite possibly you are, since your preference ranking for choice behavior may well be defined over "comprehensive outcomes," including choice processes (in particular, who does the choosing) as well as outcomes at culmination (the distribution of chairs).
>
> To take another example, you may prefer mangoes to apples, but refuse to pick the last mango from the fruit basket, and yet be very pleased if someone else were to "force" that last mango on you.[43]

Now on the face of it, this sort of chooser seems to act irrationally. Suppose one is confronted with the option {mango, apple}; given one's preference not to take the last mango, one will choose an apple. But now suppose that one is confronted with the set {mango, mango, apple}. Now one will pick a mango. This pattern of choices violates what many take to be two basic axioms of consistent rational choice—the contraction and weak expansion properties. According the *contraction* property, if x is chosen from the entire set S, it must be chosen from all subsets of S in which x is included. Our polite mango refuser violates this by selecting a mango from the set {mango, mango, apple} but an apple from the subset {mango, apple}.[44] Our chooser will also violate the *weak expansion* principle: if an option is chosen from each of two subsets, it must still be chosen when the sets are combined.[45] Suppose our person is confronted with two sets {apple, apple, mango} and {apple, mango}. Because she will not take the last mango, she will chose {apple} from the first set and {apple} from the second. But if we combine the two sets to get {apple, apple, apple, mango, mango} she will choose a mango, thus violating the weak expansion property.[46]

Supposing, as I think is clearly the case, that our "last-mango refuser" is not irrational, and so we want to allow for her preferences in an account of consistent choice, it may look as if we must follow

Sen in developing new axioms of rational choice. Sen seeks axioms that distinguish choices from menu-independent sets (where the contraction and weak expansion principles hold without modification) from choices involving options, like the choice of our mangoes, that are menu-dependent.[47] However, we need to recall our case of Talia, Horace, and the kitten (Section 2.3). Our polite last-mango refuser only violates the principles of consistent choice (contraction and weak expansion) if the choice is always viewed as over enjoyable food items. If Betty is simply picking the most enjoyable fruit, and if Betty chooses a mango when presented with the choice between a mango, an apple, and another apple, it is perplexing indeed if she then chooses an apple when confronted with the choice between a mango and an apple. It looks quite irrelevant that the first time her set included an extra apple (that she didn't want anyway). But, of course, the problem arises just because the relevant description changes (just as it did with our example of Talia, Horace, and the kitten): at one point Betty is choosing simply on the grounds of "Which fruit would I like the best?" and at the other time the relevant description is "Should I choose the one I like the best or be polite, knowing that Alf loves mangoes?" If Betty has reasons according to which, in cases like this, being polite is more important than an enjoyable fruit fest, then she is simply acting on her total set of preferences and there is no inconsistency.

The important point is that decision theory can model choices based on preferences over outcomes, where "preference" does not mean what one likes, but the outcomes that one has reason to choose to bring about. If one wishes to restrict "preference" to what one likes, or what promotes one's welfare, good, or goals, then we must follow Sen in distinguishing two preference orderings—those over "cumulative" and "comprehensive" outcomes. This in itself shows that the mere notion of a cardinal utility function says nothing about whether the maximization of one's utility is the same as the maximization of one's goals or aims (so again we see that utility theory is not a simply a version of instrumental rationality).

The upshot is that, to formally model a purely instrumentally rational economic agent, we must not only embrace the axioms of formal decision theory that we have considered in the last two sections, but we must further constrain the agent's preferences so as to conform to the features of instrumentally rational agents and *Homo Economicus* that we examined in Chapter 1. Decision theory is a theory of rational choice; while decision theory can give us a formal utility function for *Homo Economicus*, it can also give us one for a principled moral agent.

Utility theory, then, is a much broader theory of rational agency than is *Homo Economicus*. The notion of economic rationality that we examined in the first chapter is based on instrumental rationality, more is better than less, decreasing marginal utility, downward sloping demand curves, etc. Though, I argued, it is more general than is often thought (selfishness, much less wealth maximization, is by no means a necessary trait of *Homo Economicus*), it is still a pretty specific conception of rational human action, which constrains the sorts of preferences a rational agent may have. Utility theory can model such preferences (so long as its basic axioms are met), but it can also model preferences that are based on principles of fairness, civility (not taking the last mango), and so on. Moral and political philosophers, then, should not confuse their (in my view justified) doubts that *Homo Economicus* is a general model of rational human action with (in my view unjustified) doubts that utility theory can be of use in their work.

2.5 DOUBTS FROM PSYCHOLOGY ABOUT EXPECTED UTILITY THEORY

Expected utility theory provides a highly formal and developed theory specifying how rational agents choose under conditions of *risk*—that is, where they are not certain about what consequences are produced by their action-options, but can assign probabilities relating each action-option and possible consequences. (If they cannot assign probabilities they are said to operate not under *risk*, but under *uncertainty*, which leads to yet further complications about rational expectations.) We have seen, though, that many people have reservations about the axioms, especially the better prizes and better chances axioms. People often seem to choose in ways inconsistent with their requirements. In the last twenty-five years cognitive psychologists, led by Daniel Kahneman and the late Amos Tversky, apparently have uncovered ways in which normal reasoners systematically violate the requirements of expected utility theory. In this section I briefly review some of their findings and then consider what implications they have for expected utility theory.

Biases and Heuristics

Errors in Probability Judgments   The most basic and obvious problem is that most people are simply bad at making probability judgments:
that is, even people of above-average intelligence do not rank outcomes
in the way that expected utility theory would indicate. Consider:

> You are a fighter pilot who runs the risk of being killed by
> enemy fire. You can be killed in one of two ways: either by
> flak or by burns. You may also wear a jacket that will protect
> you entirely against one hazard, but is useless against the
> other, that is, you may wear a flak jacket or a burn jacket
> but not both. Two-thirds of the casualties result from flak;
> one-third from burns. You can wear either jacket all or part
> of the time. Which jacket do you choose to wear and why?[48]

Even pretty sophisticated reasoners who have taken courses in statistics tend to say "the flak jacket two-thirds of the time, and the burn
jacket one-third of the time." But that will not maximize your
chances of survival. Suppose there are 99 flights, each of which gets
hit by enemy fire (we can ignore the flights that do not get hit).
Assume all pilots wear the flak jacket two-thirds of the time: that is,
for 66 missions. On those 66 missions, two-thirds of the deaths will
be prevented (those from flak) while a third will die. So on those 66
missions, there will be 22 deaths. What about the remaining 33
missions (those for which only burn jackets are worn)? Here one-
third will be saved (11) and two-thirds will die (22). So altogether, the
two-thirds/one-third strategy will yield 22 + 22 deaths, or 44, which
clearly is worse than wearing the flak jacket all the time, which will
result in one-third of 99, or 33, deaths. But people have a strong
tendency to respond to mixed threats with mixed responses, even
though in cases like this a single response is best.

Even highly trained people make these sorts of errors, especially
when they have to calculate probabilities given base rates in the population. Consider a simple problem posed by Richard Nisbett and Lee Ross:

> The present authors have a friend who is a professor. He
> likes to write poetry, is rather shy, and small in stature.
> Which of the following is his field (a) Chinese studies or (b)
> psychology?[49]

Tversky and Kahneman's research indicates that people will over-
whelmingly select (a). The diagnostic information is *representative* of a

TABLE 2-3 Likelihood That One Has a Rare Disease after Testing Positive

	Have disease (10)	Don't have (9,990)
Test +	9.9	99.9
Test –	.1	9,890.1

professor of Chinese studies: people tend to be quite certain that the friend is a Chinese scholar. Yet, if we consider the relative size of the two populations—professors of psychology and professors of Chinese studies—the probability is very much that the person is a psychology professor. To be sure, the diagnostic information (i.e., the specific description of the friend) would justify some small departure from the probabilities given by the base rates, but the evidence indicates that in such situations people tend to wholly ignore base rate information, *even when it is supplied to them.*[50] Tversky and Kahneman conclude that "people's intuitions about random sampling appear to satisfy the law of small numbers, which asserts that the law of large numbers applies to small numbers as well."[51]

This bias can lead to serious errors when people rely solely on probability estimates of the accuracy of medical tests and ignore the base rates of the disease (or characteristic) in the population.[52] Suppose we have a relatively rare disease, say one that occurs at a rate of 1 in 1,000 (or, equivalently, 10 in 10,000). Suppose further that we have a test for the disease which is 99% accurate. We administer it to everyone in a population of 10,000. You test positive. Is it likely you have the disease? No, as Table 2-3 shows.

Of the entire randomly selected population who test positive, there is still only around a one-tenth chance that any one of them has the disease. Many people find this extremely surprising; if you do, then you will have trouble applying expected utility theory.

Another source of error in probability judgments is that "information is weighted in proportion to its vividness." Thus, for instance, concrete or emotionally salient information is more vivid, and hence is apt to play a dominant role in deliberating. Consider Nisbett's tale:

> Let us suppose that you wish to buy a new car and have decided that on the grounds of economy and longevity you want to purchase one of those solid, stalwart, middle-class

Swedish cars—either a Volvo or a Saab. As a prudent and sensible buyer, you go to *Consumer Reports*, which informs you that the consensus of their experts is that the Volvo is mechanically superior, and the consensus of the readership is that the Volvo has a better repair record. Armed with this information, you decide to go and strike a bargain with the Volvo dealer before the week is out. In the interim, however, you go to a cocktail party where you announce this intention to an acquaintance. He reacts with disbelief and alarm. "A Volvo! You've got to be kidding. My brother-in-law had a Volvo. First, that fancy fuel injection computer thing went out. 250 bucks. Next he started having trouble with the rear end. Had to replace it. Then the transmission and the clutch. Finally sold it in three years for junk."[53]

Nisbett acknowledges that this gives you a reason to make a very small adjustment in the repair rates given by *Consumer Reports*; assuming that it wasn't in the original survey, you now have one additional observation. But is it likely to be weighed that lightly? More to the point, would you have the nerve to go out and buy a Volvo? This bit of information is so vivid that it is apt to drive out the bland statistics found in *Consumer Reports*.

Prospect Theory   One of the von Neumann–Morgenstern axioms (Section 2.3) requires that people do not have preferences over whether to gamble, but only over outcomes. What has been dubbed "prospect theory" casts doubt on whether actual agents meet this condition. People show a marked tendency to accept risks about possible gains, but are much more averse to risk when it comes to possible losses. Consider the following gambles in Table 2-4.[54]

In both cases the expected utility is $5, but 55 of 132 subjects accepted one gamble and rejected the other. Of those that did so, 42 (out of the 55) rejected Gamble 1 but accepted Gamble 2. One difference seems to be that 1 invokes the possibility of loss, while 2 is about ways of gaining (something similar might be going on in the Allais Paradox in Table 2-2; given that people are sure to walk away with a million in option A, they may feel they might lose *their* money if the bet turns out badly in option B). People generally appear to put far more value on not losing x than on gaining x. If so, what gambles they take depend not just on the value of the prizes and the probabilities, but on whether the prize involves a loss or a gain.

T A B L E 2-4 An Example of Prospect Theory

1. Would you accept a gamble that offers a 10% chance to win $95 and a 90% chance to lose $5?

2. Would you pay $5 to participate in a lottery that offers a 10% chance to win $100 and a 90% chance to win nothing?

This is especially striking in what is called the "endowment" effect. In one experiment students were given a free coffee mug, and asked whether they wanted to exchange it for a Swiss candy bar of roughly equal market value. About 10% of the students elected to give up the mug for the candy. In another group, the students were given the candy, and were offered the mug in exchange; again, about 10% of the students made the trade. Finally, in a third group no initial distribution was made, and students could choose either a mug or a candy bar; they split roughly equally in their choices.[55] This is striking, and poses a real worry about the whole idea of indifference curve analysis. Recall that indifference curves chart a person's preferences between bundles of goods; a person is indifferent between any bundles on the same curve. But the endowment effect suggests that one will prefer a mug to a candy bar if one now has the mug but switch to a preference for a candy bar over a mug if one presently has the candy bar. One could see this as a case of crossing indifference curves (which violate the fundamental condition of the asymmetry of strict preference) as Figure 2-2 shows.

If one starts at C (with 1 candy bar), one is only indifferent between it and some quantity of mugs greater than 1; if one starts with a mug, then one is indifferent between it and some quantity of candy bars greater than 1. One strictly prefers a mug to a candy bar and strictly prefers a candy bar to a mug! Such indifference curves are impossible given our understanding of rationality.

Framing Effects The example of the two identical bets in Table 2-4 is also an example of "framing effects": different ways of putting the "same choice" can yield different preferences over options. Consider Table 2-5, which shows another example (the percentages in parentheses are those who select this option).[56]

The pair A,C will result in the same number of lives saved and lost; the pair B, D will also result in the same number of lives saved and lost. A and C are just different descriptions of the same program, yet when

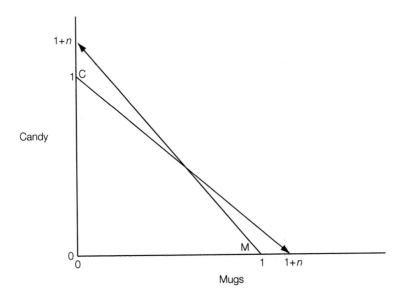

FIGURE 2-2 Crossing Indifference Curves and the Endowment Effect

the program is described in terms of saving lives, as it is in A, 72% of the respondents endorse it; when it is framed in terms of losing lives (as in C), only 22% endorse it. Similarly, although B and D are the same program, only 28% endorse B while 78% choose D. People are apt to make radically different choices depending on the way the choice is "framed" or described—saving lives or letting people die.

If one's choices are "framed" in this way—if different descriptions of the *same option* yield different utility[57]—the choices violate what Kenneth Arrow calls "extensionality":

> The cognitive psychologists refer to the "framing" of questions, the effect of the way they are formulated on the answers. A fundamental element of rationality, so elementary that we hardly notice it, is, in logicians' language, its *extensionality*. The chosen element depends on the opportunity set from which the choice is to be made, independently of how it is described.[58]

That is, the options must be stable in the sense that they describe *outcomes*, and people will have their preferences over action-options determined only by the outcomes associated with each option, not the way in which those outcomes are described.

T A B L E 2-5 An Example of Framing Effects

1. Imagine that the U.S. is preparing for the outbreak of an unusual Asian disease, which is expected to kill 600 people. Two alternative programs to combat the disease have been proposed. Assume that the exact scientific estimates of the consequences of the programs are as follows:

   A. If program A is adopted, 200 people will be saved. (72%)

   B. If program B is adopted, there is a one-third probability that 600 people will be saved and two-thirds probability that no people will be saved. (28%)

2. The same basic story is told with the following options:

   C. If program C is adopted, 400 people will die. (22%)

   D. If program D is adopted, there is a one-third probability that nobody will die and a two-thirds probability that 600 people will die. (78%)

Do These Findings Undermine Expected Utility Theory?

The findings of cognitive psychologists such as Kahneman and Tversky must give pause to any advocate of expected utility theory: they point to well-documented shortcomings in people's ability to calculate probabilities and make choices based on them. However, to evaluate just how much of a challenge they pose, we need to distinguish several different ways in which they might lead us to doubt our account of rationality.

Certainly the often-replicated findings about the systematic errors people make in probability judgments show that expected utility is an idealization that most individuals never fully approach. That, though, should not be a great surprise: to assume rational choice is to assume a certain sort of ideal chooser, which perhaps few agents ever fully achieve. The question is whether the idealization is so far removed from reality as to be useless. If people are really *awful* at probability judgments, then it will not help a lot to try to understand their actions in terms of maximizing expected utility. It is not clear, though, that the findings are as troublesome as they first appear. As Richard Epstein points out, market competition provides a feedback mechanism that helps to correct erroneous judgments.[59] There is also evidence that, while people tend to be bad at calculating probabilities, they are much better at estimating frequencies and drawing the right conclusions about them.[60] Think again of our case of testing for the rare disease in Table 2-3. People seem to have a hard time thinking of the case in terms of probability calculations involving not only the probability that the test is right but also the probability that a random person in the population has the disease. But once put in terms of Table 2-3 the reasoning is clear. So too with the flak jacket example: a case that is puzzling to many when put in terms of probability becomes much easier when redescribed in terms of frequencies. This suggests that people may be considerably better at making the probabilistically correct choices when they are able to conceive of the choice in terms of frequencies.

Endowment effects pose more of a challenge for *Homo Economicus* than for expected utility theory. Economists typically (though not always) suppose that consumers simply have preferences over goods but not preferences whether they move from a certain starting point. *If* our preferences were only over goods, then endowment effects imply the deeply irrational indifference curves of Figure 2-2, where an individual prefers a candy bar to a mug *and* prefers a mug to a candy bar. But, of course, the crux of the issue is that the individuals do not simply have preferences over goods, but prefer to keep what they have to getting something else. Such preferences may be basic to what it means to "own" something; once you see something as your property, you may be reluctant to give it up, just because it is yours. "It ain't much, but it's mine" suggests that its being yours makes it more valuable. Having such preferences may be important to living a happy life; having them is apt to make each more pleased with the goods she ends up with, which she wouldn't trade "even for a lot of money." Again, to the extent that endowment effects are strong, economists may have to weaken their assumption that preferences are only over goods, but that is not a challenge to expected utility theory per se.

We are back to Talia, Horace, and the kitten (Section 2.3). If all preferences are over outcomes characterized independently of process, then there is something odd going on. But if agents have preferences not only over outcomes but also over the processes that produce the outcomes (Was the kitten given away by a fair lottery? Was the mug something of mine that I have to give up to get the candy?), then the oddness disappears. This, finally, leads us to the most fundamental issue: *framing*. Arrow, remember, argues for *extensionality*: preferences over outcomes must be independent of our description of them, and under framing we see that our evaluation of the "same" outcome changes as the description changes. Is this so? Think of our person who refuses to take the last mango. Can we say that she *really* has a choice between eating a mango and an apple, but she responds to different descriptions and so changes her preferences, and that is why her choices violate the contraction and weak expansion properties? I think it is clear that there is no such thing as a set of brute action-options that is independent of the descriptions (intentional states) of the choosers (Section 2.1). Are Betty's true options: a mango or an apple to eat, a soft object or a hard one, a dull-surfaced object or a shiny-surfaced one, the superior piece of fruit to throw at a disliked political speaker, the superior fruit to put on the teacher's desk, or between being rude and being civil? One of the hopes of revealed preference theory, with its behavioral under-pinnings, was that we could describe an unambiguous "choice behav-ior" that had no reference to the chooser's intentional states, and so her descriptions of what she is up to. But as I have argued, this behaviorist project failed: action is inherently intentional. So "framing" cannot simply be understood in terms of different descriptions of the "same" option, for what is the "same" option depends on the relevant descrip-tion.[61] On Sen's view framing explains *inconsistent choices* but, as he points out, our person who refuses to take the last mango does not really seem inconsistent.[62]

To better to see the complexities, suppose that when possible state of the world W (spatiotemporally defined) is described as D Betty gives it μ utility, but when W is redescribed as D' she gives it μ' (where $\mu' > \mu$), even when the truth of D is consistent with the truth of D'. Under description D she sees her action-option as α; under D' she sees her action-option β (where $\beta \succ \alpha$). We cannot conclude that she has been subject to framing, for D' may have alerted her to a relevant description that changes her evaluation of W and her under-standing of the action which brings it about ("it isn't just about choosing fruit, it is also about civility"). To show Betty is in some way irrational we might show that she has manifestly relied on an *irrelevant* consideration in changing her preference, or that she chooses differently when she thinks about the good aspects of the option and when she thinks about its bad features. In this latter case we would expect that her preferences will be inconsistent (some-times $x \succ y$, other times $y \succ x$) depending on what she is thinking about: when she thinks about how many lives will be saved she prefers x to y, but when she thinks about how many lives will be lost she prefers y to x.

A full account of framing, and its relation to a plausible version of Arrow's condition of "extensionality," must then involve a notion of *irrelevant* differences in description or a criterion of choice inconsistency.[63] In our obvious framing case in Table 2-5 it seems that there is something amiss because there is apparently no good reason for drawing a distinction between A and C, or B and D, and yet the respondents do. But if there is a good reason for drawing the distinction, no framing occurs. Think about the cases in Table 2-4 which involve both the endowment effect and "framing" (the case involving buying a lottery ticket and making a bet). Suppose that the respondent supported state lotteries because they were used to fund education: now he might buy a lottery ticket for an expected payoff of $5 (he should be so lucky!) while turning down a bet with a payoff of $5, and have perfectly rational preferences. What this suggests, then, is that we need some account of which distinctions are relevant and which are not or, as John Broome says, what justifies a preference.[64] Underlying or justifying a preference ordering must be a system of principles, goals, ends, or values, and it is this that can justify distinguishing outcomes in terms of their descriptions. If this is so, then preferences over states of affairs cannot be basic. There are an infinite number of descriptions of any one state of affairs.[65] Our conviction that something is amiss in obvious cases of framing shows that we do not think every change in description makes for a different outcome. But, then, which do and which don't? It looks as if the only way to justify making a distinction is to draw on some other evaluative criteria to justify our preferences.

This shows, I think, that utility theory is a way to formalize and model rational action, but is not itself a complete theory of rational action. To employ utility theory presupposes that we know which are the relevant, and which are the irrelevant, features for evaluating states of affairs. Unless we possess such criteria we cannot distinguish framing effects from redescribing the world in such a way that we call attention to an important feature. However, only a value and/or a moral theory can allow us to do that; utility theory does not imply any specific value or moral theory, but presupposes that an agent employs one and so can rank the outcomes. One of the things I hope this chapter has made clear is that in formal utility theory, "utility" is not a sort of value, but simply a representation of one's ordering of options based on one's underlying values, ends, and principles.

SUMMARY

This chapter has explained the basics of utility theory, and I have presented my own views in regard to several controversial questions. In this chapter I have:

- *Distinguished the inherently relational idea of a "preference" from notions such as "tastes" or "likings" with which it is often confused.*

- *Distinguished preferences over outcomes from preferences over action-options.*

- *Explained and defended the axioms of ordinal utility theory, and explained what is meant by an "ordinal utility function."* To have an ordinal utility function a person must have a complete ordering of the feasible options, her strict preferences must be asymmetric, her relations of indifference must be symmetric, and her preferences must be reflexive and transitive. An ordinal utility function is a numerical representation of the ordering of the options.

- *Explained, and generally defended, the axioms of cardinal utility theory.* In order to have a cardinal utility function a person must have preferences not only over outcomes but also over lotteries. Her preferences must be continuous and satisfy the better prizes, better chances, and reduction of compound lotteries axioms. I considered several paradoxes associated with the cardinal utility axioms; I argued that these paradoxes usually are the result of ascribing too simple a utility function to the choosers, or a too-simple description of the choices they are confronting.

- *Argued that (1) utility theory does not maintain that the aim of our preferences is to achieve utility, and that (2) utility theory is not simply a formalization of instrumental rationality.* Point (1) is generally accepted; point (2) is more controversial. Utility theory is a broad theory that can model both instrumental and noninstrumental rational action. In defense of point (2) I examined the way that considerations of principle can be modeled into utility functions. We will return to this important matter in Chapter 4.

- *Explained that cardinal utility has the expected utility property.*

- *Examined some of the main findings of social and cognitive psychologists about the ways that people fall short of the predictions of expected utility theory.* It is my view that these findings generally show that people are imperfectly rational, but they do not undermine the usefulness of utility theory as a way to model human actions. Some of the findings show that people have difficulty with some ways of thinking about probabilities. Others, such as the endowment effect, once again point to the importance of not assuming too simple a view of what people's preferences range over.

■ *Emphasized the importance of "framing."* I have argued that we can only distinguish the framing effect from a relevant difference in the description of an outcome or action by appealing to a value theory, or a moral theory, that identifies the choice-relevant features of states of affairs and actions. Utility theory does not do this, and so it is best understood as a formalization of rational action that presupposes a value or moral theory.

NOTES

1. See R. Duncan Luce and Howard Raiffa, *Games and Decisions*, p. 21. They did acknowledge that this is a very rough interpretation.

2. Louis Kaplow and Steven Shavell, *Fairness versus Welfare*, p. 431.

3. Michael Walzer, "Political Action: The Problem of Dirty Hands," pp. 166–167.

4. See S. I. Benn and G. W. Mortimore, "Technical Models of Rational Choice." pp. 160–161. Amartya Sen has developed an account whereby a rational person may be said to choose her less preferred outcome. See his "Maximization and the Act of Choice."

5. Cass Sunstein writes:

   If we think of a preference as something that lies behind a choice, what is it exactly? How can it be identified or described? Internal mental states are extraordinarily complex, and the constellation of motivations that lies behind a choice in one setting may be quite different from the constellation that produces choice in a different time and place. People's decisions are based on whims, second-order preferences, aspirations, judgments, drives of various kinds, and so forth, each potentially coming to the fore depending on the context.

   All this is too complicated, Sunstein believes: it leads to all the "difficulties that the 'revealed preference' idea was supposed to overcome." Sunstein, *Free Markets and Social Justice*, p. 16. The classic formulations of revealed preference theory are by Paul Samuelson. See, for example, his

"Consumption Theory in Terms of Revealed Preference," and "A Note of the Pure Theory of Consumer Behavior."

6. For a formal account along these lines, see Peter Hammond, "Consequentialist Foundations for Expected Utility."

7. To make things more complicated we need full descriptions such as "the world in which Betty is a tax lawyer at a large firm and eats good food five times a week."

8. I am following Christopher McMahon here: "what there is best reason for an agent to do is determined by the value (from the agent's point of view) of the outcomes correlated with the available actions." *Collective Rationality and Collective Reasoning*, p. 7.

9. Alas, this is an oversimplification. Relevant here is the difference between the utility theory as articulated by L. J. Savage and that of Richard Jeffrey. The view presented in the text sounds more like that of Savage: the utility of the action derives directly from the utility of the states of affairs with which it is correlated. For Jeffrey, the act chosen may itself affect the utility of the resulting state of affairs. It would take us too far afield to go into these matters, though I do intend, by using the general idea of a "correlation" between action and outcome, to allow for conditional probabilities. For a nice summary of the difference between these two views, see Brian Skyrms, *Evolution of the Social Contract*, pp. 47–48. For an example of how the act chosen may itself affect the utility of the resulting state of affairs, see the discussion of the Newcomb problem in Section 4.2.

10. Recall Hume's statement in Section 1.1 about the relation of ends to reason; the proposals we considered that aim to "clean up" preferences are relevant here.

11. What is sometimes called a "strong" ordering has only strict preference relations (no indifference). So for all pairs of options, $x > y \lor y \lor x$.

12. Jean E. Hampton in *The Authority of Reason* takes this type of challenge very seriously. Indeed, she takes seriously the challenge "Why should I worry about being rational?" See also David Schmidtz, *Rational Choice and Moral Agency*, Chapter 1.

13. Benn and Mortimore argue that rationality itself does not require transitivity.

14. Michael Argyle, *The Psychology of Interpersonal Behavior*, 3rd edition, p. 211.

15. Benn and Mortimore, "Technical Models of Rational Choice," p. 163.

16. I discuss incommensurability as incompleteness of preference orderings in my *Contemporary Theories of Liberalism*, Section 2.3.

17. Amartya Sen, *Collective Choice and Social Welfare*, Chapter 1.

18. See John von Neumann and Oskar Morgenstern, *Theory of Games and Economic Behavior*.

19. My aim here is to give an intuitive idea of the axioms. I am primarily drawing on James Dreier, "Decision Theory and Morality," who stresses subjective utility. But see also Hampton, *The Authority of Reason*, Chapter 7; Luce and Raiffa, *Games and Decisions*, pp. 23–31.

20. See Luce and Raiffa, *Games and Decisions*, p. 27.

21. See James D. Morrow, *Game Theory for Political Scientists*, p. 34.

22. Luce and Raiffa, *Games and Decisions*, p. 27.

23. Dreier, "Decision Theory and Morality," p. 173. For other discussions of this problem, see John Broome, "Rationality and the Sure-Thing Principle," p. 90; Peter A. Diamond, "Cardinal Welfare, Individualistic Ethics, and Interpersonal Comparisons of Utility: Comment."

24. This interpretation is considered by both Dreier in "Decision Theory and Morality" and Broome in "Rationality and the Sure-Thing Principle."

25. For helpful discussions, see Daniel M. Hausman and Michael S. McPherson, *Economic Analysis and Moral Philosophy*, pp. 33–35; Broome, "Rationality and the Sure-Thing Principle."

26. See Broome, "Rationality and the Sure-Thing Principle."

27. William Riker, *Liberalism Against Populism*, p. 95.

28. See John Pollock, *Thinking About Acting*, Chapter 2.

29. Hausman and McPherson, *Economic Analysis and Moral Philosophy*, p. 32.

30. See Ken Binmore, *Natural Justice*, p. 121.

31. For an extremely insightful if contentious analysis, see Hampton, *The Authority of Reason*, Chapter 7. David Gauthier makes the error of conceiving of decision theory as instrumental in *Morals by Agreement*, Chapter 2. Morrow presents a typical interpretation: "Put simply, rational behavior means choosing the best means to gain a predetermined set of ends." *Game Theory for Political Scientists*, p. 17.

32. Cf. Morrow, *Game Theory for Political Scientists*, p. 17.

33. As Paul Anand recognizes. *Foundations of Rational Choice Under Risk*, p. 84n.

34. Hammond, "Consequentialist Foundations for Expected Utility," p. 26.

35. S. I. Benn has modeled deontological requirements in this way. See *A Theory of Freedom*, Chapter 3.

36. As John Rawls notes: "A utility function is simply a mathematical representation of households' or economic agents' preferences, assuming these preferences to satisfy certain conditions. From a purely formal point of view, there is nothing to prevent an agent who is a pluralistic intuitionist from having a utility function." *Political Liberalism*, p. 332n. I defend this idea in much more detail in "Reasonable Utility Functions and Playing the Fair Way."

CHAPTER 2

37. See Skyrms, *Evolution of the Social Contract,* Chapter 2.

38. Gary E. Bolton, "A Comparative Model of Bargaining: Theory and Evidence." Bolton treats money and fairness as substitutable. Benn and Mortimore agree that deontic preferences can be cardinalized using the lottery axioms. "Technical Models of Rational Choice," pp. 185–186.

39. See Benn, *A Theory of Freedom,* Chapter 3. If one has two absolutist principles it would seem that one would violate either completeness or asymmetry of strict preference. As Rawls notes, a strict lexicographic preference ordering prevents formulating a cardinal utility function. *Political Liberalism,* p. 332n.

40. Sen, "Maximization and the Act of Choice," p. 191.

41. See Benn and Mortimore, "Technical Models of Rational Choice," pp. 160–161.

42. Sen, "Maximization and the Act of Choice," p. 159.

43. Ibid., 161, footnote omitted.

44. See Anand, *Foundations of Rational Choice Under Risk,* pp. 56–58.

45. I consider these principles in more detail in the context of social choice in Section 5.3. I consider there in just what way this is a "weak" expansion principle.

46. See Sen, *Collective Choice and Social Welfare*; Dennis Mueller, *Public Choice III,* pp. 152–153.

47. Sen's argument is complex. He argues for a notion of maximization that is distinct from optimization, which itself has to drop consistency conditions. I cannot go into these matters here. See "Maximization and the Act of Choice," especially p. 184n.

48. This example is recounted by Richard Epstein in his *Skepticism and Freedom,* p. 229.

49. Richard E. Nisbett and Lee Ross, *Human Inference,* p. 25.

50. See Daniel Kahneman and Amos Tversky, "On the Psychology of Prediction."

51. Tversky and Kahneman, "Belief in the Law of Small Numbers," p. 25.

52. For an application to the problems in law, see Deborah Davis and William C. Follette, "Rethinking the Probative Value of Evidence: Base Rates, Intuitive Profiling, and the 'Postdiction' of Behavior."

53. Quoted in Nisbett and Ross, *Human Inference,* p. 15.

54. Daniel Kahneman and Amos Tversky, "Choices, Values and Frames," p. 15. As Kahneman and Tversky note, the "framing effect" is also at work here, something we shall presently consider.

55. Jack L. Knetsch, "Endowment Effect and Evidence on Nonreversible Indifference Curves," pp. 172–173.

56. Kahneman and Tversky, "Choices, Values and Frames," p. 5.

57. See Amos Tversky and Daniel Kahneman, "Rational Choice and the Framing of Decisions," p. 211.

58. Kenneth J. Arrow, "Risk Perception in Psychology and Economics," p. 6.

59. Epstein, *Skepticism and Freedom,* pp. 228–232.

60. See Steven Pinker, *How the Mind Works,* pp. 347–348.

61. Anand is sensitive to these issues. See his *Foundations of Rational Choice Under Risk,* pp. 93–94.

62. Sen, "Maximization and the Act of Choice," p. 168n.

63. Arrow himself refers to people being moved by "irrelevant" events in his "Risk Perception in Psychology and Economics," p. 7.

64. See Broome, "Rationality and the Sure-Thing Principle."

65. See Stuart Hampshire, *Morality and Conflict,* p. 106.

3

Efficiency

OVERVIEW

We have thus far focused on individual rationality: what is it to be a rational actor, and how can we formally model such an actor? This chapter begins with that concern, but then turns to an analysis of how rational actors interact—the subject of the remainder of the book. The main concern of this chapter is to explore the relation between rational action and the idea of efficiency: the chapter starts with efficiency of the consumption decisions of one person, and then moves to the idea of an efficient exchange: an interaction between two economically rational agents. The important ideas of *Pareto superiority* and *Pareto optimality* are introduced. The second part of the chapter briefly sketches well-known failures of efficiency, involving various notions of "externalities."

3.1 RATIONALITY AND EFFICIENCY

Everyone knows that economics is about efficiency, and most of us have some pro or con attitude about that. Some of us are all for efficiency while others insist that efficiency is a cold economic value that must not come before equity, concern for the needy, or protection of the environment. Thus it is said we need to "trade off" efficiency against other values.[1] But while most of us know whether we are "for it or agin' it," we are often not sure what "it" is. Just what is efficiency? Is it simply one value among others—one that economists but not the rest of us find very attractive—or it is somehow a fundamental idea that we cannot do without, which we ought not to sacrifice for other good things?

Efficiency and Rational Individual Choice

Let us reflect on what we know about our rational "economic man." As a fully rational chooser *Homo Economicus* has a well-formed utility function satisfying the requirements of utility theory we examined in Sections 2.2 and 2.3. His preferences are characterized by decreasing marginal utility and downward sloping demand curves (recall here the idea of decreasing rates of marginal substitution of goods in Section 1.3). Suppose, then, that *Homo Economicus* has a preference for pizza. How much pizza is it rational for *Homo Economicus* to consume? Suppose that the cost of pizza is constant at $\mu(c)$: we must remember that by "cost" we mean the total *opportunity costs* of consuming the pizza—the forgone opportunities to satisfy other preferences (see Section 1.3, point 3). It is important to stress that "cost" does not necessarily mean a monetary payment, or something that you don't like (as in "a cost of taking this course is that I have to take tests"). In the economist's sense, the "cost" of getting your first choice of a pizza is that you had to forgo your second choice of a box of chicken wings: when you have to choose between good things, the cost of your decision is that good thing you didn't choose. This can be specified in terms of *Homo Economicus*'s forgone utility—call this $\mu(c)$. It is the utility you would have received from your second choice. Now consider Alf's decision to consume the first slice of pizza. It satisfies his preference for pizza; given his utility function we can represent this by some utility benefit—call it $\mu(b)$. If $\mu(b) \geq \mu(c)$ (that is, if the utility benefits are greater than, or equal to, the utility costs), then it will be rational for him to purchase the slice of pizza. But should he buy only one slice? Well, we know that since the cost of pizza is constant per unit, the cost of the second piece will be $2[\mu(c)]$. But because of decreasing marginal utility, the benefits of the second piece will be less than twice $\mu(b)$: call this $\mu(b) + [\mu(b) - n]$ (where n is a positive number less than $\mu(b)$). The crucial idea here is that whatever the utility benefits of the first piece [$\mu(b)$], the utility of the second piece will be positive (because more is better than less) but smaller than the utility of the first piece (hence it will be $\mu(b) + [\mu(b) - n]$): that is what is meant by decreasing marginal utility.

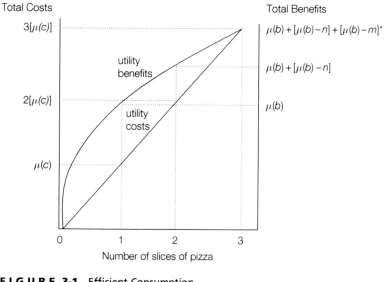

F I G U R E 3-1 Efficient Consumption

*where $\mu(b)>m>n$

It will be rational for Alf to consume two slices if the utility benefits of two slices is greater than, or equal to, the utility costs of two slices— $\mu(b) + [\mu(b)-n] \geq 2[\mu(c)]$. Because the costs are constant but the marginal benefits are decreasing, at some point it will be the case that the additional, or as economists say, "marginal" (utility) benefits that Alf gets from some slice of pizza will be less than the marginal (utility) costs he had to incur in order to get that slice; in that case it would be irrational for *Homo Economicus* to consume that additional slice of pizza because the preferences he then would be satisfying are ranked below the preferences he is forgoing. Figure 3-1 is a graphic representation of a specific example of this simple choice problem. On the left vertical axis we measure *Homo Economicus*'s total utility costs while on the right vertical axis we measure his total utility benefits. In Figure 3-1 it is rational for *Homo Economicus* to purchase three slices of pizza (but no more).

    Homo Economicus will consume up to the point where *marginal benefits equal marginal costs*. This is one definition of efficiency. *Homo Economicus* chooses in this way not because he "values efficiency" (any more than a rational actor seeks to "maximize utility" [Section 2.4])— this decision is simply required by rationality. To choose any other

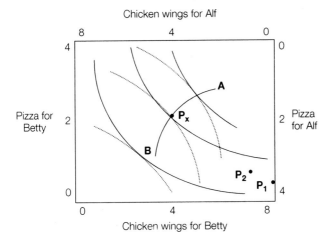

FIGURE 3-3 A Contract Curve

make either Alf or Betty worse off. Point P_x, therefore, is efficient: all the gains from possible exchanges have been exhausted. But point P_x is not unique in this regard: any bargain that occupies a point on which Alf and Betty's indifference curves are tangent is Pareto-optimal. The line A-B (which is called the *contract curve*) represents all such possible efficient bargains—ones that use all the possible gains from trade. Obviously, starting from point P_1, some of the efficient contracts favor Betty while others are better for Alf.[3]

Notice two things. *First*, the assumption of decreasing rates of substitution is crucial in explaining why economically rational people trade with each other. Because they each prefer varied to uniform bundles of goods, if Alf is pizza-rich he will want to exchange with Betty, who is chicken-wing-rich. This is a fundamental point that merits emphasis: *given decreasing rates of marginal substitution (or decreasing marginal utility), everyone can become better off through market exchange without any increase in the total number of goods. Second*, taking part in such trades is simply another example of marginal costs equaling marginal benefits. We have essentially the same story in a different form: here, rather than employing cardinal utility, we are analyzing the problem in terms of ordinal utility (i.e., preferences over bundles of goods). The marginal costs of Alf keeping those last two slices of pizza (his opportunity costs of forgoing acquiring four chicken wings) are greater than the marginal benefits that he gets from those two slices of pizza. Thus, as I have depicted the problem, it is irrational for Alf and Betty to refrain from trading: if they keep their bundles at P_1 they are satisfying lower- over higher-ranked preferences.

We are now in a position to understand the concept of Pareto, or allocative, efficiency.[4] We can say that distribution D_2 is *Pareto-superior* to (more efficient than) D_1 if and only if no person is on a lower indifference curve in D_2 than that person is in D_1, and at least one person is on a higher indifference curve in D_2 than she is in D_1. If despite the possibility of a move to a Pareto-superior distribution we stay in D_1 there is at least one person who could achieve a higher level of preference satisfaction without lowering anyone else's. Thus in Figure 3-3, the distribution identified by P_x is Pareto-superior to the distribution of P_1. As in all the cases we have discussed thus far (but see Section 4.2) there is something irrational about maintaining Pareto-inferior distributions. In addition to being Pareto-superior to both P_1 and P_2, point P_x is also *Pareto-optimal* just because there is no alternative distribution which is Pareto-superior to it. That is, if Alf and Betty have arrived at P_x, there is no way in which one of them can be raised to a higher indifference curve without the other moving to a lower curve.

Is the Pareto Criterion a Moral Ideal?

Paretian Welfarism The Pareto criterion is often understood not simply as a requirement of *rationality* qua efficiency, but as a standard by which we can judge the *moral* desirability of a distribution or, in general, a social state.[5] To many it seems clear that distribution D_2 is morally better than D_1 if (and only if) some person's welfare is "higher" in D_2 and no one's is lower than it was in D_1. Especially in politics, it is thought, what is good for people—their welfare— must be the (sole) criterion of a good policy. This view has clear roots in utilitarian moral theory, which identified promoting human happiness as the sole goal of morality and politics. Recall the remark quoted in Section 1.1 from Nassau William Senior, a leading political economist of the nineteenth century; economics, he said, could assume that everyone seeks wealth because "wealth and happiness are very seldom opposed." The ultimate aim clearly human happiness even if the proximate aim of economics was the growth of wealth. Now contemporary *welfare economics* typically understands a person's "welfare" to be measured by her utility function. If the utility of Betty is μ in distribution D_1 and $\mu+n$ in D_2, then it is said her welfare is higher in D_2 than in D_1, and D_2 is a better distribution than D_1. Here, however, things get complicated. The early utilitarians such as Jeremy Bentham and his followers believed that "utility" (pleasure) was a cardinal measure (it could be measured along a metric) and that, when contemplating a move from D_1 to D_2 we could sensibly add the utility Alf received from the move from D_1 to D_2, to the utility Betty received, and then subtract the loss of utility to Charlie (who, let us say, was better off in D_1). Having done our sums, we could then decide whether, overall, the move from D_1 to D_2 increases overall aggregate utility. But we have seen (Section 2.3) that there is no particularly good reason to add von Neumann–Morgenstern cardinal utilities of different people; unless there is a special case for some additive function, it is simply arbitrary to sum up cardinal utilities. The contemporary welfarist seems to have a problem: how to compare social states without interpersonal comparisons of utilities?

The Pareto criterion seems to offer a way out of this problem: if no one is worse off in D_2 than she was in D_1, and at least one person is better off in D_2 than he was in D_1, then D_2 is Pareto-superior to D_1. And since the welfare economist has identified a person's welfare with her utility, it looks as if we can say that D_2 does better from the perspective of human welfare. Now it is often thought that this cannot be a very useful criterion of "moral betterness": it only yields a judgment that D_2 is better than D_1 if *no one* is worse off in D_2. But how often is it the case that no one is made worse off? On the Pareto test, if in D_2 one million people are made better off than they were in D_1, but one person is worse off, we cannot say that D_2 is Pareto-superior to D_1. Is there ever, we might well wonder, a Pareto-superior move to be made? We are now in a position to see the economist's deep attraction to market transactions. Under certain idealizing conditions (e.g., full information, no third-party effects), each market transaction moves us to a Pareto-superior distribution. When people trade, they prefer what the other person has to what they offer to give up, and so we move to a Pareto-superior distribution. As long as we have not exhausted the possibilities for exchange—as long as there are trades that people want to make— we have not exhausted the possibilities for Pareto-superior moves.

Although market transactions are often moves to Pareto-superior outcomes, it is much harder to see how a collective public policy can meet the Pareto test. It is hard to think of any uniform policy that does not disadvantage someone.[6] To avoid this conclusion (i.e., that

79

the Pareto criterion must be violated by uniform public policy) some welfare economists and "Paretian" political philosophers have adopted what is known as the Kaldor-Hicks criterion: *the move from distribution D_1 to D_2 is efficient even when some lose by moving from D_1 to D_2 so as long as those who do gain from the move* could *compensate the losers out of their gains*.[7] To grasp what it means to say that a person *could* be compensated for a loss, consider Alf, who, we are supposing, is the sole person who has been made worse off by the move from D_1 to D_2 (to make the case simple, assume that everyone else is better off in D_2). To say that Alf has been made worse off means that he is on a lower indifference curve in D_2 than he was in D_1. Now imagine that after the move to D_2 the gainers transferred enough of their gains to Alf to raise him back to the indifference curve that he occupied in D_1: this would bring about a new distribution D_3, which is indeed Pareto-superior to D_1 because everyone except Alf is at a higher indifference curve in D_3 than they were in D_1, and Alf is now back on the same indifference curve (as he was in D_1). We can say, then, that D_2 is Kaldor-Hicks Pareto-superior to D_1 if there is a distribution D_3 that (1) could be produced by redistributing the gains made by moving from D_1 to D_2 and (2) D_3 is (in the normal sense) Pareto-superior to D_1. Note the Kaldor-Hicks test says that given (1) and (2) D_2 is Pareto-superior to D_1 *even though no actual compensation has been paid*. Distribution D_3 is that in which compensation actually has been made, but Kaldor-Hicks does not say simply that D_3 is Pareto-superior to D_1; it says that D_2 is Pareto-superior to (more efficient than) D_1 even though some people have actually incurred losses by the move from D_1 to D_2. Because D_2 *could* give rise to D_3, and because D_3 *would* be Pareto-superior to D_1, D_2 is Kaldor-Hicks Pareto-superior to D_1.

To many this seems very odd: the Pareto criterion, which was based on the denial that gains for some can outweigh losses for others, is now employed to justify policies that benefit some at the expense of others. The move from D_1 to D_2 makes some people worse off, yet it is justified as a Pareto-superior move! Kaldor-Hicks looks like a backdoor way of getting interpersonal comparisons of utility loss and gains within a Paretian framework.

Even if we put aside the controversial Kaldor-Hicks interpretation of the Pareto criterion, upon reflection the Pareto test is not as uncontroversial as is often thought.[8] Much of the appeal of the Pareto criterion lies in the question "Who could possibly object to an improvement that makes everyone better off?" Figure 3-4 suggests an answer.

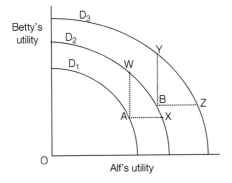

FIGURE 3-4 A Series of Paretian Moves

Suppose we start at point O, and make the Pareto-superior move to point A, which is one possible distribution along D_1—the "Pareto Frontier," the set of possible Pareto improvements from O. Once we are at A, the Pareto improvements to D_2 are limited to those between points W and X; other points on D_2 make either Alf or Betty worse off than in D_1, so are not Pareto improvements. Assume then that at some point distribution D_2 becomes a possibility: Alf and Betty make the Pareto move to point B on D_2. Suppose now that in the future D_3 becomes possible; now the possible Pareto improvements are limited to those falling between Y and Z. We can see that successive applications of the Pareto criterion move distributions along a path that is increasingly beneficial to Alf and of less benefit to Betty. If we had been able to jump to D_3 all at once, everything on it would be a Pareto improvement over O, but once we have made the intermediate moves to A and B, most of D_3 is excluded by the Pareto criterion. Perhaps, then, Betty would have good reason to object to the initial Pareto move to point A. The Pareto principle allows a wide range of moves, and it may matter a lot which of those is actually made, and in what order.

Welfare and Preferences Leaving aside these problems with the Pareto criterion, it also seems doubtful that we should accept the identification of "preference satisfaction" with "welfare." We have seen that preferences need not be about one's own good or self-interest: anytime one ranks an outcome above another, one has a preference (Section 2.1). Recall our last-mango refuser from Section 2.3; her preference is not to take the last mango, though, as Sen notes, she would like that mango and would welcome someone thrusting the mango on her. In that case it seems doubtful that we should say that her welfare is enhanced by satisfying her preference not to take the last mango, since her "civility" preference instructs her not to do what would be good for her. Those who identify "welfare" with "preference satisfaction" often simply seem driven to stipulating that in this case one's welfare *must* be advanced because one is getting what one "prefers." Here, I think, is a perfect example of the way that the ambiguity between the technical and ordinary senses of "prefer" (Section 2.1) leads to serious confusions.

Preferences regarding others also pose problems for Paretian welfarism. Suppose Alf is a prude who prefers that others do not read a somewhat racy book such as *Lady Chatterley's Lover*. It seems that according to Paretian welfarism Betty's decision to read the book cannot be approved of by the Pareto principle, since she is making Alf "worse off" when she reads the book: her reading the book (which we might normally think she has a right to do) moves him to a lower indifference curve. The way in which the Pareto principle can conflict with an individual's rights to decide what she is going to do has been analyzed by Amartya Sen.[9] Sen conceives of a person having a right as having authority to decide the social preference over at least one pair of alternatives (x,y) such that if a person chooses $x \succ y$ that is the social preference (let us call this social preference xPy); and if the person chooses $y \succ x$ then yPx (i.e., the social preference is y over x). Sen shows that attributing such rights to two persons, and assuming all possible orderings of social states are permissible, the social outcome selected by the rights can conflict with a version of the Pareto principle according to which, if for everyone $x \succ y$, then xPy. That is, if everyone prefers x to y, then the social preference must be x over y. Sen nicely summarizes his argument:

> There is a book (e.g. *Lady Chatterley's Lover*) which may be read by Mr. A ("the prude") or Mr. B ("the lascivious") or by neither. Given other things, these three alternatives define social states, *a*, *b* and *o* respectively. Consider now the following possibility. The prude A most prefers *o* (no one reading it), then *a* ("I'll take the hurt on myself"), and lastly *b* ("Imagine that lascivious lapping it up"). The lascivious [Mr. B] prefers most *a* ("it will give that lilywhite baby a nice shock"), then *b* ("it will be fun"), and last *o* ("what a waste of a good book"). On grounds of individual freedom, since B wants to read the book rather than no one reading it,

b is socially preferred to *o*; note that in *either case* A does not read the book here. Similarly, since A does not want to read it, *o* is socially better than *a*. But *a* is Pareto-superior to *b*, yielding a preference cycle.[10]

So we get *bPo* (by Mr. B's right), *oPa* (by Mr. A's right), and *aPb* (by Pareto, since in both Mr. A's and Mr. B's ordering, $a \succ b$); so we get *bPoPaPb*—an intransitive result. Sen saw this not as a case against rights, but as showing "the unacceptability of the Pareto principle as a universal rule."[11] Sometimes it seems that a commitment to Pareto efficiency can lead us astray. One way to respond to this problem is to exclude some sorts of preferences from consideration: thus we might restrict our welfare Paretianism to self-regarding preferences (preferences over different states of one's own life) and so ignore preferences that other people do rather than not do certain things (or that they not read rather than read certain books). But this certainly does not solve all the problems, for there are problematic sorts of self-regarding preferences. Consider for example the problem of expensive preferences. Suppose I always prefer expensive over cheap goods, but you prefer many cheap goods over many expensive ones. Given these preference structures, Paretian welfarism approves of distributions that raise us both to higher indifference curves—giving me expensive, and you inexpensive, goods. To many this seems unfair.[12]

Fair and Unfair Starting Points   Perhaps the most serious problem for Paretian welfarism is that it is insensitive to the distributions from which we begin. Suppose that all of Alf's and Betty's preferences are over quantities of pizza and chicken wings, but presently Alf has all the pizza and all the chicken wings and Betty has none. According to the Pareto principle, this is an efficient distribution. Since Betty has nothing to trade, there is no way to make her better off without making Alf worse off, so we have achieved Pareto optimality. But this hardly seems a moral reason to embrace the distribution. The heart of the Paretian project is to make people better off, and when no one can be made better off without lowering someone else's utility, the Pareto criterion has nothing more to say—we have achieved "optimality." But from the perspective of advancing human welfare it is hard to conceive of situations where Betty has nothing as "optimal." Plausible versions of Paretian welfarism thus seem committed to some idea of a fair starting point, and *then* can hold that Pareto-approved moves made from the initial fair starting point are moral improvements.

3.2 EFFICIENCY, EXTERNALITIES, AND PUBLIC GOODS

Externalities and Property Rights

Let us change our focus from the efficient *allocation*, to the efficient *production*, of a good. Suppose that you produce pizza: how much pizza is it efficient for you to make? The basic idea has already been explained in our analysis of an efficient consumption decision: you should produce up to the point where your marginal benefits equal your marginal costs. If you stop producing pizza while your marginal benefits are still greater than your marginal costs, it looks irrational insofar as production of an extra pizza yields more preference satisfaction than it costs (remember, our concern is opportunity costs). To produce pizza above and beyond the point where your marginal benefits equal your marginal costs means that your last pizza cost you more (in terms of preference satisfaction) than you received in benefits, which again looks to be an irrational decision. So a rational utility maximizer will produce up to the point where her marginal benefits equal her marginal costs.

The problem is that this need not be the efficient level of production for society if there are *positive or negative externalities*. An externality occurs when some person's consumption or production activity has positive or negative impact on the utility of others (where this impact is not included in the producer's or consumer's cost-benefit calculations).[13] If Alf's activity imposes negative externalities (costs) on Betty, then while as a rational economic agent Alf will engage in it up to the point were *his* marginal benefits equal *his* costs, Alf will not take account of the costs to Betty. But if Alf produces just up to the point where his marginal costs and benefits are equal, and there are additional costs to Betty, it looks as if the total social costs (the costs to Alf and Betty) of Alf's last unit of production exceeded the entire social benefits. This would violate the Pareto criterion: Alf has moved them both to a new distribution (with the extra produced unit of pizza) which benefits Alf at a cost to Betty. A similar analysis applies to external benefits: if my production has benefits to you as well as to me, then if I stop production when my marginal benefits equal my marginal costs, from a social point of view (which includes the benefits and costs to everyone) the good has been underproduced: social marginal benefits still exceed social marginal costs, since my decision has not taken into account the benefits you receive.

Externalities are a chief source of "market failure"—the failure of the market to produce efficient results. Only if Betty *fully internalizes* all the costs and benefits of her activity will she stop at just the point where social marginal benefits equal social marginal costs. So too in a trade: only if Alf and Betty fully internalize the costs and benefits of their trade can we say the trade necessarily moves us to a Pareto-superior state. If there are third-party costs (negative externalities), Alf and Betty might make trades where the social marginal costs exceed the social marginal benefits because they do not take account of the costs to Charlie; if third-party benefits exist, Alf and Betty may not trade even though the social marginal benefits exceed the social marginal costs.

Given this, the market would seem to produce efficient outcomes only if we have a scheme of property rights whereby an economic agent *internalizes all the costs and benefits of his activity*: he obtains the full benefits, and pays the full costs, of his activity. Consider the well-known case of the "tragedy of the commons" such as fisheries.[14] Many fisheries around the world are overfished, resulting in a depletion of stocks. Now it would probably be to the benefit of fisherman Alf to reduce his catch this year to secure a good yield next year *if he could be confident of obtaining all the future benefits of his reduced yield this year*. But he cannot: if Betty and Charlie fish anyway, the stocks will still be depleted. Alf will have paid a cost but will not gain the full benefits of his restraint. Conversely, Betty and Charlie do not pay the full costs of their overfishing, since the costs of depletion are transferred to other fishermen such as Alf. Thus the fisheries are overfished, and the marginal social costs exceed the marginal benefits. A scheme of property rights that internalized all costs and benefits would solve the problem.[15] Of course we have this problem just because property rights over fish in the ocean are difficult to institutionalize (fish tend to swim around a lot).

However, the ideal of a system of property rights that internalizes all benefits and costs is unrealizable unless we restrict what counts as an externality. Think about Sen's case of Mr. Prude's and Mr. Lascivious's preferences about reading *Lady Chatterley's Lover*. If Mr. Lascivious exercises his right and reads the book, there is an externality: Mr. Prude is made worse off, since Mr. Prude prefers that no one reads it to Mr. Lascivious reading it. Mr. Lascivious has negatively impacted the utility function of Mr. Prude. If people have preferences over what others do or don't do, then externalities will be everywhere. Suppose Alf prefers that people shop at Target rather than Wal-Mart; if so, every transaction at Wal-Mart involves a negative externality.

One possible solution to this difficulty might be called the *rights-based solution*, according to which Alf's action has a negative externality on Betty if and only if it violates a right of Betty's. Rights, we might say, protect a certain set of preferences: impinging on *those* preferences constitutes cost or harm to an individual. The rights-based solution is suggested by John Stuart Mill, who was especially concerned that people might be held accountable to others for every cost they impose upon them, including "costs" to others resulting from performing actions that their neighbors simply don't like. Mill argued that such "costs" should be ignored, and people should only be said to impose recognized social costs on others when they set back "certain interests, which ... ought to be considered as rights."[16] Thus, says Mill,

> Encroachment on their rights; infliction on them of any loss or damage not justified by his own rights; falsehood or duplicity in dealing with them; unfair or ungenerous use of advantages over them; even selfish abstinence from defending them against injury—these are fit objects of moral reprobation, and, in grave cases, of moral retribution and punishment.[17]

The idea, then, is that we identify a crucial set of interests (or sets of preferences over certain aspects of our life), and hold that if an action or transaction imposes costs on other parties in terms of *these preferences*, the action or transaction has a social cost (i.e., rights have been infringed). That the action involves a social cost does not show that it should be prohibited, since the social benefits may still outweigh the costs.[18]

This results in a moralistic conception of efficiency: we must first know which subsets of a person's preferences are protected by his rights before we can know what constitutes an efficient level of any activity. If, as Mill emphatically argued, no one has a right that others don't read (rather than read) books one finds offensive, Mr. Prude incurs no cost when Mr. Lascivious reads *Lady Chatterley's Lover*—there is no externality because no right was violated. There are, though, real worries about this moralistic view. For one, it does not make sense of a core argument of most liberal political economists, viz., that we should evaluate systems of property rights in terms of their efficiency-promoting characteristics. If we are to say that private property rights promote efficiency we must be able to first identify what an efficient level of production would be, and then show that private property rights are apt to result in this level. But according to the rights-based solution we must know what our property and other rights are *before* we can identify externalities, and so efficient outcomes. Say that Alf wants to build a tavern on his land and Betty objects. What is the efficient outcome? If Alf has the rights on his side, then the efficient outcome is that he builds it; if Betty has the rights on her side—she has a right not to have her property values lowered by living next to a tavern—then the efficient outcome is that the tavern is not built. If both have rights then we must still somehow weigh up the costs and benefits.

Ronald Coase proposes an analysis that is almost the reverse of the rights-based view: on Coase's view achieving an efficient outcome does not depend on the specific way that the initial rights are assigned.[19] Suppose that we live in a world free of transaction and bargaining costs, and in this world Alf has a factory that produces whatchacallits that generates smoke as a by-product; suppose that Betty has a laundry, and her costs are increased because of the smoke from Alf's factory. Alf's production, then, produces a negative externality. So if Alf produces whatchacallits up to the point where his marginal costs equal his marginal benefits, too many whatchacallits will be produced. Suppose that Alf makes $3,000 per year; Betty presently earns $24,000 from her laundry, but she would make $31,000 if Alf's smoke didn't increase her costs. Alf, then, imposes an externality of $7,000. Assuming no laws against pollution, we can still achieve Pareto efficiency: Betty can pay Alf $3,001 to stop producing whatchacallits; he will be better off and so will she, so the move is Pareto-superior.

It is important that Coase's theorem applies regardless of how the property rights are divided between Alf and Betty: a Pareto outcome can be reached whether Alf has a right to pollute or Betty has a right that he not pollute. Suppose that Alf is now making $10,000 producing whatchacallits while Betty's profits remain the same: $24,000 given Alf's pollution and $31,000 without it. Assume that Betty has the right that Alf not pollute, and so can bring suit against him. Now it is Pareto-efficient for Alf to bribe Betty not to bring suit: he can pay her $7,001 to refrain from bringing suit, and both are better off.[20]

According to Coase, then, *in the absence of transaction and bargaining costs, parties to an activity with externalities will agree to some Pareto-efficient allocation of resources regardless of the initial distribution of property rights.* Coase's theorem calls into question one of the traditional justifications for government regulation. In the absence of a perfect scheme of property rights that internalizes both costs and benefits, it has been widely argued, government is necessary to regulate the "market failure" that results from externalities. But Coase shows that market transactions can solve the problem of externalities and get us to a Pareto-optimal outcome (though the actual costs involved in negotiation, etc., may preclude this).

Public Goods

Related to the question of externalities is the special case of public goods. Public goods are defined in terms of two characteristics. *First,* they are characterized by *nonrival consumption.* Consider clean air. If it is provided at all, it can be provided to Alf without taking any of it away from Betty. Once the good is there, consumers do not compete for it; everyone can freely use it without diminishing the amount left for others. *Second,* we cannot control the flow of benefits from public goods: they are *nonexcludable.* If a public good is provided, it is provided for all to use. If we clean the air, everyone has clean air. We cannot exclude those who have not paid their share. A pure public good is one that perfectly meets these two conditions. In most cases both conditions are not perfectly met; many goods are thus *quasi-public goods.* Defense, law and order, regulation of air pollution, highways, ports, public works, and elementary education are among the goods usually cited as being quasi-public goods, though some economists have disputed the "publicness" of almost every item on this list. The classic textbook example of a public good was typically a lighthouse: a lighthouse warns all ships away from danger—one ship does not "use up" the light (so there is nonrival consumption) and it is not possible to exclude the light from the ships who did not pay for the lighthouse (so nonexcludability is met).

When we look at game theory in the next chapter, we shall explain more formally why public goods tend to be undersupplied, but the crux of the explanation appears (at least at first sight) clear. Even if everyone prefers having the public good to not having it, each of us will receive it for free if someone else pays for it. After all, the benefits are nonexcludable: if anyone gets the good, everyone does. So we typically have an incentive to *free-ride*: each, hoping the other pays, holds back from paying.

Thus the classic public good argument is for state action to fix the market's failure to generate efficient outcomes. In the interests of efficiency, it is often said, government must require everyone to contribute to the production of such goods. While powerful, the argument is not quite as simple as it seems. Three points must be kept in mind.

1. For an adequate public goods argument for state action, it must not only be the case that everyone wants the good, but that in everyone's preference ordering {contributing to secure the good & paying my share} is preferred to {not paying my share & not having the good}. If mandatory taxation to supply the good is to move us to a Pareto-superior condition, it is not enough that everyone wants the good; they must prefer having it *and* paying for it to not having it.

2. It is not the case that markets never supply public goods, or never do so efficiently. Suppose Alf's goat wanders into Betty's garden and eats her veggies, and Betty's dog wanders into Alf's property, scaring his goat so that it does not give milk.[21] A fence would be a public good. Assume that each would benefit by unilaterally building the fence (he/she would be better off building the fence alone than not having one) but, of course, each would prefer that the other build the fence. So each has the following ordering: (1) the other builds, (2) we split the cost, (3) I build, (4) neither builds. In such a case, since each would prefer to pay for the entire good rather than do without it, the public good will be provided (and, we shall see in Section 4.3, one person will pay for the entire good). Provision of public goods do not constitute a market failure until we add further conditions, such as that no one individual's utility function is such that it is rational for him to purchase the entire good at the efficient level,[22] there are a large number of people (so each is tempted to free-ride, or we do not know how many people's cooperation is necessary to secure the good), etc. As the number of individuals involved increases, the need for some sort of formal agreement about allocation of contributions becomes necessary.[23] It is, then, not simply public goods per se, but public goods that require collective action of a large number of agents that are most likely not to be adequately supplied by the market.[24]

3. Whether public goods will be voluntarily supplied, and whether universal contribution is efficient, also depends on the relation between securing the goods and individual contribution. We can distinguish three basic types of relations:

   a. *Constant Returns.* If G is the total amount of the good produced, and G_i is the contribution of any individual i, then $G = G_1 + G_2 + G_3 + \ldots G_n$. Each individual contribution adds to the amount of the public good secured. An example here is picking up after your dog in a public park: each person's contribution helps secure the good of a clean park, where all can walk without fear.

b. *Threshold at the Top.* If G is the total amount of the good produced, and G_i is the contribution of any individual i, then there exists some person k such that $G = \{G_1 + G_2 + G_3 + \ldots G_j\} = \{G_1 + G_2 + G_3 + \ldots G_j + G_k + \ldots G_n\}$. The contribution of individual k and those who follow her add nothing to the amount of public good secured. Suppose that we all support a candidate for office, and she needs 10,000 signatures to get on the ballot. After she has obtained 10,000 valid signatures, additional signatures do her no good (at least from a legal perspective)—they do not help her get on the ballot.

c. *Threshold at the Bottom.* If G is the total amount of the good produced, and G_i is the contribution of any individual i, then there exists some person k such that $\{G_1 + G_2 + G_3 + \ldots G_j\} = 0$, but $\{G_1 + G_2 + G_3 + \ldots G_j + G_k\} > 0$. Until the contribution of individual k is secured, no public good is achieved. Again, think of our candidate: until the 10,000th signature is obtained, no good at all is produced.

We can identify both pure and mixed cases (i.e., cases of public goods that combine these types). We might have, for example, a public good that gives constant returns up to a top threshold, but then no more returns thereafter, or which has a bottom threshold, and constant returns thereafter, and so on. Consider three interesting cases: (i) a simple case of constant returns; (ii) a threshold at the bottom where the k person is also the n, or last person; and (iii) a case of constant returns up to a threshold at the top. Will the good be provided by each person maximizing her own utility, or is some sort of coordination or authority necessary to secure the good?

(i) *A simple case of constant returns.* In the simple case of constant returns each individual contribution helps secure a greater level of the public good. So Alf's action always secures some of the good: he will incur some costs $\mu(c)$, but since he wants the good, he also secures some benefit from his contribution, $\mu(b)$. The problem is that while Alf's $\mu(c)$ is the total costs of his share of producing the good, his benefits $\mu(b)$ are just a small part of the total social benefits, since everyone gains from his contribution (remember, the good is nonexcludable and nonrival). As a rational economic agent Alf stops contributing when his marginal costs equal the marginal benefits *to him*. But this will not adequately take account of the overall social marginal benefits of his contribution, since all others will benefit from the higher level of the good he will provide. This is a classic case where public goods will be underprovided by uncoordinated individual choices.

(ii) *A threshold at the bottom where the k person is also the n, or last person.* In the second and very special case, *everyone's contribution is required if the good is to be secured at all.* An example is a crew of a small boat; unless everyone rows, the boat will not make headway against the strong current. No public good is secured unless everyone contributes—the public good of reaching the destination will not be achieved unless everyone does her job. Here in an interesting case where the public good is apt to be achieved by purely voluntary choices based simply on individual utility maximization, since no individual has an incentive to over- or undercontribute.[25]

(iii) *A case of constant returns up to a threshold at the top.* The third case is interesting because here it is *inefficient* to require everyone to contribute all the time. Suppose at Alf's College there is a lawn between two buildings that are located diagonally across from each other.[26] Everyone would prefer a nice lawn between the two buildings to a shoddy one. But everyone also is inconvenienced by having to walk all the way around the quad (where the walkways are). Each person would prefer {having a nice lawn *and* cutting across diagonally}—the shortest route between the two buildings—to {having a nice lawn *and* always using the walkways}. If everyone cuts across, the lawn will be ruined; but if only 10 out of a 100 people do so, there will be no problem. (Hence the threshold at the top; after the 90th person avoids walking across the lawn, no further public good is produced.) Consider three policies: (a) no one crosses, so we have a beautiful lawn but everyone is inconvenienced; (b) 10 people cross, so we have a beautiful lawn and only 90 people are inconvenienced; (c) everyone crosses 10% of the time. The second and third policies are Pareto improvements on the first. Ten people can be made better off (they can cut across the lawn) without any additional costs to others, or everyone can be made better off 10% of the time: the second and third policies achieve just as much of the public good as the first policy, but at a lower cost. As far as efficiency is concerned, if we are assuming *Homo Economicus* we have no grounds for choosing between the second and third policies (but if we assume that fairness is part of people's utility function, perhaps the third is to be preferred; see Section 2.4). We see here that a public policy based on the pursuit of efficiency does not necessarily seek to eliminate all free-riding (receiving the benefits without paying the costs); it might even (as policy b does) seek to *secure* an optimum level of free-riders (with policy b, 10).

None of this is intended to undermine the basic idea that usually the state should tax everyone to secure public goods. The point is that we should be aware that the necessity and desirability of state action to secure universal contribution is by no means an immediate inference from the mere existence of a public good and the pursuit of efficiency.

SUMMARY

In this chapter I have tried to explain the notion of efficiency and highlight its relation to rationality. This chapter has:

- *Explained why a rational consumer will consume a good up to the point where her marginal benefits equal her marginal costs.* We have also seen that a rational producer should produce up to the point where her marginal benefits equal her marginal costs.

- *Explained why rational consumers will make exchanges that are Pareto improvements.* The Edgeworth Box was explained, and we considered the relation of the contract curve to Pareto-optimal bargains.

- *Explained the idea of Pareto superiority and Pareto optimality.*

- *Considered whether the Pareto principle is suitable as a moral ideal.*

- *Analyzed the notion of an externality, and considered whether the ideal of efficient property rights that internalize all the costs and benefits of activity makes sense.* The problem, we saw, is that anytime another person negatively impacts my utility, and this is not taken into account in her decision, she imposes an externality on me. But if my preferences are about what she should and should not do, she will impose an externality on me simply by living her life as she sees fit. This problem of adequately defining an externality is a major difficulty for application of the Pareto principle.

- *Sketched the Coase theorem.*
- *Considered why public goods tend to be undersupplied by voluntary action, and described some cases where voluntary action will secure them.*

NOTES

1. See Arthur M. Okun, *Equality and Efficiency: The Big Tradeoff.*
2. Named after Francis Edgeworth (1845–1926) who depicted alternative allocations of resources, and possibilities for contracts, in this way.
3. Of course if we bring in endowment effects (Section 2.5), and Alf and Betty have a preference to keep what they already have, then they may not trade. We can now better see why endowment effects worry economists: they go to the very heart of efficiency.
4. Some distinguish allocative from Pareto efficiency; allocative efficiency is said to obtain when marginal benefits equal marginal costs, and this is distinguished from the Pareto criterion. See John C. Winfrey, *Social Issues: The Ethics and Economics of Taxes and Public Programs,* pp. 26–27. There are other concepts of efficiency employed in economics. *X-efficiency* concerns getting maximum outputs for a given level of inputs; *dynamic efficiency* concerns maximizing growth; and *technological efficiency* concerns the use of the best technology. On the different notions of efficiency see Charles Wolf, Jr., *Markets or Governments: Choosing between Imperfect Alternatives,* pp. 126ff.
5. For a careful and useful analysis of these issues, see Alan Buchanan, *Ethics, Efficiency, and the Market,* especially chaps. 1 and 3.
6. See Daniel Hausman and Michael McPherson, *Economic Analysis and Moral Philosophy,* pp. 93ff.
7. For examples of contemporary welfarists who rely on this test, see Richard A. Epstein, *Skepticism and Freedom;* Louis Kaplow and Steven Shavell, *Fairness versus Welfare.* This test is also fundamental to much social cost-benefit analysis.

8. Russell Hardin makes much of the point in this paragraph. See his *Indeterminacy and Society*, pp. 10–11.

9. Amartya Sen, "The Impossibility of a Paretian Liberal." For an extended, and accessible, discussion, see Sen's, "Liberty, Unanimity, and Rights."

10. Sen, "Liberty, Unanimity, and Rights," p. 218.

11. Ibid., p. 235.

12. See here Hausman and McPherson, *Economic Analysis and Moral Philosophy*, pp. 78–79.

13. See Dennis Mueller, *Public Choice III*, p. 25.

14. See Garret Hardin, "The Tragedy of the Commons."

15. See David Schmidtz, *The Limits of Government: An Essay on the Public Goods Argument*.

16. John Stuart Mill, *On Liberty*, Chapter 4, para. 3.

17. Ibid., Chapter 4, para. 14.

18. Ibid., Chapter 5, para. 3.

19. See Ronald Coase, "The Problem of Social Cost." My explication follows Mueller, *Public Choice III*, pp. 27–30.

20. The Coase theorem can be applied to more realistic cases, where people's activities have variable costs—the more they purchase of a good, the higher the externalities. See Mueller, *Public Choice III*, pp. 27ff.

21. I am following ibid., pp. 16ff.

22. Because the purchase of public goods has a positive externality, they will not generally be supplied at the efficient level.

23. But this is not to say that governmental, coercive action is necessary. See David Schmidtz, *The Limits of Government*.

24. Mueller gives a nice overview of the extent to which individual voluntary choices will secure public goods, and how this results in undersupply. *Public Choice III*, pp. 18ff. The discussion that follows draws on this part of Mueller.

25. See ibid., p. 22. But see the analysis of the assurance problem in Section 4.3.

26. See David Lyons, *The Forms and Limits of Utilitarianism*, pp. 69ff, 162ff. I have discussed this case in more detail in my *Social Philosophy*, pp. 182ff.

4

Game Theory

OVERVIEW

In our examination of utility theory in Chapter 2 we focused on a rational agent as one who has preferences over outcomes and a set of fixed action-options, and who can correlate outcomes with action-options; her preferences over outcomes determined her preferences over action-options. In Chapter 3 we began to consider how rational utility maximizers (who also are characterized by the additional features of *Homo Economicus*) interact, and especially how rational economic agents will engage in efficient transactions. But the analysis of rational interaction in Chapter 3 focused on Pareto-superior moves—roughly, cases in which agents' interests converged. I largely ignored the possibility of conflict. We now move to the theory of games—a general theory of what is rational when interacting with other rational agents, and especially when what is best for Betty may not be best for Alf. In this chapter I employ only the general idea of individuals as utility maximizers: the specific, additional features that are required for *Homo Economicus* are not central to this chapter. (Again we see why it is so important to distinguish *Homo Economicus* from rational utility maximizers in general.)

The chapter begins with the simplest sort of game, a "zero-sum" game in which whatever one person wins the other loses. This is a game of *pure conflict*. We then move on to the famous "Prisoner's Dilemma" and other "variable-sum" games—some will be focused on conflict, but we will also look at games in which rational players will cooperate. It is important to realize that although the theory of "games" allows us to model conflict, not all games are competitive: most games are a mixture of cooperation and conflict. The chapter concludes with a brief consideration of repeated games (in which players play a series of games), and evolutionary game theory.

4.1 STRATEGIC RATIONALITY AND ZERO-SUM GAMES

In situations of *strategic rationality* Betty, as a rational utility maximizer, is seeking to best satisfy her preferences, but now what best satisfies her preferences depends on what Alf does, and what best satisfies Alf's preferences depends on what Betty does. Modeling such interactions is known as "game theory".

Throughout we shall assume that (1) the players are rational (in the sense of being utility maximizers); (2) Alf knows that Betty is rational, and Alf knows that Betty knows this (i.e., she knows that he knows that she is rational), and Betty knows the same thing about Alf;[1] and (3) each also knows the payoffs of the other and what options he or she confronts. All of this, we can say, is *common knowledge between* them.

In this section we will focus on very simple games, in which the total gains always equal the total losses, so that the overall gains and losses always sum up to zero. Winnings minus losses equal zero. Games such as poker are obvious examples of *zero-sum* games: the only way to win is to get the money from a fellow player.[2]

Consider a simple cake-cutting game.[3] Suppose Alf and Betty are in a zero-sum game in which Alf cuts the cake, and Betty chooses the first piece, and Alf gets what is left. Suppose further that Alf knows that he can't cut the cake exactly evenly: every time he tries he always makes one piece a little larger than the other. Let us assume that Alf has two options: try to cut the pieces the same size the best he can, or cut one obviously larger. We depict the game in Figure 4-1 in *its extensive form*. The squares represent "choice nodes" of either Alf or Betty; the dots are "terminals nodes" that constitute possible outcomes. The numbers at each terminal node represent Alf's ordinal utility for each outcome (4 = best, 1 = worst); since this is a zero-sum game, *Betty's ordering is precisely the inverse*. Alf's best choice (where he gets 4 units of utility) is Betty's worst (she gets 1), and so on.

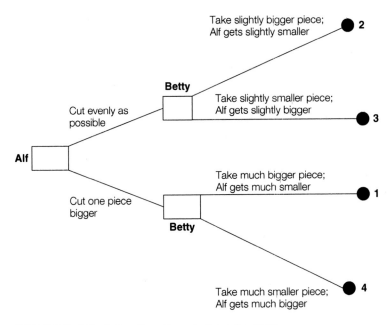

FIGURE 4-1 A Zero-Sum Game in Extensive Form

Remember, we are assuming that Alf and Betty are both rational agents, and each knows this. So Alf knows that Betty will make the best move for herself, so he knows that outcomes (4) and (3) will not occur; the only way to get to those outcomes would be for Betty to select a less rather than a more preferred option. So Alf's only choice is between options (1) and (2); to maximize his share, Alf must cut as evenly as possible, so we end up with (2). This is the solution to the game.

The same game can be put in a *strategic form* as in Figure 4-2, which lists an entire strategy (a complete series of moves) in a game and compares the outcome of every possible complete series of moves by the other player(s).

Again, the numbers represent Alf's ordinal utility; since this is a zero-sum game, Betty's are the reverse. As the cutter, Alf decides which row will be played, Betty chooses which column. Alf knows that whatever row he chooses, he will end up with the least in that row, since Betty will choose the most for her, and this is a zero-sum game. That is, once Alf makes his choice, he knows that of the remaining options, Betty will choose that which is best for her, which

CHAPTER 4

BETTY

	Choose big	Choose small
Cut almost evenly	(2) Betty gets slightly bigger piece; Alf just under half	(3) Betty gets slightly smaller piece; Alf slightly larger
Cut big and small pieces	(1) Betty gets big piece; Alf small one	(4) Alf gets big piece; Betty small one

ALF (label on left)

FIGURE 4-2 A Zero-Sum Game in Strategic Form

means that, of the remaining options, Alf will end up with that which is least attractive to him. Notice then that when he makes his move Alf's aim will be to *maximize the minimum* that Betty can leave him when she makes her choice. Given this Alf must cut as evenly as possible, knowing that Betty will leave him with the slightly smaller piece. Suppose, instead, that Betty makes the first move; in this version of the game she has to announce her choice before Alf even cuts the cake. She knows that, once she has announced her choice, Alf will cut the cake so that she gets the smallest possible slice that her choice permits; she, of course, wants to get the biggest piece possible. Given that Alf will try to counter her move, she will choose the column where his *maximum* (what Alf will try to get) *is minimized*. That means she should announce she will choose the biggest piece once the cake is cut; so once again we see that the outcome is that Alf cuts as evenly as possible and she gets the slightly larger piece.

Consider the following rather more serious game.

In February 1942 General George Churchill Kenny, Commander of the allied Air Forces in the southwest Pacific, was faced with a problem. The Japanese were about to reinforce their army in New Guinea and had a choice of two alternative routes. They could sail either north of New Britain, where the weather was rainy, or south of New Britain, where the weather was generally fair. In any case, the journey would take three days. General Kenny had to decide where to concentrate the bulk of his reconnaissance aircraft. The Japanese wanted their ships to have the least possible exposure to enemy bombers, and, of course, General Kenny wanted the reverse.[4]

98

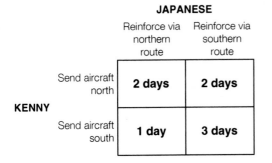

FIGURE 4-3 A Zero-Sum Game with a Weakly Dominated Strategy

Here the Japanese and General Kenny each must make their move without knowing what the other has done, so we can view them as making simultaneous moves, as in Figure 4-3.

The "payoffs" are the number of days that the Japanese fleet will be exposed to reconnaissance: for General Kenny, the higher the better; for the Japanese, the lower the better (remember, in a zero-sum game one player's payoffs are the inverse of the other's). The general will do best if he sends his aircraft along the route the Japanese take; the Japanese do best if they take the opposite route. But neither knows what the other will do. Does the general know what to do? Many game theorists have argued that the general can conclude that the Japanese will not follow *weakly dominated strategies*. To see the reasoning behind this, consider the choice from the Japanese view. If they choose the northern route the worst they can do is two days' exposure; if they choose the southern route they might have up to three days' exposure and can't do any better than two days. So no matter what the general does, it seems to many that the Japanese should choose the northern route. We can say that the southern route is (*weakly*) *dominated* by the northern route: in some cases the northern route is better and it is never worse than the southern. (Strategy A *strongly dominates* strategy B if one always does better by playing A.) Some game theorists have argued that the general would be rational to eliminate the possibility that the Japanese will take this weakly dominated strategy.[5] Given our common knowledge assumption, the suggestion is that since the General knows that the Japanese are rational, they will choose the northern route, so he too must do so. The game has a single *equilibrium* (or Nash equilibrium) *solution:*

Defender → Attacker ↓	Reinforce left	Reinforce center	Reinforce right	**MIN**
Attack left	–3	2	10	–3
Attack center	8	6 ◄—	9	6
Attack right	5	▲	–2	–2
MAX	8	6	10	

F I G U R E 4-4 An Example of the Maximin Solution

north/north. To say that the solution is a *Nash equilibrium* is to say that neither player can do better by unilaterally changing his strategy. What this means is that each player is making his *best move* in response to the move of the other. In this sense we can see strategic rationality at work: rationality is what maximizes your utility given the move of the other player. When each has made his best response to the other's move, an equilibrium results. A "solution" to a game is an equilibrium of this sort. Let us consider one more military game, involving a defender and an attacker.[6] The payoffs are for the attacker (row player); since it is a zero-sum game, the defenders' payoffs are the inverse (lowest is best for them). The game is depicted in Figure 4-4.

The solution to game is center/center. The MIN column indicates the minimum that an attacker can get: this occurs if the defender correctly anticipates the direction of attack. Attack on the center is the *maximin* choice for the attacker: it has the highest minimum. The MAX row is the maximum that the defender has to give up for any given defensive posture: how much the defender might lose for every defensive posture. The *minimax* defense strategy is to defend the center. Center/center is, then, the solution: *minimax equals maximin.* We can also see how center/center is a Nash equilibrium: neither player can do better by a unilateral change of strategy.

In some ways, to be sure, the reasoning behind minimax looks conservative. The more you assume that your opponent knows your move in advance and then offers his best reply, the more minimax is attractive.[7] If one thought one first chose the row, and one's enemy then selected the cell in the row, maximin would make perfect sense.[8] On the other hand, if both parties are really uncertain about what will

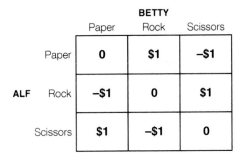

	BETTY		
	Paper	Rock	Scissors
ALF Paper	0	$1	–$1
Rock	–$1	0	$1
Scissors	$1	–$1	0

FIGURE 4-5 A Game That Requires a Mixed Strategy

happen, and cannot assign probabilities, they might select different strategies. If both players gamble in this way we cannot predict the outcome of the game.

John von Neumann (1903–1957) demonstrated that in every zero-sum finite game (a finite number of moves), between two persons, there is always at least one minimax solution: there is always some outcome that is rational for both parties to accept and that is not rational to defect from. However, this outcome need not always be a combination of "pure" strategies. A *pure strategy* is when one always makes the same response to a certain move by the other; a *mixed strategy* is when one may respond to the same move by the other in different ways.

An obvious case where a pure strategy won't do is a game of Paper, Rock, Scissors. (Paper covers [beats] Rock, Rock crushes [beats] Scissors, Scissors cut [beat] Paper; so Paper $\succ$ Rock $\succ$ Scissors $\succ$ Paper.) You should not, of course, always play Rock, because then the other player will respond with Paper to cover it; you shouldn't always play Paper, because the other player will respond with Scissors; and you should not always play Scissors, because it will be crushed by Rock. So you should play a mixed strategy: a one-third chance of either. Let's see why. Suppose we have a game of Paper, Rock, Scissors, as in Figure 4-5. The payoffs are Alf's, since this is a zero-sum game; Betty's are the inverse (if Alf wins a dollar, she loses; if he loses, she wins).

If Alf plays a pure strategy he will lose $1 per game, since Betty will respond with the strategy that always beats it. Suppose Alf plays a mixed strategy of 50% Paper/50% Scissors. Betty will respond with a pure strategy of scissors; she never can lose, and she will win half the time. Alf's expected loss per game is 50¢ (since this is a zero-sum game, Betty's expected gain is 50¢). Suppose Alf plays a mixed strategy of playing each move one third of the time. Betty's best move is the same mixed strategy, giving each an expected gain of 0. One third of the time Alf will win a dollar, one third of the time he will lose, and one third of the time there will be a draw. Thus there is an equilibrium in this game, as many ten-year-olds know. The point of mixed strategies, then, is to neutralize the other's player's choices of strategies.[9]

However, if we are talking about a single-play game, it is not entirely clear what it means to say that a combination of mixed strategies is in equilibrium; clearly over a run of games the mixing strategy is best, but in a simultaneous one-play game, any strategy that is unannounced is as good as any other. Each pure strategy is part of the best mixed strategy in the single case, so any pure strategy might be played. In the one-play case, mixed strategies can, perhaps, be seen as instructions to engage in a certain randomization process rather than a combination of strategies. Note, though, that the solution then does not involve a mix of strategies at all, but a new strategy involving a randomization device.

4.2 THE PRISONER'S DILEMMA

Three Versions of the Prisoner's Dilemma

Most interactions are not zero-sum; depending on what they do, Alf and Betty may find that their gains and losses vary. Thus we usually play variable-sum games. Let us start with the most famous game of all, the Prisoner's Dilemma.[10] The familiar story behind the Prisoner's Dilemma goes like this. Two suspects, Alf and Betty, have been arrested by the police. The police have enough evidence to convict both on a relatively minor charge. If convicted of this charge—and the police can obtain a conviction—each will get two years in prison. The police, however, suspect that Alf and Betty acted together to pull off a bigger crime, but they have inadequate evidence. They make the following offer to Alf (the same offer is made to Betty).

> Alf, turn state's evidence against Betty, and we'll let you go free; we'll demand the maximum penalty for Betty, so she will get 12 years. Of course if Betty confesses too, we're not going to let you both go free: you'll each get 10 years.

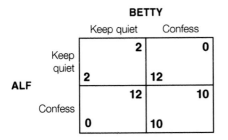

FIGURE 4-6 A Prisoner's Dilemma in Terms of Jail Time

However, if you keep quiet and she confesses, we'll let her go free, and you will be the one to get 12 years. But if neither of you confess to the big crime, we won't have enough evidence to prosecute. We will then proceed with the lesser charge, and you'll get 2 years each.

Figure 4-6 presents their problem in terms of years in jail; Alf's "payoffs" (time in jail) are depicted in the lower left of each cell, Betty's in the upper right.

Alf reasons:

If Betty confesses, and I keep quiet, I'll get 12 years; if Betty confesses and I confess too, I'll get 10 years; so I know one thing: if Betty confesses, I better confess too.

What if Betty keeps quiet? Alf reasons:

If Betty keeps quiet and I keep quiet too, I get 2 years; if Betty keeps quiet and I confess, I go free. So if Betty keeps quiet, I do best by confessing.

But now Alf has shown that confessing is a *dominant strategy*: no matter what Betty does, he does best if he confesses. And Betty will reason in a parallel way; she will conclude that no matter what Alf does, she does best by confessing. So they will both confess, and get 10 years. Hence the (sole) Nash equilibrium outcome (that they both confess) is strongly Pareto-inferior to the nonequilibrium outcome in which they both keep quiet.

This however is simply a story in terms of jail time. We have simply assumed that the players want to stay out of jail. In order to really get the result that the rational thing for them to do is to confess,

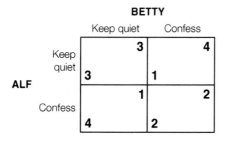

FIGURE 4-7 The Prisoner's Dilemma in Ordinal Utility (4 = most preferred outcome)

we need to say something about their *preferences* over outcomes. We can generate an ordinal utility function for (any) Alf in terms of his preference rankings for the different outcomes if his rankings satisfy the standard axioms (Section 2.2). Employing an ordinal scale where 4 is best and 1 is worst, we thus get Figure 4-7.

Again we see that "confessing" is the *dominant strategy* for both players: no matter what Betty does, Alf does best if he confesses, and no matter what Alf does, Betty does best by confessing. Confess/confess is the sole *Nash equilibrium: it is the best response by each to the move of the other—neither player can do better by unilaterally changing his or her move.* John Nash's great contribution to game theory was to show that all finite competitive games (games in which there are no binding agreements) have at least one such Nash equilibrium (there may be many). Nash's result is a generalization of von Neumann's minimax theorem: minimax solutions are also Nash equilibria.

Given the standard von Neumann–Morgenstern axioms (Section 2.3) we can convert ordinal utilities into cardinal utilities, which not only give the ordering of the payoffs but also the size of the differences in the payoffs for each (or, more strictly, the ratios of the differences). Assuming the higher the number, the better the outcome, Figure 4-8 gives the general cardinal form of the Prisoner's Dilemma while Figure 4-9 gives a specific example of how the numbers might come out.

So in Figure 4-9, Alf and Betty reason themselves into an outcome that, on each of their cardinal scales, gives him/her .1 out of 1, whereas the {keep quiet/keep quiet} outcome would give each .85 out of 1.

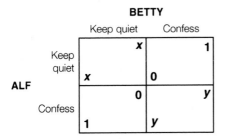

FIGURE 4-8 The General Form of the Prisoner's Dilemma in Cardinal Utility (where 1 > x > y > 0)

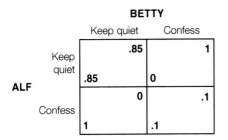

FIGURE 4-9 A Specific Example of the Prisoner's Dilemma in Cardinal Utility

Why the Prisoner's Dilemma So Captivates Philosophers

The Prisoner's Dilemma has captivated moral and political philosophers for at least a generation. It seems to raise questions that go to the heart of our understanding of rationality, morality, and politics.

The Break between Rationality and Efficiency   In the last chapter I argued that rationality and efficiency were intimately related: efficient transactions raise both parties to higher indifference curves, so such transactions are part and parcel of rational utility maximization. *But in the Prisoner's Dilemma what is rational to do leads to a Pareto-inferior result.* Even if Alf and Betty are experts in game theory, the best move that each can make in response to the other is to confess. (In fact, experts   in   game   theory   make   this   response   more   often   than nonexperts.) If one should "cooperate" (i.e., not confess), the other will get 1 out of 1 by confessing, while the cooperator will receive 0 out of 1. So these perfectly rational agents can be certain that by being perfectly rational they will end up with a utility of .1 out of 1, where "less rational" agents—those who both cooperated—would receive .85 out of 1. So tight is the connection between being rational and achieving your goals that many insist that there is a more comprehensive notion of rationality that would direct us to cooperate in the Prisoner's Dilemma. I shall presently take up two such proposals.

Self-Interest, Morality, and Politics   Many believe that the Prisoner's Dilemma offers key insights about the relation of self-interested action to moral and political rules. The Prisoner's Dilemma models a number of real-life situations in which individual efforts to best pursue one's own goals lead to competitive situations that do not benefit anyone. Contemporary philosophers often use the Prisoner's Dilemma to model the relation between the sorts of self-interested agents that Thomas Hobbes (1588–1679) is widely held to analyze in his *Leviathan*.[11] In the absence of morality and law, many argue, almost all social life could be understood as a Prisoner's Dilemma. According to Hobbes, life without common rules followed by everyone would be a state of constant war of each against all others. For Hobbes the basic problem is that humans are fundamentally equal in the crucial sense that anyone can kill anyone else. This equality gives rise to war, because each person is as hopeful as the next of obtaining her goals. But that means if they both want something, neither is apt to give way, since neither considers herself inferior to the other. And thus, Hobbes tells us, they are apt to become enemies. We can depict Hobbes's state of nature as a sort of deadly Prisoner's Dilemma, as in Figure 4-10.

The result is, as Hobbes said, a state of war:

> In such a condition, there is no place for industry; because the fruit thereof is uncertain: and consequently no culture of the earth; no navigation, nor use of the commodities that may be imported by sea; no commodious building; no instruments of moving, and removing, such things as require much force; no knowledge of the face of the earth; no account of time; no arts; no letters; no society; and which is worst of all, continual fear, and the danger of violent death; and the life of man, solitary, poor, nasty, brutish and short.[12]

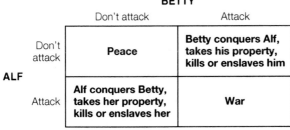

FIGURE 4-10 Hobbes's Deadly Prisoner's Dilemma

Thus far we have been considering apparently rational self-interested individuals: in what Hobbes called a "state of nature" in which there was no law or morality, they would be driven to a condition of war because they have the option to "defect" (i.e., to pursue the noncooperative strategy). Now suppose that each, seeing that this single-minded devotion to his own goals leads to a situation that is worse for everyone, agrees to live by rules of justice—rules that tell us not to attack others, not to steal, and so on. This will not solve the problem of Hobbes's state of nature: we have just landed in a new Prisoner's Dilemma, this time whether we should keep the rules of justice or break them. As long as the others keep the rules, it would be better for me to break them. This problem was seen long before Hobbes. In Plato's *Republic* one of the characters, Glaucon, tells the story of a Gyges, a shepherd who discovers a magical ring that makes him invisible: when he wears it he can go anywhere and do anything with no fear of being known, much less caught and punished. What does he do? Gyges

> contrived to be chosen one of the messengers who were sent to the court; where as soon as he arrived he seduced the queen, and with her help conspired against the king and slew him, and took the kingdom. Suppose now that there were two such magic rings, and the just put on one of them and the unjust the other; no man can be imagined to be of such an iron nature that he would stand fast in justice. No man would keep his hands off what was not his own when he could safely take what he liked out of the market, or go into houses and lie with any one at his pleasure, or kill or release from prison whom he would, and in all respects be like a God among men. Then the actions of the just would be as

the actions of the unjust; they would both come at last to the same point. And this we may truly affirm to be a great proof that a man is just, not willingly or because he thinks that justice is any good to him individually, but of necessity, for wherever any one thinks that he can safely be unjust, there he is unjust. For all men believe in their hearts that injustice is far more profitable to the individual than justice, and he who argues as I have been supposing, will say that they are right. If you could imagine any one obtaining this power of becoming invisible, and never doing any wrong or touching what was another's, he would be thought by the lookers-on to be a most wretched idiot, although they would praise him to one another's faces, and keep up appearances with one another from a fear that they too might suffer injustice.[13]

Unless we are truly worried about being caught and punished, many have argued, the rules of justice are too weak to control people. Hobbes thought so: for him the only solution to Prisoner's Dilemma–type problems is a powerful government that enforces cooperative and just behavior by punishing those who "defect." Caught in a Prisoner's Dilemma, individuals would see that they require "a common power to keep them in awe and to direct their actions to the common benefit."[14] If people are punished for non-cooperative behavior, then we escape the Prisoner's Dilemma: we replace the Prisoner's Dilemma with a different game in which non-cooperation is no longer the dominant strategy.

Note that Hobbes seems to suppose a specific motivation: the people in his state of nature are not merely rational utility maximizers, and not even *Homo Economicus:* they are selfish (see Section 1.3, point 4). The general form of the Prisoner's Dilemma, however, does not require us to assume that the players are selfish: as long as their orderings over the outcomes conform to the orderings in Figure 4-7, they are stuck in a Prisoner's Dilemma. Consider, for example, two ideologically opposed countries, each of which thinks that the other is out to oppress the human race, and so each believes that it is important for the future of humanity that their side is victorious. As Figure 4-11 shows, two such countries can be caught in a Prisoner's Dilemma. If the first choice of each is to free the world from the threat of the other, but each would prefer peace to a war that might kill millions, though even worse than war is to let the other side

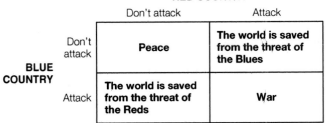

RED COUNTRY

		Don't attack	Attack
BLUE COUNTRY	Don't attack	Peace	The world is saved from the threat of the Blues
	Attack	The world is saved from the threat of the Reds	War

F I G U R E 4-11   A Prisoner's Dilemma between Crusading Countries

ALL OTHERS

		Enough others cooperate so that public good is secured	Not enough others cooperate, so that public good isn't secured
ALF	Contribute	Alf gains the public good, but has to pay part of the cost for it (3)	Alf pays the cost, but since others don't cooperate, he doesn't get the public good (1)
	Doesn't contribute	Alf gets the public good for free (4)	Alf doesn't get the public good, but at least he doesn't pay anything (2)

F I G U R E 4-12   A Multi-Person Prisoner's Dilemma

dominate the world, then our two crusading countries are in a Prisoner's Dilemma.

Public Goods   The Prisoner's Dilemma also provides a nice analysis of why public goods will not be voluntarily provided by individuals, even though everyone wants the good (Section 3.2). Let us introduce the idea of a multi-person Prisoner's Dilemma, in which each person (Alf in this case) is playing against "everyone else," as in Figure 4-12. The numbers represent Alf's ordinal utilities (4 = best).

Defection (not contributing) is the dominant strategy: no matter what the rest of society does, Alf does best by not contributing. And if everyone reasons just as Alf does public good will be undersupplied, even if everyone prefers having The public good to not having it.

Can the Prisoner's Dilemma Be "Solved"? Robert Nozick's "Symbolic Solution"

Because the Prisoner's Dilemma seems to pose a challenge to our basic ideas about rationality and acting morally, many have sought to "solve" the dilemma in the sense that they argue (1) even in a genuine Prisoner's Dilemma (2) rational people could cooperate. Let us first consider in some depth one such proposal along these lines developed by Robert Nozick, certainly one of the most innovative philosophers of his generation. If Nozick thinks that the Prisoner's Dilemma can be "solved," we are sure to learn something.

Nozick's distinctive proposal for "solving" the Prisoner's Dilemma (that is, showing that keeping quiet can be rational for both parties) depends on what he calls "symbolic utility." Nozick holds that act ϕ symbolizes value V if ϕ *stands for* V. The value of V "flows back" through the symbolizing relation to ϕ, giving "symbolic utility" (SU) to ϕ.[15] Thus an evaluation of the rationality of an act must consider not only the utility that results from bringing about preferred outcomes, but also the symbolic utility of undertaking those specific actions. Nozick writes:

> It may be thought that if an action *does* have symbolic utility, then this will show itself *completely* in the utility entries in the matrix for that action (for example, perhaps each of these entries gets raised by a certain fixed amount that stands for the act's symbolic utility), so that there need not be any separate SU factor.[16]

Nozick rejects this option; it is important to see why. Suppose that Alf and Betty not only have utility judgments concerning years in jail, but each gives symbolic utility to acting like a cooperative person, or being a cooperative person. In the Prisoner's Dilemma, says Nozick, each might see keeping quiet not simply as a way of producing the consequence of a certain number of years in jail, but as symbolizing what sort of person one is. Suppose, then, that each values being a cooperative person, but does not value being a sucker (that is, each puts symbolic value on cooperating when the other cooperates, but not on cooperating when the other takes advantage of one). Adding .2 extra units of symbolic utility, we then get Figure 4-13.

In this game {keeping quiet/keeping quiet} is in Nash equilibrium (if one player keeps quiet, the other cannot improve his/her total utility of 1.05 by confessing). However, {confess/confess} is also

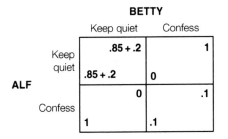

FIGURE 4-13 "Solving" the Prisoner's Dilemma by Transforming It into Another Game

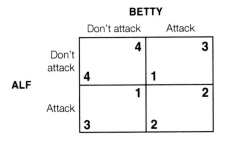

FIGURE 4-14 An Assurance Game

an equilibrium strategy: if the other confesses, one will not do better by changing one's move. Unfortunately, like so many attempts to "solve" the Prisoner's Dilemma, we have done so by converting it into another game—in this case the "Assurance Game." In an Assurance Game, Alf (and so Betty) prefers a cooperative social life to one in which he is victorious over a peaceful Betty (in contrast to the Prisoner's Dilemma, in which his first-ranked option is to is take advantage of peaceful Betty); but if they must have conflict, Alf would prefer to be quickly victorious, the next option is protracted war, and the last is defeat. So the ordinal utilities are for each (high numbers = most preferred): (4) best—peaceful cooperation; (3) victory for me; (2) continued conflict; (1) worst—defeat for me. In the Assurance Game, given in the strategic form in Figure 4-14, each prefers peace to winning, but no one wants to be the sucker.

There is no dominant strategy in this game (there are two Nash equilibria). If Alf knows that Betty will not attack, then he will not attack. But if he thinks that Betty will attack, then he will attack too. This is precisely the same ordering of payoffs that we get in Figure 4-13, derived from Nozick's addition of symbolic utility to a Prisoner's Dilemma. To truly "solve" the Prisoner's Dilemma, we cannot just convert it into a different game.[17] What Nozick needs to do is to appeal to an additional source of utility that cannot be included in the payoffs (and so the payoffs remain those of a Prisoner's Dilemma).

Nozick presents several arguments why symbolic utility cannot be integrated into the payoffs in the game (as it is in Figure 4-14). Let us focus on what might be called the *argument from utilities dependent on options*.

> [T]he symbolic value of an act is not determined solely by *that* act. The act's meaning can depend upon what other acts are available with what payoffs and what acts are also available to the other party or parties. What an act symbolizes is something it symbolizes when done in *that* particular situation, in preference to *those* particular alternatives. . . . An act's symbolic value may depend on the whole decision or game matrix. It is not appropriately represented by some addition or subtraction from utilities of consequences *within* the matrix.[18]

So the idea seems to be that a certain utility may depend not just on the value of a consequentially resulting state of affairs, but the entire game including what other options both players have. Nozick insists that this cannot be captured within, as we might say, any single "cell" but depends on the relation between the cells (the "whole game matrix"). Symbolic utility is outside of any individual box; indeed in a sense it is outside the box as a whole though it is based on the whole box.

Notice that Nozick focuses on the "matrix"—the *strategic representation* of the game. However, as soon as we become concerned about the information available at different points in a game, the strategic form is inappropriate, and we should consider the extensive form of the game. Figure 4-15 provides the extensive form of "Nozick's symbolic solution to the Prisoner's Dilemma" presented in strategic form in Figure 4-13.

Recall that squares indicate decision nodes, dots are terminal nodes that indicate the end of the game or the payoffs of the game (the utilities are given in cardinal numbers, first Alf's, then Betty's, at each terminal node). The advantage of the extensive form is that at

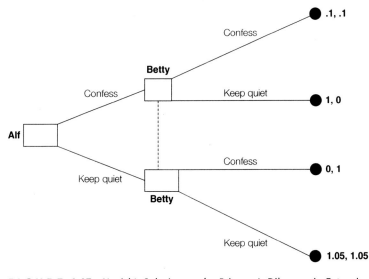

FIGURE 4-15 Nozick's Solution to the Prisoner's Dilemma in Extensive Form

each node we can identify *the information sets available to the players*. We can specify that in games of "perfect recall" information sets include knowledge of the prior moves of both oneself and the other player made at each node. The extensive form builds into games the order of the moves; in Figure 4-15 Alf makes the first move. However, in Prisoner's Dilemma–like games, the moves are simultaneous. This feature is accommodated by the dotted line connecting Betty's decision nodes; she must make her first move without knowing which node she is at (her information set at this node is thus not a singleton [i.e., it does not have one element], as she does not know which of the two nodes she occupies). Consequently, the same game could be displayed with Betty having the first move, and Alf making the second move with his information set incomplete in a similar way. Now when we think outside the box (i.e., the strategic form of the game), in this way we see how the utilities at the terminal nodes can be affected by information about what nodes the players have passed through. Alf's utility of 1.05 (the same holds for Betty) is produced (partly) by his knowledge that at choice points (nodes) where he might have ratted on Betty, he chose not to, and instead took a more

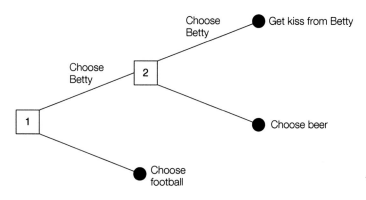

FIGURE 4-16 Alf's Reward

cooperative path, which showed something about himself (i.e., that he was a cooperative person).

In its *strategic form* Nozick's symbolic solution to the Prisoner's Dilemma is identical to the standard Assurance Game. They have the same payoffs. Still, we might think the games *seem* different—certainly Nozick insists they are. Are they? When we analyze the games in their extensive forms, we can indeed distinguish Nozick's solution to the Prisoner's Dilemma from the standard Assurance Game. To see how, compare the following two choice situations confronting Alf:

1. *Alf's Reward*: Betty says to Alf "I don't want you to go the football game this afternoon or go drinking with your friends tonight. Forgo both and you will get a kiss from me this evening."

2. *Alf's Trek to Betty*: Alf wants to see Betty this evening and get a kiss (if he turns up at her door, he *will* get a kiss), but on the way he will confront choices between seeing a football game or continuing on, and then he will confront the choice between going into the bar or continuing on to see Betty. If he goes to the football game he will be too late to drink beer or see Betty; if he goes drinking he will also be too late to see Betty.

Figure 4-16 gives Alf's decision tree for Alf's Reward and Figure 4-17 gives it for Alf's Trek.

These trees look identical; however, they differ in a crucial respect. The tree in Figure 4-17 (Alf's Trek) is *separable*, in the sense

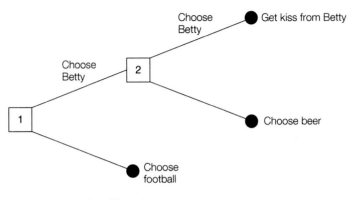

FIGURE 4-17 Alf's Trek

that if we truncate the tree, starting at node 2 rather than 1, this separated part of the tree is the same as it was when it was part of the larger tree.[19] In Figure 4-17 Alf has the exact same choice open to him at node 2, whether we begin the tree at node 1 or node 2: Betty or beer. But not so in Figure 4-16 (Alf's Reward): the payoffs there depend on passing through both nodes, so it makes no sense to truncate the tree.[20] Alf cannot start at node 2. Clearly in *some* decision trees the payoffs are necessarily conditional on confronting a series of choices and so, in such cases, a separable game cannot be started at a node that does not include one of the choices. Trees are not always simply "access routes to prospects."[21] Because in Nozick's solution to the Prisoner's Dilemma the payoffs depend on proceeding through certain nodes, the players' decision trees will have similar difficulties with separability, *since the structure of the decision tree is part of the payoffs.*[22]

Nozick's intuition is right. Just because the payoffs are the same—the games look the same in their strategic form—they may nevertheless be different games in their extensive form. The decision trees for the players may have different properties even though they lead to the exact same utilities. But this by no means justifies Nozick's claim that somehow his solution to the Prisoner's Dilemma depends on the supposition that the utilities gained by the players from their knowledge about what moves have been made cannot be integrated into the payoffs of the terminal nodes (or cannot be included "in the matrix"). All the utilities at stake in a game are part of its payoffs. As we saw in Section 2.4 *a person's utility function includes everything that matters to her.*[23] The difference between a standard Assurance Game and Nozick's symbolic solution to the Prisoner's Dilemma is not, as Nozick would have it, that some payoffs are relevant but are not included in the game, as if there is some extra utility lurking somewhere outside the matrix. But Nozick is right that looking simply at a game in its strategic form does not tell us everything about a game: *we can have two games that have identical payoffs yet the nature of their decision trees can differ.* The difference is not in the payoffs at all, but in the characteristics of the games, that is, whether the payoffs depend on passing through certain nodes. Nozick's "solution" to the Prisoner's Dilemma does not commit the simple trick of straightforwardly turning a Prisoner's Dilemma into a simple Assurance Game; he turns it into a complicated form of the Assurance Game. The solution does indeed depend on more than can be put into the matrix insofar as it also depends on the relation of the decision tree to the payoffs. Thus (as is usual with Nozick) his idea is both interesting and insightful. But his symbolic extensive form game is surely not a Prisoner's Dilemma: the ordering of the payoffs at the terminal nodes is not that which defines a Prisoner's Dilemma (see Figure 4-7). In a game, everything of normative relevance for choice—"even the structure of the decision tree itself"[24]—is part of the consequence domain. The utility at the terminal nodes sums up all the normatively relevant considerations.

An important lesson that emerges from this is that too much attention is paid by philosophers to the strategic representation of games—philosophers almost always consider games in the strategic form only. But this form conveys less information than the extensive form, especially when it is important to the analysis that the individual has been presented with certain options and has refused to take them. To some this may seem a controversial view: in Section 4.3 I will show that textbook analyses of some basic games depend on the fact that the structure of the decision tree is of relevance in determining the utility at the terminal nodes.

Can the Prisoner's Dilemma Be "Solved"? Iterated Prisoner's Dilemmas

Robert Axelrod, a contemporary political scientist, shows how rational individuals may be able to cooperate if they *face a series of Prisoner's Dilemmas.*[25] Many take Axelrod as showing that in some circumstances, "Prisoner's Dilemmas" can be solved. Axelrod argues that if we switch our attention from a single case of the Prisoner's Dilemma, where the players will never meet again, to an indeterminate series of Prisoner's Dilemmas, we can often get around the problems of order without a state.

To see this, assume that although you are in a Prisoner's Dilemma with Alf, both of you know that every day from here on you will play one Prisoner's Dilemma after another. Axelrod has shown, using a computer simulation, that you generally would do best by adopting a very simple strategy: tit-for-tat. According to tit-for-tat, your first move is the cooperative move. But if you're caught out, and Alf defects rather than cooperates, the next time around you will be uncooperative too. In short, except for the first move of the game, you decide whether to cooperate or act aggressively with respect to any person by a simple rule: *I'll do to him this move whatever he did to me the last time we met.* Essentially, a tit-for-tat player says to others "If you defect on me in this game, you will get away with it, but I guarantee that in the next game I will defect, so that we will both be losers. But I am forgiving: if you start cooperating again, I'll begin cooperating again on the move after your cooperative move." Axelrod constructed a computer program specifying a game with hundreds of moves, and a variety of actors employing different strategies. Some always act cooperatively no matter what others do, while some always defect. Each strategy played 200-move games with every other strategy, making for over 100,000 moves: tit-for-tat won.

Again, though, we have "solved" the (one-play) Prisoner's Dilemma by turning it into a different game. Now the payoffs for the first Prisoner's Dilemma game with Alf include probabilities of future beneficial or costly interactions with him. Suppose Alf and Betty play a series of games with each other. It would seem that in the first game they have two concerns: (1) what is my best response to the other in this game? and (2) will my move in this game affect future prospects with this player? The second question shows us that their considerations in deciding their present move are not focused simply on the payoffs in this game. Alf's and Betty's present decisions are also affected by what some have called "the shadow of the future." But this means that they are not playing a straightforward Prisoner's Dilemma at all. This is even clearer if we focus on the last game in the series: here the "shadow of the future" is not relevant, because Alf and Betty know there will be no future games. Suppose Alf and Betty know for certain that this is their last game. In this case they have no expectations about future interactions, so they will truly play this game as a straightforward Prisoner's Dilemma, and so they will each defect. If this is their last game it makes no sense to play tit-for-tat; they must simply give their best response in *this* game: only question (1) is relevant. So they will both defect, the dominant strategy in a one-play Prisoner's Dilemma. But now consider the second to the last game. By the reasoning we have just gone through, they will both know that both will play the last game as a simple Prisoner's Dilemma and so they will both "defect." But that means that in the second to the last game, again the only relevant concern will be (1)—the best response in *this game*, since they know that the other's move in the next game is already set. But that means that the second to the last game should also be played as a simple Prisoner's Dilemma. We can see, though, that everything we have just said about the second to the last game now applies to the third to the last game, and then to the fourth to the last, and then, eventually, to the first. So one should always defect.

This is a more serious problem with iterated Prisoner's Dilemmas than is usually thought.[26] This "backward induction" argument is often taken to be interesting but hardly of crucial importance. But "backward induction" is the typical method for solving a sequential game and is based on the crucial idea of *modular rationality*: at each possible point in the decision tree a rational chooser always takes the best option.[27] When trying to find the solution to a game we start at terminal nodes; we know that if a node is a solution to the game, the last chooser got us to that node by taking the option that maximized his utility.[28] Taking the higher- over the lower-ranked choice is, after all, what rationality is all about. Using this same assumption—that at every point in the tree the chooser took the course that maximized her utility—we can trace back through the tree the series of decisions that would lead to that outcome. Only a path along which, at every point, each chooser took the action that maximized her utility (i.e., acted on her higher- rather than lower-ranked alternative) is consistent with the assumption of modular rationality. A utility maximizer would not choose an action that satisfied lower-ranked rather than higher-ranked preferences. If, then, tit-for-tat is not verifiable by backward induction, it does not seem to be a rational solution to a definite series of Prisoner's Dilemmas *under perfect information and full rationality*. Most advocates of tit-for-tat agree, and stress that tit-for-tat depends on uncertainty about the size of the decision tree (how long the sequence of Prisoner's Dilemmas will go on). So we never are

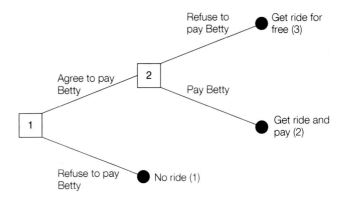

FIGURE 4-18 A Paradox for Modular Rationality

sure when we get to the last game, and so we never know when we are at the terminal nodes; thus, on this view, we cannot engage in the backward induction solution to iterated Prisoner's Dilemmas.

A more radical response to the backward induction argument rejects the idea of modular rationality altogether: on some conceptions of rationality a person may have a rational strategy that gets him to a preferred node even though at some point in his decision tree he will have to choose an action that does not maximize his utility.[29] On these views backward induction will often not find the correct strategy. Consider a simple problem. Alf's car has broken down on a deserted highway and Betty comes along. Alf has no money in his pocket, but offers to pay Betty $10 when he gets back to his apartment. He thus has the decision tree shown in Figure 4-18 (the numbers at the terminal nodes are his ordinal utilities, 3 = best, 1 = worst).

If Betty knows that this is Alf's decision tree, Betty will refuse to give him the ride. She knows that when he gets to node 2 he will take the option at that node that maximizes his utility—he will go for a utility of 3 over a utility of 2. He won't pay. Because of that, she won't give him a ride, and he can only get his worst option. Some have argued that if Alf was a *resolute chooser*, who could *sometimes make a choice that does not maximize utility*, he could end up following a sequence of moves that would give him more utility overall. If Betty knew that at node 2 Alf was such a chooser and *would opt for a utility of 2 rather than a utility of 3* (at that node he would choose a lower-ranked option), then he could get home (his second choice). To most game theorists, however, that sort of plan is irrational as it violates a basic norm of rational games: "subgame perfection." To be "subgame perfect" a series of moves in a game must be such that at each node a player makes the choice that from that point on in the game maximizes his utility.[30]

Is the Prisoner's Dilemma a Newcomb Problem, and If It Is, Does That Help Solve It?

Some have claimed that the Prisoner's Dilemma is a case of another paradox, called the "Newcomb problem."[31] In the Newcomb problem an agent confronts a situation with two boxes: the agent can choose to take the contents of one box or the contents of both. The first box is clear, and so the agent can see that it contains one thousand dollars; the second is opaque—it may contain a million dollars, or it may be empty. So far it is an easy choice—the agent should take both boxes, assuring himself of at least a thousand dollars, plus perhaps the million that might be in the opaque box. This is the *dominant strategy*. However, the agent also knows that *yesterday* an extremely reliable predictor (in some accounts a *perfect* predictor) has put the money in the boxes. She has put a million dollars into the opaque box if and only if she predicts he will choose it alone; if she predicts that he will choose both boxes, she has left the opaque box empty. Now what should the agent do—choose one box or two?

According to Nozick's important analysis,[32] if one employs a simple principle of expected utility the agent will just calculate the utility of each option's possible outcomes, weighted by their likelihood, and then add these up. Since, however, the outcomes are not necessarily probabilistically independent of the action the agent performs (the predictor has put the million dollars in the opaque box if and only if she predicts the agent will choose only it), a more adequate evidentially expected utility principle calculates the expected utility of actions by taking account of the conditional probabilities of the outcomes, given that the agent performs that action. Now, Nozick famously argued, an agent employing an evidentially expected utility principle will reason that given the information about the predictor, the probability of getting a million dollars conditional on choosing both boxes is extremely low (if the predictor predicts the agent will choose two boxes, she will leave the opaque box empty), whereas the evidential expected utility of taking only the opaque box is high, so the evidentially expected utility principle recommends choosing only the opaque box. This seems counter-intuitive to those moved by dominance reasoning: after all, at the time of choice, the million dollars is either in the opaque box or not (the predictor, remember, put the money in the boxes *yesterday*), and so the agent's decision to take one or two boxes at that time cannot causally affect what is in them. So why not still take both? We seem to be torn between two different ways of connecting outcomes and actions (think back to Figure 2-1): a causal connection that supports dominance reasoning and taking both boxes, and an evidential connection that indicates one ought to take only one box.

David Lewis argued that the Prisoner's Dilemma has the same structure. He advances a version of the Prisoner's Dilemma/Newcomb problem, which, he thinks, shows them to be the same problem:

> You and I, the "prisoners," are separated. Each is offered the choice: to rat or not to rat. . . . Ratting [in Lewis's version] is done as follows: one reaches out and takes a transparent box, which is seen to contain a thousand dollars. A prisoner who rats gets to keep the thousand. (Maybe ratting is construed as an act of confessing and accusing one's partner, much as taking the Queen's shilling was once construed as an act of enlistment—but that is irrelevant to the problem). If either prisoner declines to rat, he is not at all rewarded; but his partner is presented with a million dollars, nicely packed in an opaque box. (Maybe each faces a long sentence and a short sentence to be served consecutively; escape from the long sentence costs a million, escape from the shorter sentence costs a thousand. But it is irrelevant how the prisoners propose to spend their money).[33]

Thus we have Figure 4-19.

Note the ordering of the payoffs (in square brackets) is the same as Figure 4-7; we have a Prisoner's Dilemma. As Lewis sees it, each player in a Prisoner's Dilemma is in a Newcomb problem. On the one hand, causal reasoning identifies a dominant strategy in both the standard Newcomb problem and its Prisoner's Dilemma version: one has no causal control over what the other will do, so no matter what the other does, one does best by taking both boxes (ratting). But one has reason to suspect that if one takes the dominant strategy, one will do worse than one would by just taking one box (cooperating). After

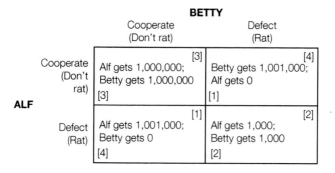

F I G U R E 4-19 Lewis's Newcomb Problem/Prisoner's Dilemma

all, you have reason to suspect that the other party will reason precisely as you do. The other party is a clone of you: you are both rational agents, and have the same ordering of outcomes—*so what you will choose is evidence of what the other party will choose.* So we are good predictors of each other's choices. Perhaps, then, your decision to defect is evidence that the other party will also defect; if so, this affects your conditional probabilities concerning possible outcomes given your choice of defecting. If so, it looks as if you should cooperate. Causal reasoning points to one connection between action and the best outcome while evidential reasoning endorses another.

There is dispute as to whether some or all Prisoner's Dilemmas are really Newcomb problems,[34] as well as what is the rational thing to do in the Newcomb problem itself. Many argue that one should follow one's dominant strategy in both cases (defect in the Prisoner's Dilemma, take both boxes in the Newcomb problem). As Brian Skyrms suggests (and I concur), to employ the sort of evidential reasoning I have described—*when one knows there is no causal connection between your choice and the choice of the other player*—constitutes a "voodoo" decision theory, a magical decision theory whereby I can determine what others choose, yet there is no causal path that links my decision to their choice.[35] Nevertheless, some insist that in both cases one should rely only on evidential reasoning (cooperate in the Prisoner's Dilemma, take one box in the Newcomb problem), while Nozick recommends a complex scheme in which one takes account of both causal and evidential reasoning. Interestingly, empirical evidence suggests that actual reasoners switch between causal and evidential reasoning depending on the values at stake (including how much money is in the two boxes).[36]

Psychological Doubts, Again

Just as psychologists have questioned expected utility theory (Section 1.5), so too have they questioned the accuracy of game theory, and especially predictions based on the rationality of defecting in the Prisoner's Dilemmas. For example, despite the backward induction argument, people do cooperate in a finite series of Prisoner's Dilemmas (though not all the way to the last game: subjects typically start defecting when they perceive that they are getting near to the end of the series).[37] More generally studies of people's behavior in games such as the Prisoner's Dilemma show that they cooperate much more than we would expect,[38] though some insist that this is often because people do not understand the game, and so they cooperate less the more they play.[39]

Consider a well-known experiment that tested people's behavior in a Prisoner's Dilemma–like game.[40] In this game there is a group of 7 subjects, and each gets $6. Each is given the choice of giving away the $6 to the group. When a subject elects to give away her $6, the experimenter will contribute $12, and this $12 will be divided equally among the *other* 6 members (each gets $2). So if you are the only one to contribute $6, you lose $6 and get nothing back. If everyone elects to pay in the $6, everyone will go away with $12 (each will get $2 when each of the other six people contribute their $6). But if all the others contribute and you do not, you get all $12 for their contribution, plus your $6. We seem to have the crux of a Prisoner's Dilemma. No matter what the others do, you will do best by not contributing (keeping your $6). If they all contribute, you do best by not contributing. If not enough others contribute (unless at least three others contribute you will lose out by contributing), you will do best by not contributing. (It takes four others to contribute for you to do better by contributing that by defecting.) It might help to think of this as a game with three outcomes as in Figure 4-20; in any event the dominant strategy appears to be to keep your $6 dollars.

In this experiment, however, 30% of the players contributed to the common pot (adopted the cooperative strategy). When asked why they cooperated these players cited "Doing the right thing"—a moral concern. In another run of the experiment, the experimenters allowed the players five minutes of discussion before the game. Cooperation jumped to 75%! Now when the cooperators were asked why they cooperated they tended not to talk about doing the right thing, but caring about the good of the group. The five minutes of

		THE SIX OTHERS	
	At least four others contribute, so you get a profit	Three others contribute	Less then three others contribute
YOU Contribute $6 to the group	You get at least $2 extra (you gain $8, but you contributed $6); you could get a profit up to $12	You get zero profit (you still have $6)	You lose money (you contributed $6, but receive less than that)
YOU Keep your $6	You get at least $8 profit, and maybe as much as $18	You get at least a profit of $6 (you keep your $6, and get $6 from the others)	You keep at least your $6, and maybe up to $4 profit

FIGURE 4-20 A Prisoner's Dilemma–like Contribution Game

discussion seemed to create a group sympathy that led them to contribute their $6.

Interesting as they are, the problem in interpreting such studies is that they typically suppose that the subjects are in a Prisoner's Dilemma because there is an ordering of monetary prizes that conforms to the Prisoner's Dilemma ordering. Think back to Figure 4-6, which depicted a "Prisoner's Dilemma" in terms of jail time; we also might give one in terms of dollar prizes. As I stressed at the outset, simply because the ordering of jail time is consistent with a Prisoner's Dilemma, we do not really get a Prisoner's Dilemma until we know the utility functions of the players.[41] If the players' utility functions do not generate the Prisoner's Dilemma orderings as in Figures 4-7 and 4-8, then the game simply is not a Prisoner's Dilemma. So if those taking part in experiments care about other things besides the monetary payoffs—such as the moral thing to do or the good of the group—then they are not really in a Prisoner's Dilemma at all. Thus, as I have argued, it is mistaken for Nozick to claim that people might cooperate in a Prisoner's Dilemma because they attribute symbolic importance to not taking advantage of others, or to being fair. If these concerns affect the ordering of options such that cooperation is preferred to defection, then we simply are no longer playing a Prisoner's Dilemma.

I have been at some pains to show that even utility that derives from the process of choosing ("I am not the sort of person who rats on others!") is part of the consequence domain (Section 2.3), and so is part of a person's utility function. People who care about being fair do not cooperate in Prisoner's Dilemmas—they avoid them, and tend to play a type of Assurance Game instead. Why, then, do so many distinguished philosophers insist that, somehow, we (really) could be in a Prisoner's Dilemma and yet end up rationally cooperating? Surely one reason—it is certainly Nozick's—is the conviction that utility theory only captures instrumental reason. If utility theory is simply a formalization of instrumental reason, and if instrumental reason is only about choosing actions as paths to good results, then if there is some reason to choose an action in addition to its power to bring about good results, such noninstrumental reasons cannot be included in the utility functions of the players. So even if their utility functions lead to a Prisoner's Dilemma, they still might cooperate for *these other reasons* that lie outside of their utility functions. It should now be clear why I was especially insistent on the distinction between instrumental reason and utility theory in Chapters 1 and 2. Utility theory is simply a way to formalize a certain conception of coherent choice based on what matters to you; it does not prejudge the question whether the only thing that should matter to you are the results that your action produces. The action itself may matter, as I have tried to show in this section. In the next section we will see that it is impossible to make sense of some classic games unless the route by which the action yields an outcome can affect the overall utility.

4.3 CHICKEN AND OTHER GAMES

Chicken

Recall our public goods story (Section 3.2) about Alf's goat and Betty's garden and dog. His goat wanders into her vegetables while her dog wanders on to Alf's property, scaring his goat so that it does not give milk. We saw that in this case the public good of a fence would be provided, since each would prefer to pay for the entire good rather than do without. We now can analyze the situation in terms of a game, as in Figure 4-21 (as always, 4 = best, 1 = worst).

This game has the same strategic representation as the game of Chicken. It is named after a game that teenagers played in the movie *Rebel without a Cause*: two teenage boys (or, as the philosopher Bertrand Russell is said to have described them, "youthful degenerates") drive toward each other with the pedal to the metal, and the

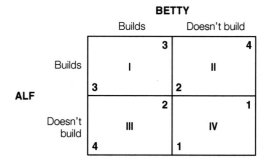

FIGURE 4-21 A Public Goods Game of "Chicken"

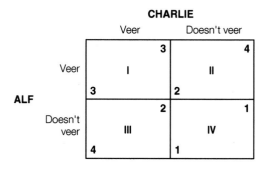

FIGURE 4-22 The Game of Chicken

first one to swerve is "chicken." So the best result is to keep driving straight while the other swerves: he chickened, you didn't. This is best for you (4), but is the second worst outcome (2) for the chicken. If both swerve their reputations take a bit of a hit, but it is better to both chicken than for one to back down when the other doesn't; so let's say this is the second-best outcome for each (utility = 3). If, on the other hand, neither swerve they both take a much bigger hit and crash (1, the worst outcome). (See Figure 4-22.)

In the game of Chicken, only two outcomes are in equilibrium (cells in II and III). Remember, an outcome is in (Nash) equilibrium when neither party can make himself better off by unilaterally changing his move. If Alf and Charlie find themselves in cell I, either can gain utility by switching moves (assuming the other keeps playing the current move); so too with cell IV. But note that this is not the case in cells II and III. If Alf continues to do what he is currently doing,

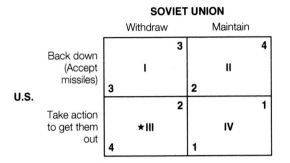

FIGURE 4-23 The Cuban Missile Crisis as a Game of Chicken

Charlie does best by also continuing to do what he is doing (and vice versa).

Chicken is often used as a way to model the Cuban Missile Crisis. In October 1962 the United States discovered that the Soviet Union was in the process of placing nuclear missiles in Cuba. This meant that Soviet missiles could reach American cities in a matter of a few minutes, giving the United States no time to launch a retaliatory strike; because of this, President Kennedy and his advisors determined the missiles destabilized nuclear deterrence and so it was absolutely imperative that they be removed. Admittedly some in the Kennedy administration thought that it was best for the U.S. to accede to the new status quo—let the missiles stay. But that was a small minority: for the most part Kennedy's team of advisors seriously considered only two options: an air strike against the missiles (perhaps followed by an invasion), which would kill Soviet technicians as well as Cubans, and a blockade of Cuba that would stop any further shipments of missiles to Cuba. This blockade would not itself force the Soviet Union to withdraw the missiles it had already installed; some further measures to apply pressure to remove existing missiles might be necessary. The Soviets had the options of withdrawing the missiles or remaining in Cuba. It was thought that, if the U.S. launched an air strike and the Soviet Union refused to withdraw, there was a very real chance of nuclear war.

Figure 4-23 presents an analysis that explains the outcome in terms of Chicken.

The standard representation is that the Soviet Union "chickened," that the U.S. got its first option (took public action and demanded that the Soviets withdraw their missiles), and that the

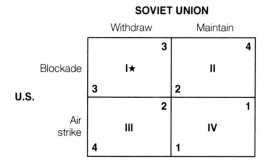

FIGURE 4-24 A Game of Chicken Where No One Chickened?

Soviets got their third (public humiliation of backdown)—the outcome identified by the star (★). But the modeling depends on the set of options we identify and how we think policy makers ranked them: some have disputed that this was a game of Chicken.[42] Consider the representation in Figure 4-24.

Here the worst outcome is air strike/maintain because that may lead to nuclear war (don't veer/don't veer). Each side would prefer that the other backs down; again the equilibrium solutions are II and III. But note that the actual outcome was I: the U.S. blockaded (took the moderate action) and the Soviet Union withdrew (the moderate action). But if these were the orderings, then although we have a game of Chicken, the actual outcome was not an equilibrium solution. Perhaps the U.S. and the Soviet Union were, after all, not playing a game of Chicken. Steven Brams argues that rather than Chicken we had another game, as in Figure 4-25.[43]

The difference in payoffs (from Figure 4-23) are underlined. First, Brams argues that it would *not* have been best for the U.S. to take the aggressive action (air strikes) when the Soviet Union backed down ("they veered"), since the U.S. would be widely condemned for its overreaction and reckless action. On the other hand, Brams argues, the danger of nuclear war was not as highly estimated as in the Chicken representation; if the U.S. had attacked an obstinate Soviet Union, the world would have generally supported its action and the Soviet Union likely would have capitulated. Notice that in the ordinal form the game does not have an equilibrium solution. Although Nash showed that all finite variable-sum games have at least one Nash equilibrium, this may require a mixed strategy, and for that we need cardinal utilities.

F I G U R E 4-25 Bram's Modeling of the Cuban Missile Crisis

The example of the Cuban Missile Crisis shows three limits of attempts to apply game theory to actual interactions. *First*, whether a game models an actual strategic interaction is highly sensitive to just how we describe the options and compare them in the eyes of the decision makers. Do we consider just "back down" or "don't," or do we consider different ways of responding such as an "air strike" or "blockade"? And what really are the orderings? *Second*, we see that if we only have ordinal utilities some games do not have solutions.[44] *Third*, in the actual world, games are played under imperfect information in which players are in doubt about both the rationality and the utility functions of their opponents. Under these conditions it is not surprising that in one-play games the outcome may not be a Nash equilibrium.

Let us leave the real world behind and return to Figures 4-21 and 4-22. I presented these as the same game—Chicken. But given our analysis of Section 4.2, we can distinguish them. In the classic game of Chicken (in Figure 4-22), the payoffs depend on the structure of the decision tree: Alf can only get his payoff if Charlie "chickens" and turns the wheel. He must have that choice node available to him: if he does not—if his decision tree does not include a turn/don't turn choice—he cannot get the utility from not turning. To better see this, suppose that Alf discovered that Charlie borrowed his mother's Swedish car which has a safety auto-swerve device such that, when another car was approaching, at a distance of 30 feet the car automatically turned away. Although in *some sense* (see Section 2.4) the consequences would be "the same" as if one player chickened (we get to a "swerve, didn't swerve" terminal node), the payoffs would change, since the swerving was not the result of the other player making a chicken choice at one of the nodes.

To approach the matter from another direction, suppose we have a modified form of Chicken "don't swerve twice": *two cars head toward Alf,* one after another, and he must not swerve for either. Clearly Alf's decision tree is not separable (Section 4.2)—he cannot start the game at node 2 (the second car), since the payoffs depend on going through both nodes, just as in Figure 4-16, Alf's Reward. This shows us that the game's payoffs include the utility of traveling through the decision tree. Contrast this to the public goods case of "Chicken" in Figure 4-21. Here the decision trees for the players are simply causal routes for constructing a fence. In the public goods case Alf and Betty receive no utility from the other being a "chicken"—they get all their utility from the fence, and none of it from the knowledge that the other "chickened out." Thus, just as in Section 4.2 where we identified two forms of the Assurance Game—that in which the utilities partly derive from the structure of the tree and that in which they do not—we can distinguish two forms of Chicken. This is enlightening. If one accepts the modeling of the Cuban Missile Crisis as a game of Chicken, one might object that Kennedy and Khrushchev were playing "macho games with the future of the world," as if they received utility from the knowledge that the other backed down. This may have been the case, but it does not follow from the "Chicken payoffs," which are consistent with all the utility being derived from the outcomes (as in Figure 4-21).

The Stag Hunt

Jean-Jacques Rousseau presents a depiction of man's natural condition in which simple people's "love of [their own] well-being" leads them to cooperate with each other, but not always in the most far-sighted ways. Such men would acquire:

> some gross ideas of mutual undertakings, and of the advantages of fulfilling them: that is, just so far as their present and apparent interest was concerned: for they were perfect strangers to foresight, and were so far from troubling themselves about the distant future, that they hardly thought of the morrow. If a deer was to be taken, every one saw that, in order to succeed, he must abide faithfully by his post: but if a hare happened to come within the reach of any one of them,

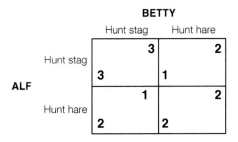

F I G U R E 4-26 The Stag Hunt

it is not to be doubted that he pursued it without scruple, and, having seized his prey, cared very little, if by so doing he caused his companions to miss theirs.[45]

Rousseau's story can be formalized into a game called The Stag Hunt as in Figure 4-26 (3 = best, 1 = worst). Best for both is if they hunt a stag together and have lots of meat. But one person cannot catch a stag: both must cooperate. One, however, can hunt a hare alone.

If the other hunts stag, you should hunt stag, but if the other hunts hare, you should hunt hare (both are Nash equilibria). Though not as interestingly paradoxical as the Prisoner's Dilemma, The Stag Hunt may serve as a better model for understanding social life. Rather than the main issue being "should we try to do each other in or live in peace?" perhaps the really important question is whether we go it alone and get something (hunt hare), or cooperate (hunt stag) and get (much) more?[46]

The Stag Hunt has no dominant strategy: Alf and Betty cannot be sure they will end up sharing a stag. When I have taught The Stag Hunt students have questioned this. If Alf and Betty have common knowledge of the payoffs, and of their own rationality, shouldn't Betty assume that Alf will hunt stag (and Alf assume that Betty will too)? After all, as rational agents they see that there is an equilibrium (Hunt Stag/Hunt Stag) that is strongly Pareto-superior to the other (Hunt Hare/Hunt Hare): why would either think the rational other would select the Pareto-inferior option? As Rousseau suggests in the passage quoted earlier, it would seem that only some sort of short-sightedness (imperfect rationality) could lead to hunting hare.

To understand why this worry is insightful, yet still not quite right, we need to grasp the distinction between *rationalizable* strategies and *common conjectures*. As my students rightly recognized, rational players can sometimes use their common knowledge to eliminate those strategies that are not "rationalizable." I can know that my rational opponent will not choose some strategies. We have already considered an example of this in our analysis of General Kenny's "game" with the Japanese (Figure 4-3). Recall that, according to some game theorists, General Kenny can eliminate the possibility that the Japanese fleet would take the southern route because it was weakly dominated by the northern route. A player can suppose that his rational opponent will not choose such a dominated strategy; by successively eliminating dominated strategies, a complicated game may ultimately have a simple solution in pure strategies. However, in The Stag Hunt both hunting stag and hunting hare are rationalizable. The problem is that, after all, Alf cannot be entirely confident that Betty will hunt stag. Why? Because it is rational for Betty to hunt stag only if she thinks Alf will do so. So for Betty to certainly hunt stag she would have to be sure that Alf will hunt stag too. Does, then, Betty *know* that Alf will hunt stag? No, because Alf will hunt stag only if he thinks Betty will hunt stag: he needs to know that she will hunt stag. So she will hunt stag if she knows he will, and he will if he knows she will. We can see that the rationality of hunting stag is contingent on the other person hunting stag, but whether each will hunt stag is contingent on whether they think the other will, which is contingent on each thinking that the other will, and on and on.

What Alf and Betty require is a *common conjecture* about how the game is to be played that allows them to hit on the "hunt stag" equilibrium: they need to play in a way that both play the desirable equilibrium. Here communication would help. If Alf and Betty tell each other that they intend to hunt stag, then they should both hunt stag: neither would have any incentive to say one thing and do the other; neither could gain by "tricking" the other into hunting stag. If Alf does decide to hunt hare, it doesn't matter to him what Betty does, so why deceive her? That hunting stag strongly Pareto-dominates hunting hare is an excellent reason to settle on stag.[47] Yet, sometimes it may be difficult to settle even on a Pareto-dominant equilibrium. Common conjecture via communication works less well in a very similar game that we have already considered, the Assurance Game (see Figure 4-27).

Sometimes this game is also called Stag Hunt (I have put the relevant hare/stag options in parentheses), but we can see that the payoffs differ from those in Figure 4-26. Unlike the true Stag Hunt of Figure 4-26, in Figure 4-27 although the best option is

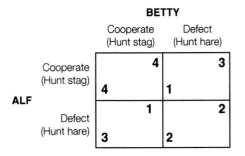

FIGURE 4-27 The Assurance Game Version of the Stag Hunt

for both to hunt stag, Betty's second-best option is to hunt hare when Alf hunts stag. Now the game has room for deception. Suppose that Alf and Betty are in the hunt hare/hunt hare equilibrium and Betty tells Alf that she intends to switch to hunt stag. Regardless of what she intends to do, it makes sense for her to convince Alf to play "hunt stag."[48] Her verbal evidence makes sense of both a decision to change her move and a decision not to. So Alf has a harder time taking her at her word: communication may help a lot less in establishing common conjectures about how the game is to be played.

Coordination Games

Having started this chapter with games in which interests are diametrically opposed, let us now consider games where the player's preferences largely converge as in Figure 4-28.

This is Luce and Raffia's (admittedly sexist) "Battle of the Sexes" problem.[49] Betty and Alf wish to go out together: he wants to go to the fights with her (I); she wants to go the ballet with him (IV). Either coordination point (I or IV) is preferred by both of them to options in which they fail to coordinate. Both are Nash equilibria. (Following David Lewis, we might employ a special idea of a *coordination equilibrium* as "a combination in which no one would have been better off had *any one* agent alone acted otherwise, either himself or someone else."[50]) There is certainly room for conflict and strategy here: Alf may simply leave a message on Betty's cell phone that he will meet her at the fights and then turn his phone off; Betty may tell Alf that she has become a pacifist and cannot witness blood sports. But they

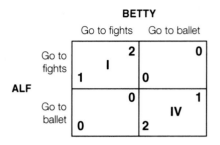

FIGURE 4-28 An Impure Coordination Game

do not wish the conflict to get out of hand so long as they prefer both coordinated to both uncoordinated outcomes.

Jeremy Waldron believes that The Battles of the Sexes game is the key to understanding politics: "the felt need among members of a certain group for a common framework or decision or course of action on some matter, even in the face of disagreement about what the framework, decision or action should be, are the circumstances of politics."[51]

> We want to act together in regard to some matter M, but one of us thinks it is important to follow policy X while others think it is important to follow policy Y, and none of us has reason to think any of the others a better judge of the merits of M than himself. . . .
>
>   In these circumstances, the following will *not* be a way of settling on a common policy: each does whatever he thinks is important to do about M. We must find a way of choosing a single policy in which [we] . . . can participate despite our disagreements on the merits.[52]

As Waldron understands politics, we will debate and discuss the merits and demerits of each of the possible coordination points (policies); since it is an impure coordination game, I prefer a different coordination point (policy) than do you, so we have something to argue about. However, we each prefer any coordination point to lack of coordination. In essence, then, Waldron argues that we need to coordinate on some single policy, even if it is not the one that both of us see as best. Politics is essentially an impure coordination game: we desire to coordinate but disagree about which coordination point is best.

It seems, though, unlikely in the extreme that every piece of legislation is an impure coordination problem: if anyone prefers even one uncoordinated outcome to even one way of acting together we no longer have an impure coordination problem: somebody can be made better off by a unilateral defection from some ways of acting together. If, say, Alf is a Millian liberal who thinks that there should be no laws concerning self-regarding acts, then what legislation we should have concerning pornography cannot be a coordination problem. Alf may benefit by unilateral defection from any policy on this matter. More plausible is to see, not each policy or act of legislation, but government itself, as an impure coordination problem. We all agree that we need some government, but we disagree about which one is best, and we cannot all go on our way. This, though, can only hold over some set of types of government. Although Hobbes may have thought that any government is better than no government, few agree. Oppressive governments that invade people's life, liberty, and property may well be worse than no government at all. So we first need to find the set of governments that everyone sees as superior to "going it alone": only in relation to selecting among them can we see political theory as based on an impure coordination game.

4.4 REPEATED AND EVOLUTIONARY GAMES

Repeated Games

If we do not confront a definite series of Prisoner's Dilemmas, we cannot utilize backward induction to solve the game because we cannot be sure about which is that "last game." While there is no single solution to an infinite (or indefinite) series of Prisoner's Dilemmas, repeated Prisoner's Dilemmas still have equilibrium—indeed infinitely many— "solutions." Two tit-for-tatters (Section 4.2) are in a Nash equilibrium when cooperating in such a series. Remember, tit-for-tat cooperates on the first game in a series of Prisoner's Dilemmas, and then will do to its opponent in the nth game whatever its opponent did to it in the $n - 1$ game. So if one tit-for-tatter defects on the $n - 1$ game, the other tit-for-tatter responds by "punishing" the defector in the nth game. If one tit-for-tatter unilaterally defects from cooperation, the other tit-for-tatter will punish, and so lower the payoffs of the defector. Knowing this, neither tit-for-tatter can gain by unilateral defection, so they are in a Nash equilibrium. But it is not just two tit-for-tatters that are in equilibrium. Consider "the Grim strategy." Grim cooperates on the first move, but if its opponent defects, Grim will punish for every move after that—forever. Two Grim players are also in equilibrium: neither would benefit from defection. The important thing here is that *punishing strategies* can achieve equilibrium: if I can punish you for defecting from a cooperative interaction, repeated Prisoner's Dilemmas allow what are essentially "self-policing contracts" to cooperate. Since we are playing infinitely or indefinitely many games, I can afford to punish you to bring you around, and you will see that, and so will not unilaterally defect. Indeed, any cooperative outcome that gives each player more (or, more formally, at least as much) as the minimum he might receive if the other player acted in the most punishing way can be an equilibrium: if we are each above this minimum point, then one party still has room to inflict punishment on the other for a deviation from the "contract." Thus the minimax payoff (Section 4.1) is the baseline: it is the payoff a person could get if her opponent treated the game as a zero-sum game in which he was intent on making sure she got as little as possible. As long as the agreement (the coordinated payoffs) is above that, room remains for punishment, so unilateral defection will not pay, and so there will be a Nash equilibrium. This result is known as "the folk theorem."[53]

We can build into repeated game theory the possibility of learning, so that the players' responses change as they learn from interacting with other players. In a fascinating recent paper Peter Vanderschraaf models a Hobbesian state of nature in which some players have cooperative ("Assurance Game" orderings) while other players have noncooperative ("Prisoner's Dilemma" orderings).[54] Vanderschraaf shows that if players tend to anticipate each others' strategies and learn from experience (change their anticipations throughout the course of a game), even a population with a small number of noncooperators easily ends up at an equilibrium of a Hobbesian war of all against all.

Evolutionary Games

The reader might have noticed that I have described tit-for-tat in two very different ways. As I presented the folk theorem, it concerned two rational players who sought to respond in the best way to the moves of the opponent. But in my description of Axelrod's tournament I considered strategies playing each other: the strategies simply ran their routine automatically, and at the end of the day Axelrod

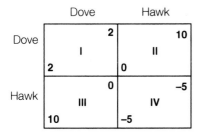

F I G U R E 4-29 Hawks and Doves (A Game of Chicken)

tallied up how well each strategy did. In this latter case we can think of each strategy as "hard-wired": the "players" simply acted out the instructions of their strategy and never modified or abandoned their strategy. We can suppose that strategies that do better are more *fit* in that environment; we might suppose that the number of players following a strategy is positively correlated with how fit that strategy is. So the fitter the strategy, the faster it grows within a population. *Notice, then, that we can thus remove reason and choice from game theory. Indeed, we can even remove the players, and simply think of the strategies playing each other.*

Consider a population that is divided between Hawks and Doves. When they come into conflict over who will occupy a territory, Hawks act aggressively, while Doves back off. When a Hawk meets a Dove, the Dove quickly retreats; when a Hawk meets another Hawk there is combat, in which one Hawk will win, but the other will be defeated and injured in a fight; let us say that any Hawk will win half the time against another Hawk. When two Doves meet they might engage in some bluffing, one randomly will back down, and no fight results. Figure 4-29 gives possible payoffs in cardinal utility (high numbers = best).[55]

Remember that we are viewing Hawk and Dove not as possible strategies for a player, but unchanging responses. Notice that Figure 4-29 has no players who choose strategies; there are only strategies that can either encounter the same strategy or a different one. So "Hawk" always plays hawk and "Dove" always plays dove—they never vary their response. When a Hawk meets another Hawk, the expected payoff is −5: they will get caught in a destructive battle. Think of this as {don't swerve/don't swerve} in a game of Chicken (Section 4.3). When a Hawk meets a Dove the expected payoff is 10 for the Hawk. Again, in the game of Chicken this is the payoff for not swerving when the other swerves: the Dove (or we might say chicken) runs away (0) and the Hawk wins (10). Let us denote the expected Hawk payoff against a Dove as $E(H/d) = 10$ (i.e., the expected payoff of Hawk playing against Dove is 10). When two Doves play each other each gets a payoff of 2 $[E(D/d) = 2]$. They have a small ritual fight, one flees and the other stays (assume that this is random, so 50% of the time each Dove gets the territory in a conflict with another Dove). In the game of Chicken, this is like {swerve/swerve}; both take the cautious option.

As I have been emphasizing, the payoffs in Figure 4-29 represent the payoffs of "Chicken," being played by our Hawks and Doves. But again, it needs be stressed that row and column are no longer individual players who can vary their strategies: when a Hawk meets another Hawk it will still play Hawk. In the game of Chicken this would not happen: if Alf knows that Betty will not swerve, he certainly will swerve. And in the Hawk/Dove game, if two Doves meet they will both "swerve," but this will not happen in Chicken; if Betty knows that Alf is a "chicken" she will not also "chicken." Because the Hawks and Doves do not adjust their moves to the anticipated moves of the other players, we cannot say that cells II and III are in equilibrium in the Hawk/Dove game (though they are in Chicken).

So if the Hawks and Doves do not vary their strategy, what constitutes "playing" or "winning" the game? In evolutionary game theory your strategy "wins" if, compared to the opponents, those following your strategy have greater reproductive fitness: (roughly) they reproduce at a greater rate such that, over many generations, they tend to dominate the population. We can assume that reproductive fitness is correlated with how many points the strategy accumulates in each generation: the more points the strategy accumulates (we can think of this as the more food and other goods it gets), the more able it is to reproduce. So as the Hawks and Doves play each other again and again, the percentage of Hawks and Doves in the population from generation to generation will vary with how many points they gather in our Hawk/Dove game.

Whether it pays to be a Hawk (or a Dove) depends on the composition of the rest of the population. Suppose that we have a population of all Hawks: for every interaction the expected payoff is -5. Imagine we introduce a Dove: its average payoff will be 0; although the average payoff of the Hawks will go up a tiny bit (when a Hawk does find the Dove the Hawk gets 10), overall, the Dove will still do better than the average Hawk. Every time a Dove meets a Hawk, it gets 0, whereas the Hawks are caught in serious fights with an expected payoff of −.5. So a mutant Dove will thrive in a population of all Hawks. If we invert the story and start with a homogeneous Dove population, it is even clearer how a mutant Hawk will thrive. The Dove population will have an average payoff of 2, but the mutant hawk will get 10 in all its interactions.

The solution to these games is when the population achieves a mix in which neither strategy can increase its share in the population at the expense of the other. This idea can be formalized in terms of an *evolutionary stable strategy* (ESS). Let us say that S is an evolutionary stable strategy if and only if, with respect to a mutant strategy S* that might arise:

Either:

(i) $E(S/s) > E(S^*/s)$

Or:

(ii) $[E(S/s) = E(S^*/s)]$ & $[E(S/s^*) > E(S^*/s^*)]$

The idea is this. Suppose that we have an S population in which one or a few S* types are introduced. Because of the predominance of S types, both S and S* will play most of their games against S. According to the first rule, if S does better against S than S* does against S, S* will not get a foothold in the population. Suppose instead that S* does just as well against S as S does against itself. Then S* will begin to grow in the population, until there are enough S* so that both S and S* play against S* reasonably often. According to the second rule, once this happens, if S does better against S* than S* does against itself, S will again grow at a more rapid rate. To say, then, that S is an ESS is to say that an invading strategy will, over time, do less well than will S.

In our Hawk-Dove case the evolutionary stable strategy is a "mixed strategy" (Section 4.1) where this does not mean that a player mixes his responses, but that the population contains a mix of strategies (of Hawks and Doves). If we call the entire population P, we can see that in this case the ESS will occur when $E(H/p) = E(D/p) = E(P/p)$. That is, the expected payoff of Hawks playing the rest of the population is the same as the expected payoff of Doves playing the rest of the population which is the same as the expected (average) payoff of the population playing against itself. Hawks and Doves do as well against the mixed population as the entire population on average does playing against itself. More intuitively, we can see that the Hawks and Doves are in equilibrium: if any imbalance is introduced (suddenly more Hawks are born), the population will return to the evolutionary stable mix. In this example the ESS is a population of 8/13 Hawks and 5/13 Doves. The Hawks will get their −5 payoff 8/13 of the time (when they play other Hawks), yielding −40/13; they will receive their 10 payoff 5/13 of the time when they play Doves, for 50/13, for a total expected payoff of 10/13. The Doves will receive a 0 payoff 8/13 of the time when they play the Hawks, and 5/13 of the time they receive 2 (when they play each other), for a total payoff of 10/13.

All this assumes a rather simple model, in which the strategies meet each other randomly and they choose what to do independently of what the other does. Our evolutionary mix of 8/13 Hawks and 5/13 Doves in our initial Hawk/Dove game corresponds to a Nash equilibrium of mixed strategies in the game of Chicken with the payoffs of Figure 4-29. If Alf and Betty were playing a game of Chicken with these payoffs, the mixed strategy in equilibrium would be to swerve 5/13 of the time and don't swerve 8/13 of the time. In this sort of mixed strategy, we can think of each player using a random device (yielding an 8/13 chance of don't swerving each time) to decide what she will do. Of course if we do this, sometimes neither will swerve and we get the lowest payoff (and sometimes both will swerve). Robert Aumann has developed the idea of a *correlated equilibrium*—the players would do better to have a single chooser; for example, one person using a random device telling them both what to do (one swerves and the other doesn't). Suppose Alf and Betty are playing the game of Chicken in Figure 4-29, but they agree to let Charlie toss a coin: if is comes up heads Alf does not swerve, if it comes up tails, Betty does not swerve. Of course, if you know the other won't swerve, you know you'd better! Given this, the expected payoff of each player is 10 half the time (5) plus two half the time (1), for an average payoff of 6—a quite nice average payoff for this game of Chicken!

Brian Skyrms and Peter Vanderschraff have applied Aumann's idea of a correlated equilibrium to evolutionary game theory. Suppose a mutant strategy arose such that its players coordinated their action according to a convention: instead of choosing their play independent of each other, they somehow agreed to a rule that says "You swerve (play Dove) if X happens, I swerve (play Dove) if Y happens." For example, consider what has been called the "Bourgeois" strategy—a "first possession" strategy, which acts like a Hawk on its own territory but a Dove off its territory. As Skyrms has shown, this is an example of a correlated convention.[56] Two Bourgeois will not fight over a territory: the Bourgeois already in possession will act like a Hawk (getting a gain of 10), and the one who is off his territory will act like a Dove (getting 0). Suppose that Bourgeois conducts half its confrontations with other Bourgeois on its own territory, so that $E(B/b) = 5$. (It gets 10 half the time and 0 the other half of the time.) We can see that Bourgeois does better against Hawk than Hawk does against itself [(H/h) = −5; $E(B/h) = -5/2$]. That is, when Hawk meets another Hawk their average pay off is −.5, but Bourgeois will only fight half the time (when it is on its own territory), so it only gets the −.5 payoff half of the time. Bourgeois also does better against Dove than Dove does against itself. When two Doves come together their expected payoff is 2 [$E(D/d) = 2$], while Bourgeois will win against Dove the half of the time that Bourgeois is in its own territory (10/2), and will draw with Dove the other half of the time (2/2), so $E(B/h) = 12/2$ (i.e., 6). So since Bourgeois does better against each than each does against itself, Bourgeois can invade both the Hawk and Dove populations. Moreover, once it takes over we can see that, according to ESS, it will be stable vis-à-vis Hawks and Doves. Recall that when it plays itself its expected payoff is 5. In comparison $E(H/b)$ would be 2.5; since half the time when a Hawk meets a Bourgeois there will be a fight (−5/2), and half the time the Hawk will win (10/ 2), we get a 5/2, or 2.5. Also we can see that $E(D/b) = 1$ (half the time the Dove gets 2, half the time 0), again less than $E(B/b)$ of 5. Thus Bourgeois does better against itself than either Hawk or Dove do against it: they could not invade a Bourgeois population.

We see, then, that an ESS may be either monomorphic, in which a single strategy takes over, or polymorphic, where more than one strategy is in equilibrium. Insofar as our interest is in morality, we may worry about polymorphic outcomes, in which the population settles into an equilibrium where people have, say, different "strategies" concerning what is just. Consider a very simple case drawn from Brian Skyrms's work.[57] Suppose we are playing a cake-cutting game in which each party makes a claim for a fraction of the cake. If their total claims are not greater than 100% of the cake, both players get their claim; if the total claims exceed the whole cake, neither player gets any cake. Suppose that there are three strategies: demand $^1/_3$, demand ½, demand $^2/_3$. It is possible for a population to end up in what Skyrms calls a "polymorphic trap"—a mixed equilibrium in which people have different demands. The population might divide into a mix of the Greedy (always demanding $^2/_3$) and the Meek (always demanding $^1/_3$). Whether they do so, or whether one strategy such as "demand ½" takes over the entire population, depends on the relative size of each strategy in the initial population *and* also on whether strategies can find the right players to play against. If "demand ½ players" have a better than random chance of meeting, it becomes far easier for them to take over the population, so that the entire population moves toward a ½ monomorphic equilibrium.

Skyrms has also employed evolutionary game theory to examine the conditions under which in The Stag Hunt (Section 4.3) the equilibrium will be on hunting stag rather than hunting hare: we find cooperative practices that make us all better off rather than each going her own way.[58] What is interesting is that for large groups hunting hare can easily take over; indeed even in small groups in which players have a modest chance of being wrong in their conjectures about how their neighbors will play (Section 4.3), hare hunting can quickly take over. An interesting aspect of Skyrms's analysis is that he distinguishes two different types of dynamics: best response and imitate the best. Best response is the crux of game theory: we consider the moves of others, and respond to them in a way that maximizes our payoffs. But since evolutionary game theory is not really about rational choice, we can analyze a very different type of dynamic: look around one, see which of one's neighbors is doing well, and imitate her behavior. In evolutionary games of The Stag Hunt, best response and imitate the best dynamics can lead to very different outcomes.

At this point, however, it is not clear whether further exploration of evolutionary game theory will enlighten us about our main concern—rationality. Evolutionary game theory might be understood as reviving Rationality as Effectiveness: our model of a "rational" agent is simply a being that engages in instrumentally effective behavior. We saw, though, that effective action can be divorced from rationality (Section 1.1), thus evolutionary game theory can devote itself simply to the study of effective behavior, be it in bacteria, birds, or humans. In an important sense, this vindicates our rejection of Rationality as Effectiveness: if we adopted it, our "theory of rationality" can apply to genes or bacteria, but that clearly must mean it is not a theory of rational action at all. As we suspected at the outset, even instrumental rationality must involve more than effective action.

SUMMARY

This chapter has surveyed some of the main types of games, and some foundational issues in game theory. The chapter has:

- *Explained zero-sum games, and how maximin is the equilibrium solution for such games.*

- *Analyzed the Prisoner's Dilemma.* I argued that it is especially important to keep in mind that, while the story of the Prisoner's Dilemma is in terms of jail time, a true Prisoner's Dilemma must include all the utility at stake in the game, and the total utility must conform to the Prisoner's Dilemma ordering.

- *Explained the idea of a Nash equilibrium in both pure and mixed strategies.*

- *Examined why the Prisoner's Dilemma so captures the attention of philosophers and social theorists.* A striking feature of the Prisoner's Dilemma is that it presents a clear break between rationality and Pareto-efficiency (which we explored in Chapter 3). Many have also thought that it models a condition of anarchy, and explains why government is necessary. In particular, it seems to model certain public goods problems, and why people free-ride on the contribution of others. On the other hand, some psychological studies indicate that people do not defect in Prisoner's Dilemmas as often as would be predicted.

- *Critically examined attempts to solve the Prisoner's Dilemma.* Because of its paradoxical nature, many philosophers have tried to show that rational individuals would cooperate even given the utility orderings of the Prisoner's Dilemma. I was skeptical of such claims. I focused on Robert Nozick's "solution," arguing that while Nozick does not solve the Prisoner's Dilemma, he does show us how the "strategic" form of the game misses crucial information that we can only capture by analyzing the game in its "extensive form." Picking up on a theme from Chapter 2 (Section 2.4), we saw that sometimes the utility of an outcome depends on the options (the "menu") that one encountered to reach that outcome.

- *Examined the idea of modular rationality, and briefly considered theories that reject modular rationality in favor of resolute choice.*

- *Examined other games such as Chicken and The Stag Hunt.*

- *Explained iterated games, and the "folk theorem."* Strategies such as tit-for-tat and Grim, we saw, can be in equilibrium in iterated Prisoner's Dilemmas.

- *Briefly examined evolutionary game theory.* We considered the idea that "hard-wired" strategies interact, with their success being determined by their reproductive fitness. We also considered the idea of correlated equilibrium, and its application to evolutionary game theory.

143

NOTES

1. And he knows she knows that he knows she is rational, and so on.

2. Notice that these games are most easily understood in terms of monetary payoffs rather than utilities. If we suppose that people only have preferences in these games over the monetary payoffs, and that their preferences are linear with money, then utility and monetary payoffs come to the same thing. As we will see in Section 4.2, paying sole attention to monetary payoffs, when they are not monotonic with utility, can lead to confusions.

3. I am drawing here on the nice discussion of such games by William Poundstone in his interesting book, *Prisoner's Dilemma*, Chapter 3.

4. Morton D. Davis, *Game Theory*, p. 13.

5. Some more recent game theorists dissent, arguing that we are not justified in eliminating weakly dominated strategies *when they are in Nash equilibrium*. See Ken Binmore, *Natural Justice*, pp. 69–70.

6. I am following here Todd Sandler, *Economic Concepts for the Social Sciences*, p. 43.

7. See Davis, *Game Theory*, pp. 44–45.

8. See John Rawls, *A Theory of Justice*, p. 152. The similarities between Rawls's maximin principle and von Neumann's are seldom appreciated.

9. See James D. Morrow, *Game Theory for Political Scientists*, p. 87.

10. The game was developed by Merrill Flood and Melvin Dresher of the RAND Corporation; the name "Prisoner's Dilemma" has been attributed to Albert Tucker. See Brian Skyrms, *Evolution of the Social Contract*, pp. 48–49.

11. See Thomas Hobbes, *Leviathan*, edited by Edwin Curley. Curley's introduction considers the Prisoner's Dilemma based interpretations of Hobbes. Especially important in developing this interpretation of Hobbes was Jean Hampton's *Hobbes and the Social Contract Tradition*.

12. Hobbes, *Leviathan*, p. 76 (Chapter 13, para. 9).

13. Plato, *The Republic*, pp. 38–39.

14. Hobbes, *Leviathan*, p. 109 (Chapter 17, para 12).

15. Robert Nozick, *The Nature of Rationality*, pp. 26–27.

16. Ibid., pp. 54–55, emphasis in original.

17. Which may well be an incoherent aspiration, but let us proceed. See Simon Blackburn, *Ruling Passions*, Chapter 6.

18. Nozick, *The Nature of Rationality*, p. 55, emphasis in original.

19. Edward F. McClennen, *Rationality and Dynamic Choice*, pp. 120ff.

20. As Peter Hammond notes, "a decision tree can hardly include, as a partial consequence, regret at missing an opportunity to have consequence y, unless there was an opportunity in the past to have had y." Hammond argues, however, that his continuity principle over choices may still apply. "Consequentialist Foundations for Expected Utility," note 4. In any event, note that denying separability here does not lead one at any node to choose what, from that node onward in the tree, would be a suboptimal outcome. Thus the core of the notion of modular rationality is retained.

21. McClennen, *Rationality and Dynamic Choice*, p. 120.

22. Ibid., p. 26.

23. Hammond, "Consequentialist Foundations for Expected Utility," p. 26.

24. See ibid.

25. See Robert Axelrod, *The Evolution of Co-operation*.

26. Russell Hardin argues that this is a "cute" argument that leads to perverse results. *Indeterminacy and Society*, p. 25.

27. For a more complete analysis of modular rationality, see Skyrms, *Evolution of the Social Contract*, Chapter 2.

28. For a helpful discussion see Morrow, *Game Theory for Political Scientists*, pp. 124ff.

29. See McClennen, *Rationality and Dynamic Choice*. Hardin, I think, comes close to advocating such a view in *Indeterminacy and Society*, Chapter 2.

30. I have just scratched the surface here. The idea of subgame perfection includes an analysis of decision trees. Again Morrow provides a very helpful discussion in *Game Theory for Political Scientists*, pp. 128ff. McClennen's work is the most sustained effort to defend resolute choosers.

31. See David Lewis, "Prisoner's Dilemma Is a Newcomb Problem." See also Philip Pettit, "The Prisoner's Dilemma Is an Unexploitable Newcomb Problem."

32. See Nozick, *The Nature of Rationality*, pp. 43ff; Robert Nozick, "Newcomb's Problem and Two Principles of Choice."

33. Lewis, "Prisoner's Dilemma Is a Newcomb Problem," pp. 251–252.

34. Jorden Howard Sobel, "Not Every Prisoner's Dilemma Is a Newcomb Problem."

35. Skyrms, *Evolution of the Social Contract*, p. 50.

36. See Paul Anand, *Foundations of Rational Choice Under Risk*, p. 41. For a doubter, see David Christensen, "Review Essay of 'Robert Nozick, *The Nature of Rationality*.'"

37. John Conlisk, "Why Bounded Rationality?," p. 691. See also Hardin, *Indeterminacy and Society*, Chapter 2.

38. Matthew Rabin, "Psychology and Economics."

39. Ken Binmore upholds this analysis in *Natural Justice*, pp. 65–66.

40. Robyn M. Dawes, Alphins J. C. van Kragt, and John M. Orbell, "Cooperation for the Benefit of Us—Not Me, or My Conscience."

41. See Binmore, *Natural Justice*, pp. 64–65; Blackburn, *Ruling Passions*, Chapter 6.

42. See Steven J. Brams, "Game Theory and the Cuban Missile Crisis."

43. Ibid.

44. Brams provides an interesting solution to Figure 4-25, relying on "the theory of moves" which we cannot explore here.

45. Jean Jacques Rousseau, *Discourse on the Origin of Inequality*, pp. 209–201.

46. For an analysis that focuses on the Stag Hunt, see Brian Skyrms, *The Stag Hunt and Evolution of Social Structure*.

47. On these matters, see Morrow, *Game Theory for Political Scientists*, pp. 94ff.

48. As Binmore argues, *Natural Justice*, p. 68.

49. R. Duncan Luce and Howard Raiffa, *Games and Decisions*, p. 90.

50. David Lewis, *Convention*, p. 15. Emphasis in original. See also Hampton, *Hobbes and the Social Contract Tradition*, p. 138.

51. Jeremy Waldron, *Law and Disagreement*, p. 102. I have considered Waldron's analysis in more depth in my *Contemporary Theories of Liberalism*, Chapter 4.

52. Waldron, *Law and Disagreement*, p. 107.

53. For an excellent discussion, see Binmore, *Natural Justice*, pp. 79ff.

54. Peter Vanderschraaf, "War or Peace?: A Dynamical Analysis of Anarchy."

55. These are drawn from John Maynard Smith, "The Evolution of Behavior." For discussion see Davis, *Game Theory*, pp. 136ff; Skyrms, *Evolution of the Social Contract*, pp. 65ff. The next few paragraphs generally follow the very useful explication of Davis.

56. Skyrms, *Evolution of the Social Contract*, pp. 76–79. See Peter Vanderschraaf, *Learning and Coordination: Inductive Deliberation, Equilibrium and Convention*, especially Chapter 2.

57. Skyrms, *Evolution of the Social Contract*, pp. 14ff.

58. See Skyrms, *The Stag Hunt and Evolution of Social Structure*, especially Chapter 3.

5

Social Choice Theory

OVERVIEW

In this chapter we continue to explore problems of rationality and social interaction. However, rather than being concerned with each agent's rational response to another as in game theory, we turn to whether a *group of rational individuals can arrive at a rational group or collective choice.* Insofar as our concern is with politics and government action, we are concerned not only with interactions of rational individual actors, but also with the rationality of collective actors.

I begin by examining two views of politics: one denies that economic analysis can enlighten us about the political sphere, and the other maintains that the problem of aggregating rational individual preferences into a collective preference is the very heart of politics. If we do think something like the latter, then *axiomatic social choice theory* enlightens us about the conditions under which rational individual preferences can be aggregated into a rational collective preference. I begin in Section 5.2 with a finding of axiomatic social theory that endorses the rationality of democracy, and then consider a series of related results that cast doubt on the rationality of collective choice and, apparently, democratic choice.

5.1 THE MARKET AND THE FORUM

Rationality, we have seen, can either lead us to efficient outcomes (Chapter 3) or get us stuck in Pareto-inferior outcomes such as the Prisoner's Dilemma (Chapter 4). And, in any event, although efficiency is a value closely connected to our notion of rationality, it is not itself a moral value, and other values may clash with it. All these considerations have led political theorists to justify government as a coercive organization that can move society to valuable or worthy social states that cannot be brought about by market transactions. Sometimes the problem is that the market has failed to yield efficient results—government, it is said, is necessary to move us to social states in which we enjoy public goods, and regulate negative externalities (given non-zero transaction costs). At other times government pursues values in addition to efficiency, as when it seeks a fairer distribution of resources. More basically, we need government to define property rights.

But what values is government to pursue? If we all agreed that government is to supply exactly the same set of public goods (in agreed-upon precise amounts), there would be no great problem. If we look at a 2×2 matrix of the Prisoner's Dilemma it is obvious what we would want government to do—get us to the cooperate/cooperate payoff (by changing the game so that defection is no longer the dominant strategy). Clearly, though, this is to ignore the very fact on which economic analysis builds: our orderings of outcomes usually differ. In market transactions we benefit from the diversity of preference orderings: it is because you order the outcomes differently than do I that we can engage in mutually beneficial trade. You prefer a chicken wing to another slice of pizza, and I prefer a slice of pizza to another chicken wing, so we trade. But diversity of preferences is much more of a challenge to most government policies: in most cases, when the government acts we must all do the same thing even though our preferences differ.

There are two very different responses to this problem: let us call them (very broadly) *preference respecting* and *preference transforming* views of the political. On a preference respecting view, we suppose that each person has an ordering over possible political outcomes that expresses his overall values, goals, and so on: we can call these his "normative criteria." As we have seen, utility functions can accommodate all the normative criteria relevant to choice: I have been at pains to argue that they need not be about what promotes your self-interest, or wealth, or whatever. On this view, the basic data of politics should be the same as the basic data of economics: people's orderings of the outcomes capturing all that they see as normatively important for making a choice. The difference between the market and the political forum is that in the market each person makes her own choice, based on her preferences and option set, whereas in the political setting we come together with our individual preference orderings and seek to make a uniform collective choice. Just as we have been concerned with rational individual choice, and the axioms that individual choice must meet to be rational, we can develop axioms of rational collective choice.

Jon Elster, a proponent of the preference transformative view, thinks that this preference respecting view

> embodies a confusion between the kind of behavior that is appropriate in the market place and that which is appropriate in the forum. The notion of consumer sovereignty [in the market] is acceptable because, and to the extent that, the consumer chooses between courses of action that differ only in the ways it affects him. In political choice situations, however, the citizen is asked to express his preference over states that also differ in the way that they affect other people. . . . [T]he task of politics is not only to eliminate inefficiency but also create justice. . . . [1]

We should clearly distinguish two lines of criticism of the preference respecting approach suggested by Elster's remarks. First, Elster insists that political choice is not simply about efficiency but about justice, and that is why aggregating individual preferences into a social choice is inappropriate. But while this may be true if we suppose that political agents are simply *Homo Economicus* (see Chapter 6), we have seen that utility functions can include the entire range of normative considerations, including notions of justice. So the mere idea of starting out with individual preference orderings to determine a social choice about what is just is not "incongruous."[2] The second criticism, though, has considerably more bite: once we are concerned with collective choice, we can't simply rest content with the idea that a person's preferences are his own business. Recall Prude and Lascivious (Section 3.2). Each has a preference about what books the other is to read: should our collective political choice take these external preferences into account?

In response to these worries preference transformative views see politics as a way of coming together in the public forum, arguing, and changing each other's minds. It is not enough to simply assert "this is my preference"—preferences that were not formed by a properly reflective process, or some sorts of external preferences, or preferences that could not be publicly revealed (say, racist preferences), should be transformed (or eliminated) in reasoned political discussion. In one sense, the transformative view is clearly correct: we do not think that discriminatory external preferences should be the basis of a social choice. Still, the contrast between the market and the forum is not quite so sharp as the advocate of the transformative view suggests. For one thing, we have seen that all desires or goals can be criticized as not sufficiently reflective, or formed by nonautonomous processes (Section 1.2). There is no reason intrinsic to market analysis to prevent arguing that some desires, say those for addictive drugs, should not be met by the market. Indeed, Cass Sunstein, an influential legal theorist, has offered a wide-ranging criticism of many market outcomes because they satisfy preferences that ought not to be respected.[3] And even in the market some sorts of external preferences are a worry: can one claim that others have inflicted a negative externality on you because they have read a book you don't like? Is reading such a book inefficient? So the debate between preference respecting and transformative views occurs within analyses of the market itself.

Another reason that the contrast between preference respecting and preference transformative views of politics is not as clear-cut as one might think is that, even after debate and transformation in the forum, we can still expect an extremely wide range of preference orderings about what is the best social choice. To be sure, some contemporary political theorists, known as "deliberative democrats," seem to hope for significant consensus on political issues, but this does not look terribly plausible in extensive and diverse polities such as the United States, the United Kingdom, and the European Union.[4] Even after deliberation and discussion we are apt to be left with a diverse set of preferences which, presumably, the social choice mechanism then will have to respect, thus leading us back to the preference respecting view of the forum.

In this chapter I explore political choice on the preference respecting view. If one upholds the pure preference respecting view of politics—Elster's "market" view—then the following analysis should be of great interest. Insofar as one endorses the transformative view of the political, some of the problems explored in this chapter will be of less concern, as some of the worries about collective choice will stem from allowing citizens to hold any ordering over outcomes that their normative criteria recommend, and respecting these orderings in the social choice process. However, even for the transformative theorist, many of the problems we discuss—such as path dependency and strategic voting—must remain a deep concern.

5.2 AXIOMATIC SOCIAL CHOICE THEORY AND MAY'S THEOREM

According to Thomas Jefferson, in collections of people self-government requires following a collection of wills expressed by the majority; the majority, typically although not always through voting, articulates this collection of wills.[5] Thinking of democracy as taking a collection of wills (or individual preference orderings) and generating a social will (or social preference ordering) is a long-standing and, in many ways, attractive idea. We might think of this "democratic collecting of wills" in two ways. (1) Most ambitious is to aim at a *social preference ordering*. It seems safe to suppose that we would want our social preference ordering to conform to the axioms of ordinal utility (Section 2.2): asymmetry of strict (social) preference, symmetry of (social) indifference, reflexivity, transitivity, and completeness all seem as important for a social ordering as they were for an individual ordering. Let us call a social outcome with these properties a *social ordering*. Let us say that a social welfare function (SWF) takes as *inputs* individual preference orderings and yields as *outputs* a social ordering. (2) Less ambitiously, we might aim only at a *collective choice rule* (CCR) that, from a set of options, selects the best choice. A CCR takes as inputs people's individual preference orderings and yields a selection of the socially best option. Let us call $(p_1 \ldots p_n)$ a profile of individual preference orderings (p_1 is the ordering of person 1, etc.) of a set options $(w, x, \ldots, z)$. The aim is to apply a CCR to take $(p_1 \ldots p_n)$ and select some "best" member of the option set $(w, x, \ldots, z)$. The aim of a SWF is to take $(p_1 \ldots p_n)$ and yield a social ordering of $(w, x, \ldots, z)$.

Axiomatic social choice theory considers the formal properties of social welfare functions and collective choice rules. Consider, for example, the important 1952 theorem by K. O. May.[6] The power of May's proof, which concerns a CCR between two options (x, y),[7] depends on the acceptability or reasonableness of the conditions that he imposes on any acceptable CCR.

> (i) *Universal Decisiveness.* The CCR will yield a decision between x and y for all possible configurations of individual preferences, such that either xPy, yPx, or xIy (read as: x is socially preferred to y, y is socially preferred to x, or x and y socially tie). All possible permutations of x and y must yield a single definite

social choice. We cannot have $[(xPy)$ & $(yPx)]$ or $[(xPy)$ & $(xIy)]$ or $[(yPx)$ & $(yIx)]$.[8]

(ii) *Undifferentiatedness.* The identity of the voters has no effect whether xPy, yPx, or xIy. For a given preference profile among voters $\{p_1 \ldots p_n\}$, that preference profile will always yield the same decision when the identities of the voters are permutated. If the social choice mechanism is undifferentiated, it doesn't matter what names are attached to the votes: the CCR counts the votes without paying attention to the voters' identities.

(iii) *Neutrality.* If for a given profile of individual preferences $\{p_1 \ldots p_n\}$, xPy (or xIy), and, keeping that profile, if x is relabeled as w, and y is relabeled as z, then wPz (or wIz). A collective choice rule should be neutral between alternatives in so far as neither alternative has a built-in advantage, and so the labels attached to the proposal don't matter. For example, a rule that a 2/3 decision is required to pass a proposal, otherwise it fails, violates neutrality: it is biased in favor of the status quo. The rationale behind neutrality is that we do not want our social decision-making procedure to work to the advantage of some options ("no change from the status quo") and to the disadvantage of others ("change the status quo"). Under the 2/3 rule just discussed, the decision-making rule favors those people with conservative preferences and places an extra obstacle in front of those with reformist preferences.

(iv) *Strong Montonicity.* This includes two conditions: non-negative responsiveness and positive responsiveness. According to *non-negative responsiveness*, if already xPy, and one or more voters change their previous vote for y to a vote for x, then still xPy. A social choice mechanism is weakly monotonic if it always is the case that if some one individual changes her preferences such that she is more favorable to x than previously; then if there is any change at all in the social choice, it is an outcome more favorable to x. Non-negative responsiveness seems a minimum requirement for an acceptable CCR (or SWF). If we were deciding on what mechanism to adopt to produce a social choice out of individual preference orderings, we would insist that whatever social choice mechanism we adopt, it will never be the case that someone's becoming more favorable to an alternative itself, with no other changes on anyone else's part, causes that alternative to be rejected. According to *positive responsiveness* ties can be broken by just one voter changing her mind. If xIy and one y voter changes to x, then xPy. That is, the social choice mechanism positively responds to the decision of a single voter in the case of a tie. The rule used by most juries is not positively responsive. Say that a jury is deadlocked 6 for conviction, 6 for acquittal. This might be called a tie: $\neg(xPy)$ and $\neg(yPx)$. Now say that one person changes his mind such that 5 jurors are for conviction, and 7 for acquittal. This doesn't break the tie. If a system fails to be positively responsive, it says that there is nothing to choose between two alternatives even though some one individual changes his preferences to support one while everyone else's preferences remain the same. In effect, such a system ignores this person's change of preference.

These are the conditions that, May believes, any reasonable CCR (collective choice rule) should meet. May's theorem shows that one, and only one, CCR satisfies all four conditions when deciding between two options: *simple majority voting*. The basic reasoning runs like this. The first three conditions imply that if the number of votes for y equals the number of votes for x, then xIy. To see why this is so, suppose that it was false, and so even though x and y had the same number of votes, xPy. We now appeal to neutrality, and re-label x as w, and y as z. So we then have wPz. Now appeal to undifferentiatedness and change the identity of the voters, so that everyone who voted for x becomes a z voter, and everyone who was a y voter becomes a w voter. Undifferentiatedness requires that the identity of the voters doesn't matter, just the number of votes, so it must be the case that if previously xPy, now zPw. But we have defined z as a re-label of y; so on the same set of preference profiles the rule has selected both x and y, and that violates decisiveness. Therefore it is not consistent with our first three axioms to suppose that if x and y have the same number of voters, xPy. We can see that this reasoning will lead us to conclude that if the number of votes for y equals the number of votes for x, then xIy. We now invoke positive responsiveness: if one voter changes to x, then positive responsiveness requires that xPy. At this point we have arrived at the simple majority rule. 50% + 1 generates a winner. We also can show that non-negative responsiveness is satisfied by simple majority rule. Suppose that x beat y by k votes; then suppose that one y voter changes to x, so that x now wins by $k + 1$ votes. This change cannot reverse the outcome of xPy.

May's original theorem, though limited to choices between two options, is still important. At some point or another we are apt to wonder "What is so special about making decisions by a vote where over 50% wins? Why over 50% and not over 45% or 60%?" May provides an answer: out of every conceivable CCR, majority voting between two alternatives alone satisfies these four reasonable conditions. Moreover, the limits on May's theorem are not as severe as was previously thought: recently Robert Goodin and Christian List have offered a version of May's theorem that extends it to instances involving three or more options, where it provides a case for plurality voting (but see Section 5.3).[9]

5.3 ARROW'S THEOREM

Condorcet Voting and Its Paradox

May's theorem shows that majority rule uniquely satisfies his conditions when choosing among two options. Let's now consider choices among three or more options. Of all the ways of choosing between three or more policies, candidates, etc., the *Condorcet method* seems the most direct extension of simple democracy between two choices (x,y). Simple majority vote handles pairwise choices very nicely; it puts a question to the voters "x or y?" Things get complicated by the introduction of a third alternative, z. We often use plurality, or "first past the post," asking "which do you want, x, y, or z?" But plurality need not give us a majority winner: x can win a plurality contest with 40% of the vote (with y and z both getting 30%). The Condorcet method stays truer to the core idea of simple majority rule by taking a vote between each pair of alternatives: now we have three questions rather than just one: x or y?, y or z?, x or z? In each case the winner will be by simple majority: if one option beats every other alternative, then we can say that the majority prefers this

TABLE 5-1 Condorcet Paradox
Preferences

Alf	Betty	Charlie
x	y	z
y	z	x
z	x	y

option to every other; it is always preferred by a majority when compared against each other alternative, one at a time.

Condorcet voting gives rise to the Condorcet Paradox, as in the preferences in Table 5-1. If we take a series of pairwise votes, we get: xPy, yPz and zPx—an intransitive result. Thus out of a set of individual preferences that meets all axioms of a rational ordering, we generate an intransitive social "ordering."

Arrow's Conditions

Arrow's theorem can be understood as a generalization of the Condorcet Paradox. As with May's theorem, we first postulate a set of conditions that we would want our social welfare function (SWF) to meet.

Universal Domain (U). The SWF must yield a social ordering for a set of options for all logically possible individual orderings of the options.

Pareto Principle (Pr). For any pair of options (x, y), if for all individuals $x \succ y$, then xPy. [Read: if every individual prefers x to y, then the social preference is x over y.]

Pairwise Independence of Irrelevant Alternatives (I). The basic idea here is that the social choice between x and y should not depend on the presence or absence of a third (irrelevant for this pairwise choice) alternative, z. One way to formalize this idea is to suppose that we have a SWF, and we apply it to two different sets of individual preferences orderings $\{p_1 \ldots p_n\}$, $\{p'_1 \ldots p'_n\}$. Suppose that x and y are in both sets, and every individual orders x and y the same in both sets. That is, whatever individual i's preference is between x and y in the first profile, he has the same pairwise preference in the second profile. An individual might vary all other preferences over other options between the two profiles, and the set of options in the two profiles may otherwise differ. Condition I requires that whatever social preference our SWF yields between x and y in the first profile must be the same in the second.

Nondictatorship (D). There is no individual i such that for every option, whatever i prefers is the social preference. That is, it cannot be the case that there is some i, such that for all (x,y) if $i{:}x \succ y$, then xPy.

The theorem, then, is that there is no SWF that satisfies these conditions. The key to the proof is that the conditions entail a contradiction. We begin by assuming that there is no dictator, but Arrow's proof shows that one can be uncovered. The core idea underlying the proof is that given unrestricted domain (all possible sets of individual preferences orderings are allowed), when we have two pairs of social preferences (xPy) & (yPz), transitivity can commit us to third social preference of xPz even if this preference is held by only one person: so, in essence, transitivity pushes us to a social preference even when just one person holds that preference.

The First Stage of the Theorem: From Local Semi-Decisiveness to Global Decisiveness

One way to understand Arrow's proof is as a two-stage argument.[10] First it is shown that *if* an individual has the power to decide between any one ordered pair of options (his individual preference is the social preference even if no one else agrees), he becomes the overall dictator. Second, it is shown there *really is* such a person; hence both steps together establish a dictator. The first stage of the argument, then, is to show how (roughly) if some individual has the sole power to make the social choice between two ordered options, this can give him the power to decide between all other pairs.

We must first introduce two more definitions:

Def 1: Semi-decisiveness. A set of individuals S is *semi-decisive* for x over y if xPy (that is, the social preference in x over y) when for every individual in S $x \succ y$, and $y \succ x$ for every individual not in S. Note two things. First, that S is semi-decisive for x over y does not entail that S is semi-decisive for y over x. Second, we can see that semi-decisiveness is rather odd: S determines the social preferences only when everyone in it prefers x to y *and* everyone not in S has the opposite preference, y over x.

Def 2: Decisiveness. A set of individuals S is decisive for x over y if xPy when for every individual in S, $x \succ y$. So if S is decisive, when it agrees that $x \succ y$, then xPy regardless of what those outside of S prefer. Decisiveness is a stronger condition than semi-decisiveness, so if S is decisive for x over y, S is *semi-decisive* for x over y.

We first can show that *if* there is some individual Alf, who is semi-decisive between any pair (x,y), then Alf must be a dictator. Starting with Alf's semi-decisiveness over just one pair, he becomes decisive over every pair—a dictator.

So our supposition is that Alf is semi-decisive for x over y. Let z be any other alternative. Suppose that Alf's preference ordering is $(x \succ y)$ & $(y \succ z)$, and for everyone else in society (call these The Others): $(y \succ x)$ & $(y \succ z)$. Remember, given the unlimited domain condition, we can specify any preferences we like. Note that the preference relation between x and z is only specified (via transitivity) for Alf. We have, then, for Alf $x \succ y$, and for The Others $y \succ x$; Alf's semi-decisive power over the (x,y) pair implies that xPy. The Pareto principle now can be invoked to determine the social preference between y and z; since for Alf $y \succ z$, and for The Others $y \succ z$, then by the Pareto principle yPz. We also know that a SWF must yield a transitive social preference, thus given (xPy) & (yPz), it must follow that xPz. Again, we know that xPz even though we have not supposed anything about any nondecisive individual's preference between x and z. We have only assumed that for The Others, $y \succ z$ and $y \succ x$. Here the independence condition comes in: by pairwise independence of irrelevant alternatives we know that the preferences of The Others over y and z, and over y and x, cannot affect their preferences over x and z. So nothing in the assumptions we have made about the preferences of The Others has any implications for their preferences of x and z; it is only Alf for whom we have specified $x \succ z$. Hence for Alf $x \succ z$ implies that xPz regardless of how The Others order x and z. Alf's semi-decisive power for x over y has led to his decisive power for x over z. So now he is decisive over (x,z) too: *his original semi-decisiveness has spread to decisiveness over a new pair.* So we have our first conclusion:

1. *If Alf is semi-decisive over* (x,y), *he is decisive over* (x,z).

And we can see that his decisiveness will spread even further. Suppose Alf's preferences are $(z \succ x)$ & $(x \succ y)$; that of The Others is $(z \succ x)$ & $(y \succ x)$. The Pareto condition implies that, since for everyone $z \succ x$, it must be zPx. And since Alf is semi-decisive over (x,y), his preference $x \succ y$ implies xPy. Since we have (zPx) & (xPy), transitivity entails zPy. Again, note that we have no information about what The Others think about the preference relation between z and y; all we know is that Alf holds $z \succ y$ (by transitivity); so now Alf's semi-decisiveness over (x,y) has given him decisiveness over (z,y). So:

2. *If Alf is semi-decisive over* (x,y), *he is decisive over* (z,y).

Now let's use our result from step (1). Recall that we discovered that (1) if Alf is semi-decisive over (x,y), he is decisive over (x,z). Given definitions 1 and 3, if Alf is decisive over (x,z) he is also semi-decisive over that ordered pair. Let's now see how the semi-decisiveness over (x,z) spreads. Suppose next that Alf's preferences are $(y \succ x)$ & $(x \succ z)$, while for all The Others $(y \succ x)$ & $(z \succ x)$. Since Alf is semi-decisive over (x,z), it must be xPz. Again, since everyone holds $(y \succ x)$, the Pareto principle implies yPx. Invoking transitivity, if (yPx) & (xPz), then yPz. We again see that we have no information about the preference of The Others between (y,z), but do know that (by transitivity) Alf holds $y \succ z$. So the mere fact that Alf holds $y \succ z$ implies yPz. Thus:

3. *If Alf is semi-decisive over* (x,z), *he is decisive over* (y,z).

By the close of the third step Alf's semi-decisiveness over (x,y) has spread to decisiveness over the ordered pairs (x,z), (z,y), and (y,z). The same general reasoning can be repeatedly invoked to show that Alf's decisiveness keeps on spreading until he is decisive over every ordered pair among (x,y,z): (x,y), (y,x), (x,z), (z,x), (y,z), and (z,y). Table 5-2 summarizes the necessary steps.

Once Alf is decisive over all combinations of (x,y,z), we can see that he will be decisive over *all alternatives from the full set of options* (that is, he is a dictator). To see this, take two options out of the larger set at random: call them (v,w). If (v,w) happened to be our original (x,y) alternatives, then we have already shown that Alf is

TABLE 5-2 The Steps of the First Part of Arrow's Theorem

If Alf Is Semi-Decisive Over	Alf's Preferences	The Others' Preferences	Social Preferences	Alf Is Then Decisive Over
1. (x,y); assumption	$(x > y)$ & $(y > z)$	$(y > x)$ & $(y > z)$	(xPy) & (yPz), so (xPz)	(x,z)
2. (x,y); assumption	$(z > x)$ & $(x > y)$	$(z > x)$ & $(y > x)$	(zPx) & (xPy), so (zPy)	(z,y)
3. (x,z); from (1)*	$(y > x)$ & $(x > z)$	$(y > x)$ & $(z > x)$	(yPx) & (xPz), so (yPz)	(y,z)
4. (y,z); from (3)*	$(y > z)$ & $(z > x)$	$(z > y)$ & $(z > x)$	(yPz) & (zPx), so (yPx)	(y,x)
5. (y,x); from (4)*	$(z > y)$ & $(y > x)$	$(z > y)$ & $(x > y)$	(zPy) & (yPx), so (zPx)	(z,x)
6. (x,z); from (1)*	$(x > z)$ & $(z > y)$	$(z > x)$ & $(z > y)$	(xPz) & (zPy), so (xPy)	(x,y)

*Decisiveness over an ordered pair implies semi-decisiveness over that pair.

decisive over them. Suppose that one of them was y, but the other was different, so we have a triple (x,y,w). But we have already shown that if Alf is semi-decisive for x over y, he is decisive for all pairs in the triple containing x and y, so again Alf is decisive over all. Lastly, suppose that v and w are different from x and y. Take just v; we have the triple (x,y,v). We have already shown that Alf is decisive over every pair in a triple containing x and y, so Alf will be decisive for x over v. Now add to the (x,v) set w, giving us the triple (x,v,w). Now we have already shown that if Alf is semi-decisive over two options in a triple, he is decisive over all the options; since we have said that he is decisive for x and v (and so he must be semi-decisive between them too), he must be decisive for all ordered pairs of (x,v,w). But now we have shown that Alf's semi-decisiveness over two options leads to an "epidemic":[11] if he is semi-decisive over one pair he is decisive over all pairs. That makes him a dictator.

TABLE 5-3 Condorcet Paradox Orderings in Arrow's Theorem

Alf	V-Alf	O
x	z	y
y	x	z
z	y	x

The Second Stage of the Theorem:
Finding the Dictator

The first stage was hypothetical: it holds that *if* there is a person like Alf who has semi-decisive power over one pair (x,y), he will be a dictator. We now have to show that there is at least one pair over which Alf is semi-decisive; if we do that, given the first part of the proof, we will show he is a dictator. We know that there has to be some decisive set for every ordered pair, even if that S is the entire society. It follows by Definition 2, remember, that any set which is decisive is also semi-decisive. So let us examine all the decisive sets over all pairs, and choose the smallest such set (the smallest decisive set over *any* pairwise choice), and call it V. Assume that V is decisive for (x,y). We have said that V is the smallest decisive set; either it contains one person or more than one. If it contains one, we have found our dictator. Suppose, then, that it contains more than one person. Divide V into two groups, Alf and "V minus Alf" (*V-Alf*). Call those outside of V, The Others, O. Unrestricted domain allows us to suppose any possible preference ordering, so we choose our Condorect Paradox orderings, as in Table 5-3.

Since for all members of V $x \succ y$, it must be that xPy: this follows from the definition of V being the decisive set over (x,y). What about y and z? We see from Table 5-3 that only *V-Alf* holds $z \succ y$; if zPy, then *V-Alf* would be the decisive set for z over y. But we have supposed that V is the smallest decisive set; since *V-Alf* is a proper subset of V, it cannot be a decisive set. So we know $\neg(zPy)$. By completeness, then, it must be that y is socially at least as preferred (strictly preferred, or indifferent) to z (call this relation yRz).[12] If, though, xPy & yRz, transitivity implies xPz. If x is preferred to y, and y is at least as good as z, then x must be preferred to z. However Alf is the only person who holds $x \succ z$, so Alf is semi-decisive for x over z. So we have located a single person who is semi-decisive over one pair. But, by the first part of the proof, that shows him to be decisive over all options, so he is a dictator. But we have assumed nondictatorship: hence we have contradicted our original assumptions. All the conditions cannot be met.

Arrow's proof is sometimes said to reveal a conflict between "representation" and "coherence." We can obtain coherent social preferences if we are willing to abandon the requirement that the social preference reflects the preferences of the body of citizens (we can accept a dictator or abandon the Pareto principle); or we can ensure that the social preference reflects the preferences of the citizens, but then, as the Condorect Paradox shows, we can end up with an incoherent social preference. One can easily see why Arrow's theorem is seen as challenge to the rationality of democracy. If the aim of democracy is to generate a social decision that (1) represents the preferences of the citizens no matter what their preferences, and yet (2) is coherent, it seems that democracy aims at the impossible. Not all the conditions can be met; the set is contradictory.

How Much of a Challenge Is Arrow's Theorem to Democracy?

There is a good deal of debate about how much of a threat Arrow's theorem is to democracy. Interestingly, some insist that it is absolutely central, and must cause us to question whether democracy can be said to be a way to generate a reasonable social choice, while others dismiss the theorem as interesting, but not crucial. There are four important ways to challenge it.

First, we might dispute whether Arrow's conditions are really intuitively compelling: to the extent that we do not mind dropping one of the conditions, the proof should not cause worries. The pairwise independence condition has been subject to considerable debate, and many are happy to drop it. However, violating any of Arrow's conditions entails significant costs, often more than his critics appreciate. SWFs that violate the independence condition, for example, tend to be subject to manipulation (see Section 5.5).

Second, it is sometimes argued that Arrow's theorem is concerned with mere "preferences" but democratic decision making is about rational judgments about what is in the common good; so, it is said, Arrow's problem of how to aggregate individual preferences into a social preference is irrelevant to democratic decision making. This challenge is, I think, misguided, for at least two reasons. (*a*) As I have stressed throughout, a "preference" is simply a ranking of one option over another—it does not necessarily involve a liking, any sort of selfishness, etc. If democratic politics is about asking people to choose among candidates or policies (for whatever reasons), the idea of a preference is entirely appropriate. (*b*) Second, Christian List and Philip Pettit have presented an Arrow-like impossibility theorem that concerns the aggregation of judgments based on several reasons. So even if we understand democratic politics as a "forum" in which people debate (and vote on) the reasons for their political judgments rather than simply reporting their conclusions (rankings), a result very much like Arrow's obtains.[13]

Third, some insist that in democratic politics we do not aim at a social ordering, but only a social choice (we see democracy as a CCR, not a SWF), and thus, again, we need not worry about the theorem. I consider that reply in the next section.

Fourth, it can be argued that Arrow relies on the Condorcet Paradox preference orderings in finding the dictator, but if this pattern of orderings does not, as a matter of fact, often arise, then we won't actually confront the inconsistency at the heart of the proof. Again, it is important to realize that unrestricted domain does a lot of work in the theorem.

There is a nice answer to when we can expect Condorcet Paradox sorts of orderings to arise. Let us call a *dimension* an option space along which each person has some ideal point, and in each direction, the further you get from the person's ideal point, the less preferred is the option. Right to Left in politics; Dove to Hawk on war issues; pro to con on civil rights—all these are examples of an option dimension. Consider a voter, Alf. Say he sees the options (x, y, z) as arranged along the Left/Right dimension in politics. Alf is a middle-of-the-road independent, so he prefers y as the best; x and z are worse than y. But let us say he thinks that z is better than x. Betty too sees the options in terms of a Left/Right dimension, but being a Leftist, she ranks x as the best, Alf's middle-of-the-road y as the second best, and z as the worst. Charlie also sees the options along this dimension, but as a conservative he orders them $z \succ y \succ x$. We thus get Figure 5-1.

In this case, although Alf, Betty, and Charlie disagree on the best option, because they order their options along the same dimension, all their preference curves are *single-peaked*. If all the preferences are single-peaked, Condorcet Paradox preference orderings cannot arise. Assume, though, that Betty no longer sees the options in terms of

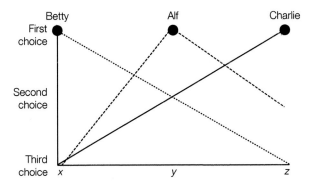

FIGURE 5-1 Single-Peaked Preferences

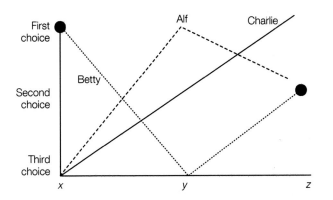

FIGURE 5-2 A Double-Peaked Preference: Condorcet Paradox
Preferences

Left/Right, but in terms of free-market/anti-market. And suppose
that she sees x, the option of the Left as most anti-market, but her
second choice is z, the option of the right, since the conservatives too
have doubts about "liberal economics." She thus changes her ordering and we get Figure 5-2.

Betty no longer orders her preferences along the x-y-z dimension; we can see that her preference curve is *double-peaked*: this is not
the relevant dimension along which she orders her options. Even
though y is closer to her ideal point than is z, she prefers z to y. And
now we have a Condorcet Paradox ordering. *Thus when voters do not*

agree on the relevant dimension of the option space, Condorcet Paradox orderings can arise. How often do cycles actually arise? There is spirited debate about this in the literature on democracy: some think that uncontrived cycles are rare, while others think them more common.[14] As we will see, however, the main importance of Condorcet Paradox type cycles may be the way they lend themselves to various sorts of contrived manipulation.

5.4 COLLECTIVE CHOICE RULES

It is hard to have faith in any SWF in the light of Arrow's theorem. To be sure, as I have stressed, SWFs can, under some profile of preferences, satisfy the Pareto principle, nondictatorship, and the independence of irrelevant alternatives. But when the preference profiles of the citizens display considerable multidimensionality, Arrow-type problems come to the fore. Moreover, as we shall see, minorities can generate voting cycles by misrepresenting their true preferences, thus magnifying the problems to which Arrow points.

At this point, though, students of democracy may insist that social welfare functions are not really of much interest. After all, we do not want a social ordering, just a social *choice*: for any set of options, we only want to pick out the *best*. Our interest should be in collective choice rules, not social welfare functions.[15] At first blush this looks inviting: some CCRs meet all of Arrow's conditions, so the proof does not preclude all CCRs. The difference between a SWF and a CCR is, of course, the transitivity requirement: Arrow requires strict transitivity of the social ordering of all options. What does a CCR require? Let us follow Sen in requiring of any collective choice rule that, for any set of options (w,x,y,z), the CCR can select one option as best. Now Sen shows that so understood, such a CCR requires social preferences that are reflexive, complete (Section 2.2), and *acyclical* over the entire set of preferences.[16] Preferences are acyclical if (wPx, xPy, yPz) then wRz—w must be, socially, at least as good as z. We can easily see how cyclical preferences mean that there may be no best choice from some sets. Consider the Condorcet Paradox preferences in Table 5-1, and consider what is the best choice from the set (x,y,z). There is, of course, no best choice from the entire set: we get xPy, yPz, zPx, so we cannot choose. So if we are going to guarantee that a choice can always be made we must ensure that we do not have cycles;

thus we require that the results be *acyclical*. To get a better idea of a CCR, consider an example of a rule that Sen discusses:

> *Pareto Choice or Indifference*: if for everyone $x \succ y$, then xPy; if it is not the case that for everyone $y \succ x$, then xRy (that is, x is socially at least as good as y).

So on this rule, x is socially preferred to y if and only if everyone prefers it; and, of course, the same goes for y *vis-à-vis* x. If there is any disagreement in people's strict preference profiles about x and y (for some $x \succ y$, for others $y \succ x$), then (xRy) and (yRx)—x is socially at least as good as y, and y is socially at least as good as x. And that means that socially x and y are indifferent (xIy). Using this CCR, our Condorcet Paradox orderings in Table 5-1 yield a "choice" of xIy, yIz, xIz. But in this case the rule satisfies all of Arrow's requirements. Suppose instead we just consider Alf and Betty's preferences from Table 5-1. For Alf ($x \succ y \succ z$) and for Betty ($y \succ z \succ x$). Since for both $y \succ z$, then the CCR yields yPz; since they disagree on the other pairings we get social indifference—xIy, yIz. Now, however, transitivity is violated. Given (xIy) & (yPz), we should get (xPz): if society is indifferent between x and y, but y is better than z, transitivity would hold that x is better than z. Instead our CCR says xIz. However, acyclicity does still hold: we get a "best" (even if it is a tie) from every possible set. We also can see that Pareto Choice or Indifference satisfies all the rest of Arrow's conditions. It obviously satisfies the Pareto condition, since it is defined never to yield a choice against it. It does not violate the independence of irrelevant alternatives, since we can see that in deciding between x and y, it is only concerned with people's preferences over x and y; we have a good inkling that unrestricted domain will not cause trouble, since we have used Condorcet Paradox orderings; and we can never have a dictator, since xPy only if everyone agrees.

However, while Arrow's theorem does not apply to CCRs (since they do not require transitivity), they have their own Arrow-like problems. Arrow, it will be recalled, showed that a SWF meeting the pairwise independence condition (I), unrestricted domain (U), and the Pareto principle (Pr) always has a dictator; it has been shown that any CCR that meets I, U, and Pr will always have something very much like an *oligarchy* (a subgroup) that can always veto a social choice.[17] That is, the dynamic of Arrow's theorem, in which decision-making power becomes concentrated in one person, also obtains for CCR, though in a somewhat mitigated form. Instead of a dictator, we find subgroups that are able to impose their will by blocking whatever others want or (given slightly different conditions) actually imposing their will.

Recall that earlier I considered contraction and expansion principles (Section 2.4). According to the *contraction principle*, if from a set (x,y,z) a person chooses (x), he must choose x from the other subsets in which it enters (x,y), (x,z). If it is the best in the entire set, it must be best in every subset it is in. It would be odd indeed if, thinking that x is the best choice when confronted by two options, one no longer thinks that x is best if one considers it in relation to just one of those options. According to the *expansion principle* (roughly), if x is chosen as best in the set (x,y,z), and if there is a set (w,x,y,z), y or z cannot be the social choice from the larger set; if x is better than y and z in the small set, it must be better than they are in the larger set. This expansion principle implies the *weak expansion principle* I considered in Section 2.4. If x is chosen from the set (x,y,z) and x is chosen from the set (v,w,x), it must be chosen from the union of those two sets.

These seem reasonable conditions of consistent choice: collective choice rules that violate them yield inconsistent choices about what is the best depending on how we cut up the options. If we violate these principles, then an option that is best in a large set may not be best in a smaller set; an option that beats another in a small set may lose to that same option in a larger set. However, it can be shown that the expansion property applied to CCRs that always yield a social choice essentially turns them into SWFs, and so Arrow's theorem can then be appiled to such CCRs. Thus, roughly speaking, if we wish to avoid Arrow's theorem by adopting a CCR we must abandon the expansion principle as a principle of rational choice. And that involves some cost.

Path Dependency and Agenda Manipulation

Arrow stressed the importance of a final choice being independent of the path to it.[18] The crux of *path independency* is that the best choice from the set $\{w,x,y,z\}$ should not vary depending on the order we take up the options, or the subsets we first consider in our path to a final choice. Path independency assures us that when our CCR selects a "best option" from a set, this selection is not an artifact of the order in which we considered the options—the path by which the final choice was reached. If we considered the same options in a different order, we would have arrived at the same choice from the same set. If, then, we aim at a CCR that really uncovers what is the best social choice given a profile of individual preferences, we would insist on a path-independent choice rule. When we employ a path-*dependent* choice rule, we must accept that while our CCR selected y as best from the set, it could have selected some other option from the same set if we had considered the options in another order. In that case our choice is to some extent an artifact of the path. However, it turns out that full path independence requires the *contraction* and *weak expansion principles*; given this, a path-independent CCR is subject to Arrow-like problems of concentration of decision-making power in some oligarchic-like group.[19]

The basic point is roughly this: to entirely avoid Arrow-like concentration of power problems we must embrace some sort of path-*dependent* CCR. So, we might ask, what is so bad about path-dependent CCRs? Why not avoid Arrow-like problems by simply rejecting the contraction and weak expansion principles? Consider most closely what follows from path dependency, such as the procedure used to decide on bills in the U.S. Congress. First a proposal (call it y) is brought before Congress; amendments (call one x) are then proposed, and a vote is taken between x and y. Finally there is a vote between no bill at all (call it z), and whatever bill won the x versus y contest. This means that one of the pairs—either (x,z) or (y,z)—is never voted on. Since the outcome depends on the order in which the options are considered (or, we might say, the way the total option set is divided up in decision making), those who control the agenda— the order in which the options are considered—have great power in determining the outcome. A committee chair who sets the agenda may well be able to determine the outcome. Path-dependent CCRs thus allow for *manipulation of the agenda.*

Again, there is lively dispute about how pervasive path dependency and agenda manipulation are. William Riker famously argued that they were the stuff the politics. Consider, for example, Riker's account of the aid to education bill in the late 1950s and early 1960s.[20] The Democratic leadership in the U.S. House of Representatives put forward a bill that would provide the states with federal funds for building schools. The Democrats were generally in favor of such aid while the Republicans opposed it. However, each time the bill was proposed, Adam Clayton Powell, an African-American member from Harlem, offered an amendment, requiring that aid would only be given to states whose schools were "open to all children without regard to race." Southern Democrats—who supported federal aid to education, since they would be net recipients—opposed the amendment, since under the amendment the South would not receive aid, having segregated school systems. In contrast, urban Democrats from the North supported the amendment; but the Democratic leadership opposed the amendment, primarily because it would make the school aid bill harder to pass. The Republicans, who were generally against the expansion of the federal government, opposed federal aid to education. To analyze the voting, let:

$x = $ the bill with the Powell amendment

$y = $ the original, unamended bill

$z = $ the status quo (no federal aid to education)

Let us distinguish four groups in Congress:

The Powellians: $x \succ y \succ z$. These members preferred the amended bill to the original bill, and preferred both to no bill at all. Northern Democrats would form the core of this group.

The School Aiders: $y \succ x \succ z$. This group preferred school aid to anything else. This included democrats following the Democratic party leadership (who saw the Powell amendment as killing school aid) and some Republicans.

The Southerners: $y \succ z \succ x$. As the story indicates, they were for school aid but strongly against the Powell amendment.

Republicans against Aid: $z \succ x \succ y$. This probably is not quite right; Riker argues that the Republicans split into two groups, as we will see later on. But for now, I will treat them as one group with this preference order.

Riker advances the following estimate of the relative strengths of the groups:

The Powellians $(x \succ y \succ z)$: 132

The School Aiders $(y \succ x \succ z)$: 67

The Southerners $(y \succ z \succ x)$: 130

Republicans against Aid $(z \succ x \succ y)$: 97

Given this estimate, the result of Condorcet voting would be xPy (229 to 197), yPz (329 to 97), zPx (227 to 199)—a cycle. Note that the original bill (y) easily defeats no bill (z) by a large margin of 329 to

**T A B L E 5-4   The Condorect Paradox Preferences and the Borda
Count**

	x	y	z
Alf's ranking	1	2	3
Betty's ranking	3	1	2
Charlie's ranking	2	3	1
Total in three-way contest	6	6	6

97. But because of path dependency, z was selected. Recall that given the path-dependent process followed by Congress, once y was defeated by x it was eliminated from consideration, leaving only x to survive and confront z, with x losing to z. We see, though, that y would have defeated z, since we are in a cycle.

Gerry Mackie has investigated Riker's examples (including the case just presented) and has argued that careful investigation does not support Riker's conclusions. He makes two distinct claims. *First*, he challenges Riker's estimations of the voting strength of these groups. If y (the original bill) met z (no bill), Mackie argues that, based on another similar vote, z would have defeated y, hence there would have been no cycle.[21] Whereas Riker holds that y would have beaten z by a large margin, Mackie argues that z would have beaten y by a smaller one. So there is dispute about the true strengths of the groups, and whether there was a cycle—Riker himself suggests that there may not have been a "real" cycle, but that some of the Republicans voted "strategically" (Section 5.5). *Second*, Mackie argues that even if Riker's estimates of the strength of the groups are correct, Riker's conclusion that there is no coherent way to combine preferences still does not follow. "Does an alleged cycle," Mackie asks, "show once again that the aggregation of preferences is incoherent?" "No," he answers, because there would be other ways to choose among these preferences that would not result in a cycle. "If there was a cycle, then the problem is not with the preference rankings, the problem is with the voting procedure."[22] What can this mean? Consider again our Condorcet preference orderings, presented in Table 5-4 (in a different manner than we have displayed them previously).

We know that pairwise voting yields a cycle, xPy, yPz, zPx. But, as Mackie suggests, we might employ another procedure such as the

T A B L E 5-5 Borda's Violation of Independence (I)

	x	y
Alf's ranking	1	2
Betty's ranking	2	1
Charlie's ranking	1	2
Total in two-way contest	4	5

Borda Count: each option gets one point for being first, two for second place, and three points for third; that with the lowest total is socially most preferred. In this case we get a three-way tie, with all three options scoring six. In other cases the Borda method can yield a strict social preference even when pairwise voting yields a cycle. This seems the basis of Mackie's rather confusing claim that the problem is pairwise voting, not the preference rankings—some other system of voting would yield an answer. *Of course!* But recall Arrow's theorem: the problem is that *every system of voting violates one of the conditions* (Section 5.3). In Table 5-4 pairwise voting violates transitivity; but if we use Borda then we violate pairwise independence of irrelevant alternatives (Mackie is not impressed by this condition, and that explains his attractions to the Borda count). To see how the Borda count violates the pairwise independence condition, eliminate z from the list, so now there are only two options, x and y. Borda changes from xIy to xPy (x now gets four points while y gets five), as shown in Table 5-5.

Thus Borda gives a different pairwise judgment of the relative merits of x and y depending on whether a third, irrelevant alternative (to the pairwise choice) exists: no one has changed her relative evaluation of x and y, yet the SWF has changed its relative evaluation—a clear violation of the independence condition. We can see in this case why violating the pairwise independence condition is troubling: society's preference between x and y has changed even though no individual's preference between them has altered. But how can society "change its mind" when no individual has? The change appears arbitrary. The lesson of Arrow's theorem is that, as it were, we must choose our poison: will it be intransitivity, violation of the pairwise independence condition, the Pareto principle, unrestricted domain, or nondictatorship? We can always avoid cycles, but then we must violate some other condition. The "incoherence" of aggregation systems is not that they must yields cycles (that is clearly not the case, and Riker never thought it was), but that they must violate some basic axiom. Yet in a way Mackie is right: there is nothing wrong with the preference orderings; the problem is that there are only imperfect ways to aggregate them.

5.5 STRATEGIC VOTING

The problems I have thus far been exploring all have assumed that each individual is reporting her "true" preference. Of course on revealed preference theory it does not make any sense to distinguish what a person truly prefers from her behavior; we have seen, however, that revealed preference theory is inadequate (Section 2.1). So we suppose that people can indeed misreport their preferences; by doing so they often can obtain their favored outcome. The most obvious case of strategic voting involves multi-stage votes (such as votes on amendments and bills in Congress) and run-off elections. For example, in the Aid to Education Bill just discussed, Riker notes that the Democratic leadership in the House was convinced that the Republicans were not really in favor of the Powell amendment, but were voting strategically just to help kill the aid to education bill.[23] That is, the Democratic leadership was convinced that the Republicans' true preference ordering was: $z > y > x$ (no bill, original bill, amended bill). If that was the true preference ordering of even half the Republicans, the amendment would have failed, and Congress would have voted on the unamended bill, which would have passed. By misreporting their true preferences (voting for their third choice over the second choice when the amendment was initially proposed), these Republicans helped to secure their first choice. This of course is just an example. However, it has been shown that, roughly, non-random, nondictatorial voting procedures that are sensitive to the voter's full statement of preferences are subject to strategic manipulation. The Borda Count discussed in Section 5.4 is subject to strategic voting, as is voting is path-dependent procedures.[24]

Another case of voting against one's true preferences occurs when legislators vote against their preferences on Issue 1 (which they care less about) to achieve their preferred outcome on Issue 2 (which they care more about). Sometimes this is called "log rolling" or "vote

TABLE 5-6 An Example of Strategic Voting as Vote Trading (Based on Display 6-5, William Riker, *Liberalism Against Populism*.)

Rustbelters	Sunbelters	Others
$\neg y$	$\neg x, y$	$\neg x, \neg y$
x, y	x, y	$\neg x, y$
$\neg x, \neg y$	$\neg x, \neg y$	$x, \neg y$
$\neg x, y$	$x, \neg y$	x, y

trading." Assume that we have two issues to be decided in a legislature split into three factions.

x: whether to provide increased federal funds for urban renewal projects, which will mostly benefit the Rustbelt States. Someone *against* this we can say is for not-x, which will be designated $\neg x$.

y: whether to increase expenditure for defense. Those in the Sunbelt states will primarily benefit from this. Someone against this is for $\neg y$.

Our three groups are, then: Rustbelters, Sunbelters and Others. Each has 100 votes in our imaginary legislature. Their preferences are ordered in Table 5-6.

According to *Rustbelters'* preferences, they would prefer the urban aid, but don't want to also incur the costs of increased defense spending; perhaps they hope to fund the aid to urban areas with defense cuts. But they would prefer both the urban aid and increased defense spending to no urban aid at all. If they can't get their urban aid, they want to at least hold the line of federal spending so that their economies might improve. The last thing they want is increased federal spending and no urban aid. According to the *Sunbelters'* preferences, they not only want to resist defense cuts, but also want some increases in defense spending to spur growth in their states, many of which rely on defense contractors. They would prefer not to increase the federal deficit with urban renewal expenditure; however, they would prefer to have both urban renewal and increased defense spending to no increase in defense spending. But if they can't get the increase in defense spending they want, they certainly want to at least hold the line on other new expenditures, so they can go back to their districts arguing that they were in favor of keeping the lid on federal expenditure. The worst thing that could happen for them is for the Rustbelters to get their urban renewal aid, thus increasing the deficit but leaving them empty-handed. The *Others* are not enamored of either project; they are worried about the deficit, and see no pressing need for either expenditure. But if there has to be expenditure, it always sits better with their constituents if it is for defense. They don't, however, want to fund both projects at the same time—that would lead to terrible strains on the budget; so they prefer to fund the Rustbelters alone than to pay for both projects.

If we suppose sincere voting on the issues separately, both x and y are defeated, leaving us with $\neg x$, $\neg y$. However, there is clear possibility here for vote trading: The Rustbelters will agree to vote for the defense spending when that vote comes up (even though they prefer $\neg y$ to y), and the Sunbelters will agree to vote for urban aid when that vote comes up, even though they prefer $\neg x$ to x. If they do so, the decision in favor of $\neg x$, $\neg y$ is changed to x,y. They each get their second preference instead of their third: here the strategic vote against their first preference gained them their second choice. Yet in one sense society ends up with a result that would be clearly rejected if the votes were not linked. As we shall see in the next chapter, this dynamic might lead to the society making choices that are worse for everyone.

SUMMARY

This chapter has examined axiomatic social choice theory, focusing on its implications for democracy. Axiomatic social choice examines the formal properties of procedures that take a set of individual preferences over options and seek a social preference or group decision. In this chapter I have:

- *Argued that, even if we understand democratic politics as a "forum" rather than market, so long as citizens deeply disagree about how to order the options, we have the basic problem that axiomatic social choice theory investigates: how to take a set of diverse individual preferences and reach a rational social decision.*

- *Explicated May's theorem, which shows that, for choices between two options, majority rule uniquely satisfies a set of reasonable conditions.*

May's conditions are universal decisiveness, undifferentiatedness, neutrality, and strong montonicity.

- *Explicated Arrow's (much more complex) theorem.* We have seen that Arrow shows that in cases with three or more options, there is no social welfare function that meets a set of reasonable conditions. In the version of Arrow's theorem we considered, the conditions are universal domain, independence of irrelevant alternatives, nondictatorship, and the Pareto principle.

- *Considered the relevance of Arrow's theorem for democracy.* Many think that Arrow's theorem shows that any procedure for aggregating individual preferences into a social decision is either irrational or nonrepresentative. I stressed that, when preferences are multi-peaked, Condorect Paradox preferences can arise, and this leads to the sorts of problems Arrow explores.

- *Investigated whether the general sorts of problems Arrow identifies can be avoided if we aim only at a rational "social choice" rather than a "social ordering."* I argued that most of the problems remain. Rational collective choice rules ought to meet certain conditions, such as the contraction and expansion principles. If a collective choice rule satisfies the expansion principle, it is essentially a social welfare function.

- *Argued that if we do not satisfy reasonable conditions such as the contraction and weak expansion principles, our procedure is path-dependent.* If a choice is path-dependent, the order in which the options are considered can determine the outcome.

- *Examined an example of a path-dependent procedure—voting in the U.S. Congress.* We saw that path-dependent procedures can yield decisions even when we confront Condorcet cycles because some pairwise comparisons are not made. But it looks as if, in the case we considered, a different answer would have been reached if the options were considered in a different order (though, some observers have a different analysis of this case).

- *Considered the way in which misrepresentation of one's true preferences, what is called "strategic voting," can affect the outcome of a decision procedure.*

NOTES

1. Jon Elster, "The Market and Forum," pp. 10–11.

2. Ibid., p. 11.

3. Cass R. Sunstein, *Free Markets and Social Justice*, especially pp. 18ff. I defend preference respecting views of the market against Sunstein's criticisms in "Backwards Into the Future: Neo-Republicanism as a Post-Socialist Critique of Market Society."

4. I have argued this in *Contemporary Theories of Liberalism*, Chapter 5.

5. *Thomas Jefferson on Democracy*, edited by Saul K. Padover, p. 15.

6. K. O. May, "A Set of Independent, Necessary and Sufficient Conditions for Simple Majority Rule." For a statement of the formal proof, see A. K. Sen, *Collective Choice and Social Welfare*, pp. 71–72. I follow here Dennis C. Mueller, *Public Choice III*, pp. 133–137.

7. It should be clear how we could also see this as a SWF over two options. The distinction between a social welfare function and a collective choice rule only becomes important when we have three or more options in our option set.

8. This, of course, follows if we are aiming at a social ordering.

9. Robert E. Goodin and Christian List, "Unique Virtues of Plurality Rules: Generalizing May's Theorem."

10. My explication follows Sen's in *Collective Choice and Social Welfare*, Chapter 3. Wulf Gaertner also provides a nice explication of Sen's version of the proof, as well as two others in *A Primer in Social Choice Theory*. See also John Craven, *Social Choice*, Chapter 3; Mueller, *Public Choice III*, Chapter 24.

11. See Craven, *Social Choice*, pp. 36ff.

12. The social preference equivalent of $y \geq z$.

13. See Christian List and Philip Pettit, "Aggregating Sets of Judgments: An Impossibility Result." See also Philip Pettit, *A Theory of Freedom*, Chapter 5. The List-Pettit result is relevant to contexts in which the several reasons are relevant to a conclusion. Suppose that a legal doctrine says that a person is responsible for his action ϕ at law if and only if conditions A, B, and C *all* hold. Instead of taking a vote among jurors and asking each for their final decision ("Do conditions A, B, and C all hold?"), we might take a series of votes: "Does condition A hold?," "Does condition B hold?," and "Does Condition C hold?" After taking a series of votes on these three questions, we might say that the person is liable if and only if a majority of jurors have answered "yes" to all three questions. The answer generated by this procedure can differ radically

from the answer that would be generated by asking each juror "Do all three conditions hold?"

14. Reporting of the work of Richard Niemi, Riker tells us that if three fourths of voters in groups as small as 45 agree on the dimension along which issues range, then cycles will not occur. William H. Riker, *Liberalism Against Populism*, p. 128.

15. This section draws on Sen, *Collective Choice and Social Welfare,* Chapter 4, and Riker, *Liberalism Against Populism*, pp. 132–136.

16. Sen, *Collective Choice and Social Welfare*, pp. 14–16.

17. I am simplifying here. If one adopts a condition slightly stronger than acyclicity, called "quasi-transitivity" (transitivity of strict preference only), then there will always be an oligarchic group who can impose their preferences; if one adds positive responsiveness to the conditions, then such a CCR will have a dictator. The results for a CCR that only meets acyclicity are weaker, uncovering a vetoer, who is very similar to an oligarch group. See Riker, *Liberalism Against Populism*, p. 131, and especially note 18.

18. See Sen, *Collective Choice and Social Welfare*, p. 48n.

19. See Riker, *Liberalism Against Populism*, p. 135.

20. My account comes from William Riker, *The Art of Political Manipulation*, Chapter 11. All quotes are from this chapter.

21. Gerry Mackie, *Democracy Defended*, p. 201.

22. Riker, *The Art of Political Manipulation*, p. 200. Mackie also disputes this claim of Riker's (and just about every other claim Riker ever made!). See *Democracy Defended*, pp. 201ff.

23. Riker, *Liberalism Against Populism*, pp. 152–153.

24. See Mueller, *Public Choice III,* pp. 593–594.

6

Public Choice Theory

OVERVIEW

I began the last chapter with Jon Elster's distinction between the market and the forum. Social choice theory, Elster maintained, employs an economic model based on fixed preferences and wrongly applies it to politics, which is about deliberation and preference change. Leaving aside the validity of the charge, social choice theory is only "economic" in a very weak sense: it employs ordinal utility based on given preferences and analyzes ways to aggregate these preferences. Social choice theory does not, however, rely on *Homo Economicus*: as I have stressed, *Homo Economicus* makes specific assumptions about utility functions. Recall, however, James Buchanan's challenge that I discussed in the Introduction: if economics can explain so much of what people do in the market, why should it be barred from explaining how they act in the political sphere? It is time, finally, to take up this idea. In this chapter I examine "public choice theory" which models politics on a much more robustly economic conception of rationality. The chapter begins with an examination of Anthony Downs's classic "economic model" of democracy, in which he depicts politicians as entrepreneurs and voters as consumers. We then consider a basic problem for any economic conception of politics: it is not clear how the act of casting a vote could be rational for *Homo Economicus*. But, we shall ask, is this a problem for the economic model, or is it a problem for democracy? I then consider some of Buchanan's own classic work on the inefficiencies of majoritarian decision making, and how we might formulate rules that will induce *Homo Economicus* to act in a way that produces efficient public policies.

6.1 DOWNS'S ECONOMIC THEORY OF DEMOCRACY

Political Rationality

Although political science has subsequently developed much more sophisticated "spatial" theories of voting,[1] Anthony Downs's classic *An Economic Theory of Democracy* is still the best introduction to the economic approach to politics.[2] Downs offers an economic theory of democracy in the sense that voters are modeled as self-interested consumers of policies and politicians as self-interested producers, seeking to maximize their market share. As with the general model of *Homo Economicus* (Section 1.3), Downs goes beyond the basic model of rational instrumental behavior to further specify the nature of voters' and politicians' aims.

Downs's conception of rationality has three main elements. *First*, he assumes the basic preference satisfaction model of rational action and that cardinal utility functions can, at least ideally, be developed (see Chapter 2 in this book). *Second*, Downs explicitly draws on instrumental rationality (see Chapter 1): as he conceives of it, political rationality is inherently about producing favored outcomes. Although, as we shall see in Section 6.2, a person might vote just because she has a brute preference for voting, Downs is *not* concerned with voting as an act of pure consumption (see Section 1.1). For him political activity is always a way to bring about results that one wants. *Lastly*, Downs adopts the view that *Homo Economicus* is self-interested (Section 1.3). According to what Downs calls the "self-interest maxim" a rational political act always aims at "selfish ends."[3] Downs is aware that this is false; not everyone in politics is selfish—there are benevolent voters and politicians. But like those who endorse the self-interest axiom for *Homo Economicus* in general, Downs holds that this simplifying assumption allows more determinate applications of the model.

It is not clear, though, that Downs really needs to make any *general* selfishness assumption. In many ways it is unfortunate that he did so, since many reject the economic theory of democracy because they reject the idea that people are generally selfish in politics. It seems that Downs only needs two, more modest assumptions: a specific assumption about the motivation of politicians, and a very general assumption about the nature of voters.

Downs's assumption about *politicians* is indeed a sort of selfishness assumption: their aim is to seek to win elections and so reap the rewards of office. Their goals are power, income, glory, and the thrill of political office. As Downs says: "Parties formulate policies in order to win elections, rather than win elections in order to promote policies."[4] So all that politicians care about is staying in office; they will formulate whatever policies are necessary to achieve this goal. Roughly, just as the firm seeks to maximize profits, political parties seek to maximize their share of the vote. The second group that Downs considers is the *voters*. Voters are also, he says, selfish, but it is not clear that he actually relies on such a strong assumption. Rather, the Downsian model supposes simply that voters are utility maximizers—hardly anything needs to be supposed about the content of their preferences. Alf's aims may center on world peace, Betty's on high income, and Charlie's on good sanitation: each can act to satisfy his or her own preferences, but it doesn't follow that these are selfish. All that Downs actually supposes is that these voters have non-tuistic preferences. Recall that if one is non-tuistic one acts to satisfy one's own set of preferences rather than the preferences of others (Section 1.3). Alf may have the preferences of a saint, and still be non-tuistic; all that non-tuism requires is that our saint, Alf, acts to further his own preferences, and not the preferences of Betty. If non-tuism holds, Alf's actions can always be explained as an attempt to maximize his own preferences, which are independent of Betty's. If so, then we would never explain why Alf did something by saying that doing this satisfies Betty's preferences; Alf's actions always are based on what Alf prefers, though he may prefer to be a generous saint. Non-tuism in no way whatsoever assumes selfishness; all it assumes is that each satisfies her own preferences, however selfish or selfless these preferences may be. We can follow Downs in putting this in cardinal rather than ordinal terms: each voter has a cardinal utility function that sums up the utility he receives from each of the policy options offered. And, once again, it must be stressed that we are not supposing that maximizing utility is anyone's aim: it is a measure of how well their aims and other normative criteria are satisfied.

Uncertainty and Ideology

If we suppose voters have full information and can compute the benefits and costs of policies, they would simply tally up the total utility they would receive from Party A's package of policies, compare it to the utility they would receive from Party B's package, and vote for the political party that gives them higher utility. There are some complications even here—voters have to make expected utility calculations about likely policies each political party will pursue in the *future* (after the election) using the best information available, i.e., what sort of policies the current government has offered in the *past* (during its last term in office). But the real interest in Downs's theory is when he brings costs and ignorance into the analysis of democratic politics. Voters may be uncertain about what party gives them the most utility because:

1. They may be aware that their total utilities have altered but may be uncertain about what caused them to alter: was it government policy or private parties that caused a change in utility?
2. Voters may not know how some proposed government policy will affect their utility.
3. Voters may be unaware that the government has adopted some policies that affect their utility.
4. Voters may not know the extent to which their own views affect public policy.
5. Voters may be uncertain as to how other citizens plan to vote.[5]

As Downs sums it up: "In short, voters are not always aware of what the government is or could be doing, and often they do not know the relationship between government actions and their own utility. . . . "[6] Our model of democratic politics is transformed when uncertainty enters the scene. Perhaps the most important new element is the rise of *ideologies*.

In a world of complete certainty—where the voters knew just what they wanted and whether the present party has given it to them—there would be little room for ideologies. To be sure, political parties would still compete, but this competition would be only on the level of packages of policies. Each political party would simply frame its overall package of policies to attract the most votes. But ideology enters into the picture once we include voters' uncertainty. "Voters do not know in great detail what the decisions of government are, and they cannot find out except at significant cost. Even if they did know, they could not always predict where a given decision would lead."[7] Under such conditions voters will find political ideologies a useful guide. Party ideologies free the voter from having to evaluate the detailed policy packages: a party's ideology gives the voter useful evidence of the general way in which the party's political aims relate to his general political preferences. They are short-cuts that save voters time and energy; by identifying a certain party as having the ideology closest to yours, you can end your investigations and vote for it.

The Simple Spatial Model

Ideologies are short-cuts for voters. Of course, they are also ways for political parties to try to win over voters; parties wish to depict their ideologies in a way that will attract the maximum number of voters. Remember that in Downs's model politicians only wish to maximize their share of votes so they can attain or retain office. Offering a party ideology, then, is simply a way to attract voters: they will shift their ideology in order to maximize their share of the vote. If the politicians want to attract enough voters so that they can win, how should they pitch their ideology?

To answer this question, let us suppose that political preferences are all single-peaked on a left-right dimension (Section 5.3). Consider Figure 6-1.

Suppose there is one citizen at each point along a political spectrum from 1 to 100. There are two parties, A and B. Initially, Party A adopts an ideology that conforms to position 25, whereas B adopts an ideology that can be placed at 75. What will happen? The hypothesis of Harold Hotelling, an economist who first explored spatial theory in economics in the 1920s, was that parties A and B would converge at the center.[8] Why? Because Party A knows that none of its extreme voters (those, say, in the 0–10 range) will vote for B; as long as it is to the left of Party B, it will get those votes. And Party B knows that as long as it remains to the right of Party A, it will keep its extreme voters. The battle is over the voters between 25 and 75. So, each party will move toward the middle ground, trying to pick up votes in the middle while ensuring it will keep its extreme voters. To see this better, assume that Party A moves to the 45 position, while Party B moves to 50. Party A would be assured of support from all the voters in positions 0–45, while B would get voters 50–100; those between 45 and 50 would, given the assumption of single-peaked preferences, vote for the party that is nearer to their preferred position; so (roughly) A and B will split these voters equally (46 and 47 will vote for A, 48 and 49 will vote for B). So B wins with over 50% of the vote. Party A must also move toward the center, getting as close as possible to B without, of course, "jumping" over it and becoming the right-wing party. Hence, it was suggested by Hotelling's analysis that parties' ideologies would converge at the middle in their quest for votes.

This reasoning underlies the *median theorem* in political science, according to which if *I* is a single-dimensional issue, and all voters

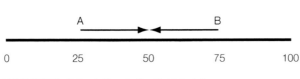

F I G U R E 6-1 A Simple Spatial Model

have single-peaked preferences defined over issue *I*, then the *m* voter, the median voter, cannot be outvoted under majority rule. To see this consider any voter *z* who is not *m*, and suppose first that *z* is to the left of *m*. By definition, all voters to the right of *m* prefer *m* to *z* (*m is nearer their ideal points*), and the number of voters to the right of *m* (including *m*) is at least N/2; so *m* could not lose to *z*. Now suppose instead that *z* is a point to the right of *m*. By definition, all voters to the left of *m* prefer *m* to *z*, and the number of voters to the left of *m* (including *m*) is at least N/2; so *m* could not lose to *z*. Thus under majority rule the median voter's position cannot lose to ideal points either to the right or left of it. Thus the median voter cannot lose under majority rule.

Complicating the Spatial Model

The simple spatial model is about convergence of two political parties in the middle of the ideological spectrum. The median voter theorem supports this, showing that the party that captures the median voter cannot lose. However, the *median voter* only occupies the *median ideological position* under special circumstances, such as when voters are equally distributed along the ideological dimension. We also have been assuming that everyone votes (the median voter theorem is, of course, explicitly about *voters*). As another economist, Arthur Smithies, showed, the spatial model becomes more complicated if we allow that the extreme "voters" might become disenchanted with this movement toward the center and so abstain.[9] Although the extreme followers of A will never vote for B, they may decide to not to vote at all; they may no longer see the choice between A and B as one that makes any difference. Now, if every movement toward the center (which, we have seen, gains new centrist voters) causes an equal loss of voters at the extremes, the convergence toward the center of the *ideological spectrum* will stop. But, as Downs shows, even with abstentions, the movement toward the center of the ideological

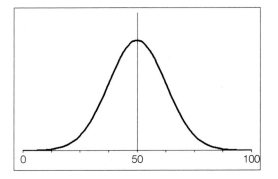

0   50   100

F I G U R E 6-2   Voters Distributed Normally on a Single Dimension

spectrum will continue if the voters are distributed along the line of Figure 6-2.

If political views approach a normal distribution, there will be many more people in the center than at the extremes. If political opinions are distributed in this way, political parties will converge toward the center once again. The pickings in the center are so good that even if you lose extremists, you stand to pick up a lot more voters by occupying the middle ground. So, in Figure 6-2 under a two-party system, the political parties will converge and present very nearly identical ideologies. Both ideologies will stress the satisfaction of the broad middle ground, although they will be different in that they will make some appeals to different extremes. Consequently, if the political opinions of voters are distributed in the way indicated by Figure 6-2, the party platforms will be almost identical. Hence the complaint in two-party systems that the voters have no real choice, since the parties are offering essentially the same policies. But it is not inevitable that in a two-party system the ideologies will converge; as we have just seen, it all depends on the distribution of voters. Figure 6-3 presents a different distribution, one that, Downs conjectures, encourages the growth of multi-party systems rather than two-party systems.

In Figure 6-3 there is no strong pull to occupy the center because movement toward the center is likely to lose as many votes as it gains; in this case it makes sense for each party to occupy a clear position on the ideological spectrum and not converge with its opponents. In Figure 6-3 parties A, B, and C occupy a position on the spectrum: A

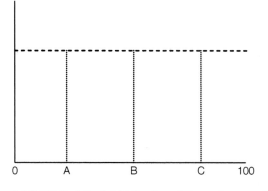

FIGURE 6-3 A Distribution of Voters Encouraging a Multi-Party System

caters to those voters on the left, B to voters in the middle, and C to voters on the right. Now assume that B tries to move toward C; whatever it takes away from C, it will lose to A.

6.2 IS VOTING RATIONAL?

Political Rationality

Recall Downs's notion of political rationality: people vote as a way to secure their favored outcomes. If this is so, an act of voting is rational only if the benefits exceed the costs (Section 3.1); otherwise it is a waste of effort.

Now if it costs Alf nothing at all to vote, and if all Alf cares about is whether his own goals are advanced, then Alf will vote for the party that he expects to better advance his goals; if he expects precisely the same utility from both parties, Alf will abstain. But time is scarce, and so it costs people to vote. At first sight these costs may appear so small that they could not possibly make a difference; how much cost is involved in missing fifteen minutes of TV, getting into the car, and going out to vote? Although these costs are very low, so is the expected return from voting. Some are surprised at this. A committed Democrat or Republican will say that it matters very much to her who wins: a great deal is at stake, so the expected returns must be high. Not so. Your vote only makes a difference if it is the decisive vote. Say that it matters tremendously to you that the Democrats win the election, and they do, by a mere 250,000 votes. Now what did your vote gain you? Nothing: whether or not you voted, the result would have been the same. You would have received the same payoff (Democrats win) even if you did not vote, so your vote could not have made a difference. And if it made no difference you paid those small costs for nothing at all. And no matter how small, it is not rational to pay something for nothing.

The expected utility from voting [$E\mu(V)$], then, can be understood as the probability (p) that your vote will be decisive in electing your favored party, Party A (call casting the decisive vote for A, "D_A") times the utility that you will gain from Party A winning over what you would have had if the other Party B had won (call this "μW_{A-B}"): that is, the *difference* in utility between your favored party winning and the other party winning. It is important that you cannot simply calculate on the basis of how much utility you would receive if your favored party wins, since you would get much of that utility even if the other party was victorious: at stake in the election is *only the difference* in the utility you receive if your favored party wins. So, assuming a purely instrumental account of political rationality, we get equation 1:

eq 1: $E\mu(V) = p(D_A) \times (\mu W_{A-B})$

If $E\mu(V)$ is less than the costs of voting (C), voting is irrational on this account. Voting then is instrumentally irrational if $E\mu(V) < C$.

The probability that your vote will be decisive [$p(D_A)$] depends on two factors: (1) the number of other people voting and (2) the anticipated closeness of the election. Table 6-1 is drawn from the work of Geoffrey Brennan and Loren Lomasky.[10] Suppose that we say it costs $1 to vote (that includes all the time you give up, gas, etc.). Suppose that you are planning on voting for candidate A: how much utility would you have to receive from candidate A winning (rather than B winning) to make the expected utility of voting exceed the cost $1? Assume we can give a monetary measurement of μW_{A-B}— the utility you would gain by A winning. Table 6-1 shows what this value must be if the expected benefits are to exceed the $1 cost.

To calculate the probability that you will be decisive you must know the expected number of voters and the anticipated size of the majority. Brennan and Lomasky's important work shows how these two variables—the expected number of voters and size of the antici- pated majority—interact to show that the expected payoff "ranges between vanishingly small and infinitesimal."[11] Because expected benefits are so low it is almost always irrational to vote as a way of securing one's favored outcome.

T A B L E 6-1 **Expected Gains from Your Party Winning That Makes It Rational to Cast a Vote Costing $1**

Size of electorate	p that a random voter will vote for candidate A* is .5	p that a random voter will vote for A is .5001	p that a random voter will vote for A is .501	p that a random voter will vote for A is .51
2001	$56	$56	$56	$56
20,001	$177	$177	$179	$481
200,001	$560	$566	$619	12.3×10^6
10 million	$4,000	$6,533	$60,000	$\rightarrow \infty\$$
100 million	$12,500	1.9×10^6	6×10^{25}	$\rightarrow \infty\$$

*That is, the election is an absolute dead-heat.

Source: Adapted from Geoffrey Brennan and Loren Lomasky, *Democracy and Decision* (Cambridge: Cambridge University Press, 1993), p. 66.

Once we discount the possibility that you will be the decisive voter, the question of whether to vote is simply a multi-person Prisoner's Dilemma as in Figure 6-4 (in ordinal utility, 4 = best).

As in all Prisoner's Dilemmas, "defect" is the dominant strategy: no matter what others do, Alf should not vote. And of course each voter occupies the role of Alf, playing this Prisoner's Dilemma against everyone else. Thus it seems that if all voters are rational, no one will vote. Few find this an inviting result. Can the rationality of voting be "saved"? Let us briefly consider several suggestions.

Nonelectoral Utility

Downs worried about the apparent irrationality of *Homo Economicus* voting—it certainly seems to undermine a theory of democratic politics based on rational *Homo Economicus*! Downs proposed adding another value to voting—the advantage that accrues to people living in a democracy: it is a system of government that ensures that the policies of government respond to the utilities of the citizens. In the previous chapter we explored social welfare functions (SWF) and collective choice rules (CCR) that take the set of individual preferences and yield a social decision. We all think that making decisions on the basis of a CCR or SWF that represents the preferences of the citizens is better

ALL OTHERS

		Enough others vote for Party A, so that it wins	Not enough vote for party A, so that it loses
ALF	Votes	Alf gains the utility from Party A winning, but has to pay part of the cost for it (3)	Alf pays the cost of voting, and does not gain utility from the election result (1)
	Doesn't vote	Alf gains the utility from Party A winning, and paid nothing (4)	Alf doesn't get utility from the electoral result, but at least he doesn't pay anything (2)

FIGURE 6-4 The Decision to Vote as a Multi-Person Prisoner's Dilemma

than having a dictator: one of the reasons that Arrow's theorem is so worrisome is that only a dictator can formulate a SWF (which requires a transitive ordering) that always satisfies unrestricted domain, the Pareto principle and the independence condition. For all of that, few readers of Arrow become fans of dictatorship. As Downs recognized, we all get some utility from living in a democracy where the social choice reflects a wide range of individual preferences. So we don't want a dictatorship—the result of everyone defecting (no one voting). We don't want the democratic CCR to collapse. But if no one votes, it will collapse.

Downs thus argues that there can be some utility gained by the mere act of voting regardless of the outcome: it can help ensure that the democratic CCR carries on, and that is to one's advantage. There is, he would like to say, utility simply from casting a vote—it doesn't matter for whom: it is the utility one gains by supporting democratic institutions. Writes Downs:

One thing that all citizens in our model have in common is the desire to see democracy work. Yet if voting costs exist, pursuit of short-run rationality can conceivably cause democracy to break down. However improbable this outcome may seem, it is so disastrous that every citizen is willing to bear at least some cost in order to insure himself against it. The more probable it appears, the more cost he is willing to bear.[12]

Since voting is one form of insurance against this catastrophe, every rational citizen receives some return from voting per se [call this the utility from casting a ballot, $\mu(B)$]. So Downs proposes what amounts to equation 2:

$$\text{eq 2: } E\mu(V) = [p(D_A) \times (\mu W_{A\text{-}B})] + \mu(B)$$

The expected value of one's vote is the probability that one will be decisive times the utility at stake in the election, plus the utility of casting a ballot to help keep democracy alive. On this view, the total utility that a person expects from voting is a function of four factors:

1. how much he values living in a democracy
2. how much he cares which party wins
3. how close he thinks the election will be
4. how many other citizens he thinks will vote

The problem with Downs's proposal is his claim that this utility attaches *to the mere act of casting a ballot*. Rather, it seems a *consequence* that one is seeking to bring about: a functioning democracy. Downs is aware that a person can get the benefit of living in a democracy without voting. As he says: "[The voter] will actually get his reward even if he does not vote as long as a sufficient number of other citizens do."[13] Living in a democracy thus is a public good (Section 3.2). If the democracy survives the election—that is, if some people vote—then not only the voters, but the nonvoters as well, get the benefits of living in a democracy. Any rational agent would prefer to be a free-rider than a contributor.

Two possibilities must to be distinguished: (1) saving democracy requires many people to participate in an election; and (2) democracy would be saved even if only one person voted. If (1) is the case we have the same problem all over again about decisiveness; the odds that your vote will be the one necessary to save democracy are almost zero. What if (2) is the case—democracy will be preserved if even a single person votes? Then we are in a public good game of Chicken: someone should vote, but not everyone (Section 4.3). Of course it is unlikely in the extreme that anything I alone could do would affect whether democracy is saved or not saved, healthy or not healthy, etc. The most plausible account is that saving democracy is just another multi-person Prisoner's Dilemma as in Figure 6-5 (in ordinal utility, 4 = best). The same reasoning that leads people not to vote to secure

ALL OTHERS

		Enough others vote so that democracy is saved	Not enough vote to save democracy
ALF	Votes	Alf gains the utility from living in a democracy, but has to pay part of the cost for it (3)	Alf pays the cost of voting, and does not get the utility of living in a democracy (1)
	Doesn't vote	Alf gains the utility of living in a democracy, and paid nothing (4)	Alf doesn't get utility from living in a democracy, but at least he doesn't pay anything (2)

F I G U R E 6-5 The Decision to Vote Is Still a Multi-Person Prisoner's Dilemma

the victory of their party leads them not to vote to secure the continuation of democracy.

If our concern really is saving democracy, letting M be the utility of living in a democracy, it looks like what Downs is really advocating is what is shown in equation 3:

$$\text{eq 3: } E\mu(V) = [p(D_A) \times (\mu W_{A-B})] + [p(D_M) \times (\mu M)]$$

That is, the total expected utility of your vote is the utility you gain by your party winning, times the probability that your vote is decisive in causing its victory, plus the utility you gain by living in a democracy, times the probability that your vote will be decisive in securing a democracy. If democracy is not a threshold public good but a constant returns one (Section 3.2), things are more complicated; regardless, it seems quite clear that you simply are not in a position to do anything significant.

Operating within a pure Downsian theory of political rationality as purely instrumental, there is one easy way around these problems: follow Australia and other countries by attaching a small monetary penalty to not voting. The problem that we have been exploring is generated by the small costs of voting being outweighed by the tiny expected benefits. But if there are costs to *not* voting, say a $50 fine,— then clearly it will be rational for almost everyone to vote. Note, though, this would not make it rational for them to become informed voters, who spend time understanding the issues and candidates. Given that their aim is to simply avoid the monetary fine for not voting, the rational thing to do is to show up at the polls and cast a blank ballot (thus saving the time it takes to check the various boxes!).

Noninstrumental Rationality: The Intrinsic Utility of the Act of Voting

At this point in the book it should be clear that utility theory and instrumental rationality are quite distinct conceptions of rational action. Recall our analysis of Nozick's view of the Prisoner's Dilemma in Section 4.2: people who otherwise would be in a Prisoner's Dilemma can find themselves in a sort of assurance game if they place utility not simply on the outcomes but on their actions within the game. Placing value on the actions one takes is to reject pure instrumental rationality: our actions are not always simply ways to produce results. The apparent irrationality of voting depends on a purely instrumental conception of rationality. If the act of voting itself is valued—if it is itself one of the elements in our utility function—then voting may well be rational. So equation 2 is just about right after all, though not for the reasons that Downs advanced about saving democracy, but because we can put value simply on the act of voting.

Why might one do so? One reason is Nozick's symbolic utility: one values symbolizing that one is a cooperator (a good citizen) who does one's bit. Or, more generally, a person might simply value being a cooperator—the sort of person who pulls her weight in cooperative endeavors. Some put this concern in terms of a person's integrity: she lives up to her own view of what she considers is the proper thing to do. Any utility that a person attaches to engaging in the cooperative act, doing the right thing, doing her bit, and so on, is apt to be sufficient to make voting rational. Again, remember that the costs are small, so it does not take a great deal of positive utility to outweigh them.

These proposals certainly show that rational utility maximizers can vote—but do they show that *Homo Economicus* would vote? Brennan and Lomasky think that voting is *expressive* behavior, like that of a fan at a ball game: "The fan's actions are purely expressive ... *Revealing a preference is a direct consumption activity, yielding benefits to the individuals in and of itself.*"[14] Expressive actions are genuinely noninstrumental. Given that the probability of decisiveness is so low, Brennan and Lomasky argue that one votes knowing that how one casts one's ballot is almost sure to make no difference—one votes from behind a "veil of insignificance." Thus each may vote, say, to express his anger rather than with the aim of selecting the best candidate: I can afford to simply let off steam when I vote if I know it does not really make a difference how I vote. If we all express our anger, everyone might vote in a way that produces a result that no one wants.

We see here that insisting on the distinction between instrumental and consumption rationality (Section 1.2) can help us understand that *Homo Economicus* has more explanatory power than we might have first thought. If voting is like eating a pizza (something that is itself a basic aim), *Homo Economicus* certainly can do it. Still, it seems a bit of a stretch to see voting as consumption behavior. Over a wide range, *Homo Economicus* prefers more rather than less of a consumption good (Section 1.1). Although given marginal decreasing utility the demand for a good decreases the more one has of it, voting seems to have a very odd demand curve. In parliamentary systems where governments decide when to call an election, for example, governments are often "punished" for calling an early election, even just a year early. Now on Brennan and Lomasky's view this is puzzling. As they see it, those who vote are those who particularly enjoy voting—they are already a self-selecting set of citizens who have a pretty high demand for this sort of thing. It would seem that, if anything, they should reward governments for frequent elections. The costs of elections are spread out over the whole population, and so the voters' consumption is being subsidized. This must be one of the few cases where voters turn on a government for providing a subsidized good! Certainly pizza eaters would not be so hard on governments subsidizing their favored good.

6.3 MAJORITARIAN INEFFICIENCIES

Market exchange, at least under some conditions, is mutually beneficial: both parties gain. Many find this hard to believe; we often think of the world in terms of zero-sum games (Section 4.1): every winning must come out of the pocket of someone. The importance of the Edgeworth Box (Figure 3-2) is in clearly showing how two parties can both benefit from exchanging even a fixed stock of goods. If the total stock of goods is increasing it is obvious how all can benefit, but even under static conditions exchange can make each person better off. Market efficiency is an attractive idea: rational economic agents, caring only about their own aims, can produce conditions that are an improvement from everyone's point of view. However, in the political sphere, *Homo Economicus* can often gain by taking away from others. It is in the sphere of politics that, on the public choice view, we typically witness real zero-sum and, even worse, negative-sum games. In politics groups seek "rents": group-specific payoffs that do not contribute to efficiency.[15] Often these payoffs are extracted from others. This is not because people in politics are nastier than they are in the market, but because the mechanism of politics provides incentives for *Homo Economicus* to gain by exploiting others rather than by benefiting them.

The most obvious zero-sum game is, of course, when the majority uses its power to transfer resources to itself from the minority. Or, what comes to essentially the same thing, when the majority passes legislation that benefits only it (say, funding for public universities), but makes everyone pay (including those who already pay tuition for private universities). Wealth is being transferred from the minority to the majority to fund the majority's consumption of public university education. More interesting and less obvious is, as James M. Buchanan and Gordon Tullock showed in their path-breaking *Calculus of Consent*, that majority decisions can make everyone worse off, including the majority itself.[16] To see this, consider a small town of 1,000 voters who meet to democratically decide on expenditures. Say the town is composed of five equal-sized groups (each has 200 of the voters):

(YF) Young Families who want to spend money to improve the primary schools. They would pay $600 each if they had to purchase the improvements themselves.

(OW) Older and Wealthier citizens, who want to improve the local golf course. They too would pay $600 each if they had to purchase the improvements themselves.

(YP) Yuppies, who want to close off the main street and pave it with cobblestones. Again, it is worth $600 to each Yuppy to do this.

(TC) Those with Teenage Children, who support improved facilities at the town recreation center. These improvements are worth $600 to each of this group.

(OR) Outlying Residents who want to have some side roads paved. These improvements are worth $600 to each Outlying Resident.

Suppose the Young Families put forward their proposal. They need the support of two other groups if the proposal is to pass. Say they agree to trade votes (Section 5.5) with OW and YP. The Young Families agree to support the proposals of those other two groups in exchange for their support of school improvements. Now each of the families knows that the school improvements are worth $600 to them, but they also know that they will have to support the OW and YP groups when they propose their own plans; they do not wish their total tax bill for all three projects to exceed $600, since that is what their own project is worth to them. Say, then, that they are willing to bear $200 in tax in support of their own project, $200 to support golf course improvements, and $200 to pay for the Yuppies' paving of the pedestrian mall, for a total of $600. But if everyone in the community is taxed $200 to support school improvements, the community can raise $200 × 1,000, or $200,000 for school improvements. By themselves the 200 in this group were willing to pay $600, for a total of $120,000. So they seem to get an additional $80,000 worth of improvements for free. So they agree. The coalition is formed, and the measure passes.

At the next meeting the Older and Wealthier group (who favor golf courses) put forward their proposal. The Young Families are committed to supporting it, so it already has 400 votes. But they need additional votes. The pro-golf course adults decide to trade votes with the Outlying Residents (good roads are always a good idea). The calculations are precisely the same as with the YF. The pro-golfing adults are willing to bear $200 in tax in support of their own project, $200 in tax to support the school improvement they already have voted for, and the $200 they are expecting to pay for paving roads as part of their vote trading with the Outlying Residents. But if everyone in the community is taxed $200 to support the golf course, the community can raise $200 × 1000, or $200,000 for the improvements. By themselves the 200 in this group were willing to pay $600, or only $120,000. So they seem also to get an additional $80,000 worth of improvements for free. So they too agree.

Now the Yuppies come forward. They want their paved pedestrian mall. They have the promise of the Young Families, but they need another group's support, so they enlist those with Teenage Children. Another deal is done. Again if everyone is taxed $200, the Yuppies can get $200,000 for their project, even though they would only pay $120,000 if they privately purchased it.

T A B L E 6-2 Vote Trading Leading to Overexpenditure on Politically Secured Goods

	Coalition Partners	Tax
Young Families (YF)	OW, YP	$200
Older and Wealthier (OW)	YF, OR	$200
Yuppies (YP)	YF, TC	$200
Families with Teenage Children (TC)	YP, OR	$200
Outlying Residents (OR)	OW, TC	$200
Total Tax		$1,000

Now the families with Teenage Children (TC) come forward. They have the promise of the Yuppies but they need another group's support, so they enlist the Outlying Residents. Another deal is done. Again if everyone is taxed $200, the TC can get $200,000 for their project, even though they would only pay $120,000.

Finally the Outlying Residents come forward. They already have the promises of the golf course group (OW) and the teenage parents group (TC), so their measure also passes.

Table 6-2 sums up the bargains and total tax rates. Notice that each ends up paying $1,000 even though, if each had purchased the good themselves, they only would have spent $600. Because some of the cost could be pushed onto the dissenting minority, each group bought more improvements than they thought worthwhile, ending up with a too-expensive package of improvements. Insofar as each person had more preferred ways to spend the additional $400, each is worse off under this form of collective provision.

The problem is shifting coalitions: as coalitions are reformed, adding new members, vote trading deals proliferate and ever more projects, with ever more taxation, get approved. Buchanan and Brennan showed that this problem, which concerns coalitions existing at roughly the same time, also arises with what we might call intertemporal coalitions.[17] Suppose that I am worried about the federal budget deficit and would like to vote for strong budgetary constraints. Now this is essentially a decision on my part to forgo present consumption and invest in the future—i.e., pay off debt so that future governments can tax less and leave more funds available for investment. But for the benefits of this policy to exceed the opportunity costs (in terms of forgone consumption), it requires constraint over a relatively long period of time. If the budget is constrained only this year, there will be no significant overall decrease in the deficit, and I will have lost an opportunity to consume. Now say that in election e_1 there is a coalition in favor of severe restraint that needs an additional member. Should I join? Well, only if I can be confident that the coalition will stay together at elections e_2 and e_3. But it is very hard to be confident. Some members of the coalition at e_1 may be simply rabid Party A members who will constrain the current Party B government; but should Party A win government, they will then wish to spend a great deal on Party A policies. Since coalitions are not permanent and contain members with different ultimate ends, I probably should not expect the coalition to stay together at elections e_2 and e_3. So even though I take a long-term view and prefer savings to present consumption, I have strong grounds to vote for present consumption, since it is doubtful that the coalition will stay together long enough to obtain the savings. Hence majority rule tends to be focused on short-term rather than longer-term policies, and so is biased in favor of present consumption over long-term savings and investment.

6.4 CONSTITUTIONAL POLITICAL ECONOMY

Assuming that Pareto efficiency is still our guide, we need to analyze different ways of making collective decisions in terms of whether they will achieve Pareto-efficient outcomes. Let us begin by assuming "direct democracy"—that each citizen takes part in the collective decision procedure that yields the social decision. I will then briefly consider representative democracy, where citizens choose their representatives, who in turn make the collective decisions.

Knut Wicksell proposed the following method for making collective decisions: in order for the state to supply public good G, there must be unanimous consent to its provision, including the tax that will pay for it.[18] To see how unanimity rules relate to efficiency, think back to Figure 3-3, and the line A-B, the contract curve. Each point on A-B is Pareto-efficient; at each point the indifference curves are tangent—there is no eye, and so there is no way for one party to gain without the other losing. Now between two persons, a unanimity rule and a contract are the same. So suppose that we have a two-member public composed simply of Alf and Betty, and they are considering public good tax proposals for G. Given what we have learned about the contract curve, Alf and Betty will accept such proposals until the line A-B is reached—i.e., until a proposal somewhere on that line is accepted. Until that point is reached Pareto gains can be achieved, so new proposals can be devised that are Pareto improvements. Once a proposal on this "contract curve" is accepted, no further agreements will be accepted by both parties, since the opportunity for Pareto-superior moves has been exhausted. Now if we consider larger groups, the result is still achieved by a unanimity rule: in principle it mimics market transactions and can get us to the Pareto Frontier—the place where no further Pareto improvements are possible.

However, given non-zero transaction costs, and lack of full information about other people's preferences, decision making via unanimity has great costs, and may well not lead to Pareto-optimal results. One of Buchanan and Tullock's important contributions was to analyze the relative costs of different voting rules. We have seen that a unanimity rule can lead to Pareto optimality. Let me stress the importance of this: if one of the reasons why we construct a state is that a market will not achieve Pareto-optimal results given externalities (Section 3.2), a decision rule that leads to Pareto-optimal outcomes is just what we need. But it is not only the market that involves externalities: political decisions do too. Some voters (call them the majority) impose costs on others (call them the minority). The minority may have to pay taxes for goods that they don't want and can't use, as people without children are forced to pay for public education. So one thing we would want a decision-making rule to do is to minimize these externalities of collective decision making, which are depicted by the external cost curve in Figure 6-6. If only one person's vote is required for passage, the external costs—the costs that one group of voters can impose on the rest—are extremely high. If, on the other hand, in an N-person population, all N votes are required, we have the unanimity rule, and so no one should be able to impose uncompensated costs on anyone else. But, of course, as the number of voters required for passage rises, so too do the decision-making costs. Call these the "internal costs" of decision making: the time necessary for passage, bargaining, bluffing, and so on. As the internal cost curve in Figure 6-6 shows, these costs are greatest under unanimity (in which one holdout can veto an agreement) and least where one person is dictator and decides for all. The optimal set of rules would be one that minimizes the combined costs, as depicted in the total cost curve in Figure 6-6.[19]

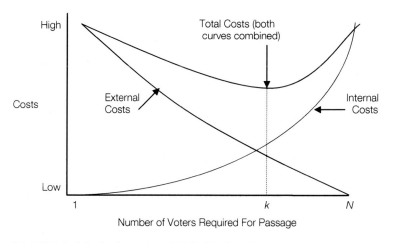

FIGURE 6-6 Buchanan's and Tullock's Cost Curves

According to Figure 6-6 the k rule (requiring less than the entire population) is most efficient. Now, Buchanan and Tullock argue, there is no reason to think that $k = N/2+1$ (i.e., the majority rule). The way the cost curves are drawn, the k rule is between simple majority and unanimity. However, if there is a kink in one of the curves (either the internal or external cost curves) at $N/2+1$, then there may well be a case for majority rule as uniquely optimal. Here is one reason for a kink: for any rule where the required number is less than a majority, there is the possibility that inconsistent collective decisions will be made by the group. If only 20% is required for passage, different fifths might pass laws that contradict each other. So we would expect the internal decision-making costs to be quite high until we get to $N/2+1$. Figure 6-7 depicts Dennis Mueller's revision of Buchan and Tullock's cost curves, a revision that provides a case for majority rule.[20] In Figure 6-7, overall costs are minimized at majority rule.

Bicameralism

Public choice theorists were by no means the first to worry about the imposition of "external costs." The prevention of "factional legislation," in which one group imposes costs on others, is the dominant theme of *The Federalist Papers*, written by Alexander Hamilton, John

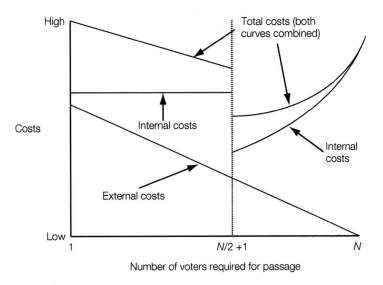

High

Total costs (both curves combined)

Costs

Internal costs

Internal costs

External costs

Low

1   N/2 +1   N

Number of voters required for passage

FIGURE 6-7 Mueller's Revision of Buchanan and Tullock's Cost Curves

Jay, and James Madison in support of the U.S. Constitution. One of the devices employed in the U.S. Constitution to minimize external costs is bicameralism (a two-house legislature). According to *Federalist 62* bicameralism is an "impediment it must prove against improper acts of legislation."

> No law or resolution can now be passed without the concurrence, first, of a majority of the people, and then of the majority of the States. It must be acknowledged that this complicated check on legislation may in some instances be injurious as well as beneficial ... [but] as the facility and excess of lawmaking seem to be the diseases to which our governments are most liable, it is not impossible that this part of the Constitution may be more convenient in practice than it appears to many in contemplation.[21]

Publius (the pen name under which James Madison, Alexander Hamilton, and John Jay published the papers) is clear that requiring two chambers to concur for legislation to be passed makes it more difficult to enact legislation, and in this way at least protects the people from bad legislation:

District							
Rep 1	V1	V2	V3	V4	V5	V6	V7
Rep 2	V1	V2	V3	V4	V5	V6	V7
Rep 3	*V1	*V2	*V3	*V4	V5	V6	V7
Rep 4	*V1	*V2	*V3	*V4	V5	V6	V7
Rep 5	V1	V2	V3	V4	V5	V6	V7
Rep 6	*V1	*V2	*V3	*V4	V5	V6	V7
Rep 7	*V1	*V2	*V3	*V4	V5	V6	V7

FIGURE 6-8 Showing How a Minority Can Control a Unicameral Legislature

a senate, as a second branch of the legislative assembly distinct from and dividing the powers with a first, must be in all cases a salutatory check on the government. It doubles the security to the people by requiring the concurrence of two distinct bodies in schemes of usurpation or perfidy, where the ambition or corruption would otherwise be sufficient.[22]

Buchanan and Tullock provide a public choice defense of bicameralism. A bicameral legislature with each house employing majority rule is equivalent to a unicameral legislature operating under a supermajority rule. Consider a unicameral, or one-house, legislature. Assume that we have 49 voters divided up into seven districts, each of which elects one member to a single-house, seven-seat legislature. We thus have a distribution of voters as in Figure 6-8.[23]

In this case 16 voters can form a winning coalition. Four voters can form a majority in four districts (in this case, the voters with asterisks in districts 3, 4, 6, 7), thus electing four representatives; and four representatives are a majority in our seven-house legislature. So 16 out of 49 voters can form a faction that enacts legislation.

Now suppose that we introduce a second house, as in Figure 6-9.[24] (I have deleted the voters with whom we are not concerned—but they haven't died; they are still there.)

In the two-house legislature in Figure 6-9, our winning coalition stays the same; our original 16 voters can control both houses. So, on the face of it, we haven't provided any barrier to a minority faction controlling the legislature. But things are more complicated than this. In this coalition, each member is hard to replace. For example, in the single-house case in Figure 6-8, even if Alf (voter 3 in the 6th district)

District	Sen 1	Sen 2	Sen 3	Sen 4	Sen 5	Sen 6	Sen 7
Rep 1							
Rep 2							
Rep 3	*V1	*V2	*V3	*V4			
Rep 4	*V1	*V2	*V3	*V4			
Rep 5			?V3 Sue				
Rep 6	*V1	*V2	*V3 Alf	*V4		?V6 Joe	
Rep 7	*V1	*V2	*V3	*V4			

F I G U R E 6-9 The Difficulty of Maintaining Minimum Coalitions in a Bicameral Legislature

were to drop out, voters 5, 6, or 7 could take his place. But in this new coalition no one voter can replace Alf, because he is uniquely placed as being in both the sixth representative district and the third senate district. No other single voter could replace him if he chooses to defect. Indeed, if Alf drops out of the coalition, and the faction wants to stay as small as possible, it will have to construct a very different coalition, for now either the third senate or the sixth representative district will have to be dropped, thus dropping some of the underlined voters along with Alf. There is no hope of capturing both of these districts with a minimum coalition without Alf. This may lead Alf to increase his claims on the coalition: since he is so valuable to the coalition, he may insist that the faction do more for him. The remaining faction members will either have to give in to Alf or try to form a new and very different coalition. This gives an incentive for all the coalition members to bargain for as much as they can possibly get, making the maintenance of the minimum faction of 16 a difficult affair indeed.

There is, though, another option: to replace Alf with two different voters, Sue and Joe. If the coalition takes on Sue and Joe to replace Alf, it can keep all the other underlined coalition members; the faction does not have to start a radical rebuilding. The problem, of course, is that now it is a 17-member coalition rather than a 16-member coalition. In addition, there are now two classes of members of the coalition: those who are necessary to win in both the house and the senate, and those (Sue and Joe) who are only necessary to winning in one or the other. Other members will demand more payoffs than Sue or Joe receive. Suppose the coalition says that, regardless of how important anyone is to winning, everyone will have equal payoffs (in terms of getting the legislation that is most desired). That is, Sue and Joe get as much from the coalition as anyone else. But then some original member, needed to win in both the house and the senate, will say: "Look, to replace me you will have to recruit two new members to the coalition. And these two new members will each demand an equal payoff. So the coalition is better off giving me 1.99 times what Joe gets (because my replacements will each get the payoffs Joe gets, $1 + 1$)."

But if the leaders of the coalition are stuck with demands for extra payoffs from the old coalition members, there will not be a significant difference between keeping one old member or replacing her with two new members. The result, argue Buchanan and Tullock (and I have only sketched their argument here), is that the winning coalition will increase in size. It could go as high as 32 in this case, in which case it would be more than a majority of voters. But it is likely that at least some voters will be required for the coalition in both houses, so the coalition will probably be less than twice that necessary to control a single house.

Bicameralism greatly increases the minimum size that a faction must obtain in order to pass its favored legislation. For example, Buchanan and Tullock calculate that assuming a total population of 39,601 split into 199 districts, 10,000 voters could form a winning coalition in a unicameral legislature. But if there are two houses, each with a 199 seats, and if voters are distributed randomly, it would require 17,500 voters to form a minimum coalition.[25] Interestingly, if a unicameral legislature operated under a rule that legislation required the assent of 7/8 of the representatives, the minimum coalition in this case would be the same—17,500 voters. And if a 3/4 majority were required of each house in a bicameral legislature, the minimum coalition in this case would be 24,000 voters—which is a larger minimum coalition that a unicameral legislature operating under a unanimity rule.

We can see, then, how the public choice analysis of the inefficiencies of majoritarianism leads to a project of constitutional design that seeks to identify rules and procedures that minimize the ability of some voters to extract resources from others and, instead, channel politics to efficient, mutually beneficial policies. Of course this project is "conservative" insofar as it is trying to find rules that prevent coercive redistribution from some to others. Those who believe that distributive justice requires redistribution balk at constitutional devices to push us toward mutual benefit. In politics, they say, it is appropriate to take from the rich to give to the poor. Issues of distributive justice are outside the scope of this book. We need, though, to remember Buchanan's insistence that *Homo Politicus* is simply *Homo Economicus* operating in politics. That is why he is so deeply suspicious of redistributive politics: given the power to redistribute, Buchanan insists that *Homo Economicus* will use it for his own benefit, wasting efforts on zero-sum games when he could be engaging in mutually beneficial exchanges.

SUMMARY

In this chapter I have explored some of the main themes in public choice theory, which might be called "the economic theory of politics." It is not an economic theory of the political in the sense that it maintains that economics drives politics; rather, it claims that the basic assumptions of economics (about *Homo Economicus*) explain political behavior. This chapter has:

- *Explained Anthony Downs's classic version of the economic theory of democracy.* Downs's theory assumes that politicians are entrepreneurs, offering policies that will get them elected, and voters are "consumers" seeking to maximize their utility by voting for the most attractive package. Downs views democracy in spatial terms; voters' views are arranged along a "spatial" dimension such as right/left. In Downs's simple version there is only one dimension; more complex versions consider N-dimensions. Downs holds that given "normal" distributions of voters over the left/right spectrum, a two-party system will emerge, with parties offering almost identical platforms.

- *Analyzed the apparent instrumental irrationality of voting.* Unless there are special penalties for not voting, voting appears to be an instrumental irrational act. We considered attempts to salvage the instrumental rationality of voting by adding other considerations such as "saving democracy": I argued that these do not help. In order for voting to be rational, noninstrumental considerations must be important.

■ *Explored an example of how majority rule leads not only to Pareto-inefficient results, but also to outcomes that make everyone worse off.* The crux of the example was that each person, hoping to get others to subsidize some government-supplied goods that she wants, ends up subsidizing government-supplied goods that others want (and she does not), with the result that her total tax bill exceeds the price she was willing to pay for the goods she does want.

■ *Sketched some considerations for and against the efficiency of supermajoritarian (k) rules.*

■ *Considered how bicameralism is equivalent to supermajoritarian voting rules in a unicameral legislature.*

NOTES

1. For a good overview see James M. Eneow and Melvin J. Hinch, *The Spatial Theory of Voting: An Introduction.*
2. Anthony Downs, *An Economic Theory of Democracy.*
3. Ibid., p. 27.
4. Ibid., p. 28.
5. Ibid., p. 80.
6. Ibid.
7. Ibid., p. 98.
8. See Harold Hotelling, "Stability in Competition."
9. Arthur Smithies, "Optimum Location in Spatial Competition."
10. Geoffrey Brennan and Loren Lomasky, *Democracy and Decision*, p. 56.
11. Ibid., p. 66.
12. Downs, *An Economic Theory of Democracy*, p. 257.
13. Ibid., p. 270.
14. Brennan and Lomasky, *Democracy and Decision*, p. 33. Emphasis added.
15. See Todd Sandler, *Economic Concepts for the Social Sciences*, p. 230.
16. James M. Buchanan and Gordon Tullock, *The Calculus of Consent*, Chapter 10.
17. Geoffrey Brennan and James M. Buchanan, *The Reason of Rules*, pp. 75ff.
18. I am following the discussion in Dennis Mueller, *Public Choice III*, Chapter 4.
19. Adapted from Buchanan and Tullock, *The Calculus of Consent*, Chapter 6.

20. Adapted from Mueller, *Public Choice III*, p. 77.

21. James Madison, Alexander Hamilton, and John Jay, *The Federalist Papers*, *Federalist* 62.

22. Ibid.

23. Adapted from Buchanan and Tullock, *The Calculus of Consent*, p. 237.

24. Adapted from ibid., p. 238.

25. This concerns Buchanan and Tullock's "complete diversity" assumption which I haven't considered. See ibid., p. 242.

Concluding Remarks: Two Economic Approaches

Our survey of the main economic approaches to the study of social and political interaction reveals a "broader" and "narrower" understanding of "the economic approach." The broader understanding dominated Chapters 2, 4, and 5. In utility theory, game theory, and axiomatic social choice theory, the "economic approach" is to understand the individual as having preferences over outcome-options and correlated actions that meet at least (for an ordinal utility function) the conditions of asymmetry of strict preference, symmetry of indifference, reflexivity of preference, transitivity, and completeness. As we saw, a great deal of game theory, and all of axiomatic social choice theory, requires only ordinal utility functions. Other parts of game theory (any games that employ expected utility) require cardinal utility functions. We saw that to some extent the assumptions of utility theory are controversial. Many have questioned the von Neumann–Morgenstern axioms (Section 2.3) that yield cardinal utility, though I have argued that they are more compelling than critics would have us believe. And in any event, the use of cardinal utility does not require these axioms: they are only necessary to derive cardinal from ordinal utility. As I pointed out in Chapter 2, John Pollock has recently argued that, given our cognitive limitations, we store our value information in cardinal form and convert *that* to ordinal information when we need it; on Pollock's view, cardinal is the primary form of utility.

Leaving aside these debates, I have stressed that utility theory is ecumenical in what sort of underlying normative considerations it can model. Selfish goals, unselfish ones, the value of fairness, the importance of following moral principles, the symbolic value of being a cooperative person, caring about doing your bit, caring about what options the other person has taken up—all these can enter into a person's utility function. I have stressed (I hope not *too* often) that many people are suspicious of utility theory because they do not realize this, and assume that only a very restricted set of considerations (e.g., self-interested or instrumentalist ones) can be formally modeled by it. Once we understand just how broad utility theory is, it is clear that it allows a more formal and rigorous understanding of social interactions without biasing the analysis toward normative considerations of a certain sort. Moral and political philosophers and political scientists should not shy away from utility theory, game theory, or social choice theory because they are too "economic."

Who should shy away from them? Well, if one thinks that as a rule people are either irrational or unconcerned with rationality, one will not think utility theory, game theory, and social choice theory are of much use. These theories do not appeal to one who is convinced that people generally: cannot order their options, do not pay attention to such ordering when they act, do not seek to anticipate what others do, do not think that everyone's ordering should be respected in social decision making, or do not care whether social decision making in some way rationally reflects the orderings of citizens. All these beliefs suggest a conviction that people are not sufficiently rational, or they do not sufficiently care about the rationality of their social decisions, to make the idea of rationality the core of understanding social interaction and political processes. As I suggested in the Introduction, at the heart of all "economic" analysis is the conviction that social explanation supposes that the actions of others can be made intelligible qua rational. One can reject that, but few moral and political philosophers do, and neither do most political scientists.

In its narrower sense, the "economic" approach employs *Homo Economicus* as a general model of rational action. We have seen that this narrower approach itself exemplifies a range. The narrow interpretation of *Homo Economicus* (we might think of this as the narrow interpretation of the narrow approach) conceives of *Homo Economicus* as a wealth maximizer (the *ultra* narrow view) or as always selfish (the narrow view). We saw in Chapter 6 that Downs explicitly claims the latter, as does a good bit of public choice theory. When people complain about the narrowness of the economic approach, I think it is this narrow view of *Homo Economicus* that they have in mind. The narrow view is not without merit: often people *are* selfish, and many economists do think that a great deal can be explained by simply assuming that people are self-interested. Still, it is obviously a very specific, and often erroneous, supposition. As James Madison pointed out, it is indeed true if we were all angels we would not need government, but it is also true that if we were all knaves, free government would be impossible.[1]

More broadly (the broad version of the narrow approach), *Homo Economicus* is understood, as in Chapter 2, as characterized by utility functions according to which more is better than less, utility is marginally decreasing, and demand curves slope downward. We might add "non-tuism," but even that might be unduly narrowing. *Homo Economicus* thus understood is an interesting creature, and is probably a good model of all of us a lot of the time. We saw in Chapter 3 how *Homo Economicus* will be driven to efficient exchange, and why public goods will be undersupplied and public bads will be oversupplied. All this sets up many of the parameters of social life, and sets the stage for many of the problems of politics. Any student of social interaction must, I think, have a basic understanding of how this broader *Homo Economicus* acts and the social patterns that result. And that is why so much of the economic approach—even narrowly conceived—is relevant to moral, social, and political philosophy, and to political science.

NOTE

1. James Madison, Alexander Hamilton, and John Jay, *The Federalist Papers*, edited by Clinton Rossiter, *Federalist* 51, 55.

Bibliography

Anand, Paul. *Foundations of Rational Choice Under Risk.* Oxford: Oxford University Press, 1993.

Argyle, Michael. *The Psychology of Interpersonal Behavior,* 3rd edition. Harmondsworth: Penguin, 1978.

Arrow, Kenneth J. "Risk Perception in Psychology and Economics." *Economic Inquiry,* vol. 20 (1982): 1–9.

Aumann, Robert. "Subjectivity and Correlation in Randomized Strategies." *Journal of Mathematical Economics,* vol. 1 (1974): 67–96.

Axelrod, Robert. *The Evolution of Cooperation.* New York: Basic Books, 1974.

Becker, Gary. *The Economic Approach to Human Behavior.* Chicago: University of Chicago Press, 1976.

Benn, S. I. *A Theory of Freedom.* Cambridge: Cambridge University Press, 1988.

Benn, S. I., and G. W. Mortimore. "Technical Models of Rational Choice." In S. I. Benn and G. W. Mortimore, eds., *Rationality and the Social Sciences.* London: Routledge and Kegan Paul, 1976: 157–196.

Bentham, Jeremy. "Introduction to the Principles of Morals and Legislation." In Alan Ryan, ed., *Utilitarianism and Other Essays.* Harmondsworth, UK: Penguin, 1987.

Binmore, Ken. *Natural Justice.* Oxford: Oxford University Press, 2004.

Blackburn, Simon. *Ruling Passions.* Oxford: Clarendon Press, 1998.

Bolton, Gary E. "A Comparative Model of Bargaining: Theory and Evidence." *The American Economic Review,* vol. 81 (1991): 1096–1136.

208

Brams, Steven J. "Game Theory and the Cuban Missile Crisis." *Math Plus*, Issue 13 January 2001 (http://plus.maths.org/issue13/features/brams).

Brennan, Geoffrey, and James M. Buchanan. *The Reason of Rules: Constitutional Political Economy*. Cambridge: Cambridge University Press, 1985.

Brennan, Geoffrey, and Loren Lomasky. *Democracy and Decision: The Pure Theory of Electoral Preference*. Cambridge: Cambridge University Press, 1993.

Broome, John. "Rationality and the Sure-Thing Principle." In Guy Meeks, ed., *Thoughtful Economic Man*. Cambridge: Cambridge University Press, 1991: 74–102.

Bruni, Luigino, and Francesco Guala. "Vilfredo Pareto and the Epistemological Foundations of Choice Theory." *History of Political Economy*, vol. 33 (Spring 2001): 21–49.

Buchanan, Alan. *Ethics, Efficiency, and the Market*. Oxford: Clarendon Press, 1985.

Buchanan, James M., and Gordon Tullock. *The Calculus of Consent*. Ann Arbor: University of Michigan Press, 1965.

Christensen, David. "Review Essay of 'Robert Nozick, *The Nature of Rationality*.'" *Noûs*, vol. 29 (1995): 259–274.

Coase, Ronald. "The Problem of Social Cost." *Journal of Law and Economics*, vol. 3 (1960): 1–44.

Conlisk, John. "Why Bounded Rationality?" *Journal of Economic Literature*, vol. 43 (June 1996): 669–700.

Craven, John. *Social Choice*. Cambridge: Cambridge University Press, 1992.

Davis, Deborah, and William C. Follette. "Rethinking the Probative Value of Evidence: Base Rates, Intuitive Profiling, and the 'Postdiction' of Behavior." *Law and Human Behavior*, vol. 26 (April 2002): 133–158.

Davis, Morton D. *Game Theory*. Menola, NY: Dover, 1997.

Dawes, Robyn M., Alphins J. C. van Kragt, and John M. Orbell. "Cooperation for the Benefit of Us—Not Me, or My Conscience." In Jane J. Mansbridge, ed., *Beyond Self-Interest*. Chicago: University of Chicago Press, 1990: 97–110.

Diamond, Peter A. "Cardinal Welfare, Individualistic Ethics, and Interpersonal Comparisons of Utility: Comment." *Journal of Political Economy*, vol. 75 (1967): 765–766.

Downs, Anthony. *An Economic Theory of Democracy*. New York: Harper and Row, 1956.

Dreier, James. "Decision Theory and Morality." In Alfred R. Mele and Piers Rawling, eds., *The Oxford Handbook of Rationality*. Oxford: Oxford University Press, 2004: 156–181.

Elster, Jon. "The Market and Forum." In James Bohman and William Rehg, eds., *Deliberative Democracy*. Cambridge, MA: MIT Press, 1997: 3–34.

Elster, Jon. "The Nature and Scope of Rational-Choice Explanation." In E. LaPore and B. McLaughlin, eds., *Actions and Events: Perspectives on Donald Davidson*. Oxford: Blackwell, 1985: 60–72.

Eneow, James M., and Melvin J. Hinch. *The Spatial Theory of Voting: An Introduction*. Cambridge: Cambridge University Press, 1984.

Epstein, Richard. *Skepticism and Freedom*. Chicago: University of Chicago Press, 2003.

Freud, Sigmund. "The Disposition to Obsessional Neurosis." In Angela Richards, ed., *On Psychopathology*. Harmondsworth: Penguin, 1979: 129–144.

Freud, Sigmund. "Inhibitions, Symptoms and Anxieties." In Angela Richards, ed., *On Psychopathology*. Harmondsworth: Penguin, 1979: 229–315.

Freud, Sigmund. *Introductory Lectures on Psychoanalysis*, translated by James Strachey. Harmondsworth, UK: Penguin Books, 1973.

Gaertner, Wulf. *A Primer in Social Choice Theory*. Oxford: Oxford University Press, 2006.

Gaus, Gerald F. "Backwards Into the Future: Neo-Republicanism as a Post-Socialist Critique of Market Society." *Social Philosophy & Policy*, vol. 20 (Winter 2003): 59–91.

Gaus, Gerald F. *Contemporary Theories of Liberalism*. London: Sage, 2003.

Gaus, Gerald F. "Reasonable Utility Functions and Playing the Fair Way." *Critical Review of International and Social Philosophy*, vol. 10 (2008), forthcoming.

Gaus, Gerald F. *Social Philosophy*. Armonk, NY: M.E. Sharpe, 1999.

Gauthier, David. *Morals by Agreement*. Oxford: Clarendon Press, 1986.

Goodin, Robert E., and Christian List. "Unique Virtues of Plurality Rules: Generalizing May's Theorem." *American Journal of Political Science*, vol. 50 (2006): 940–949.

Hammond, Peter. "Consequentialist Foundations for Expected Utility." *Theory and Decision*, vol. 5 (1988): 25–78.

Hampshire, Stuart. *Morality and Conflict*. Oxford: Basil Blackwell, 1983.

Hampton, Jean E. *The Authority of Reason*. Cambridge: Cambridge University Press, 1998.

Hampton, Jean. *Hobbes and the Social Contract Tradition*. Cambridge: Cambridge University Press, 1986.

Hardin, Garret. "The Tragedy of the Commons." In Garret Hardin. ed., *Managing the Commons*. New York: W.H. Freeman, 1977.

Hardin, Russell. *Indeterminacy and Society*. Princeton: Princeton University Press, 2003.

Hausman, Daniel M. *The Inexact and Separate Science of Economics*. Cambridge: Cambridge University Press, 1992.

Hausman, Daniel M., and Michael S. Macpherson. *Economic Analysis and Moral Philosophy*. Cambridge: Cambridge University Press, 1996.

Hobbes, Thomas. *Leviathan*, edited by Edwin Curley. Indianapolis: Hackett, 1994.

Hotelling, Harold. "Stability in Competition." *Economic Journal*, 39 (1929): 41–57.

Hume, David. *A Treatise of Human Nature*, edited by L.A. Selby-Bigge. Oxford: Clarendon Press, 1896.

Jeffrey, Richard. *Subjective Probability*. Cambridge: Cambridge University Press, 2004.

Kahneman, Daniel, and Amos Tversky. "Choices, Values and Frames." In Daniel Kahneman and Amos Tversky, eds., *Choices, Values and Frame*. Cambridge: Cambridge University Press, 2000: 1–16.

Kahneman, Daniel, and Amos Tversky. "On the Psychology of Prediction." In Daniel Kahneman, Paul Slovic, and Amos Tversky, eds., *Judgments Under Uncertainty: Heuristics and Biases*. Cambridge: Cambridge University Press, 1983: 48–68.

Kaplow, Louis, and Steven Shavell. *Fairness versus Welfare*. Cambridge, MA: Harvard University Press, 2002.

Knetsch, Jack L. "Endowment Effect and Evidence on Nonreversible Indifference Curves." In Daniel Kahneman and Amos Tversky, eds., *Choices, Values and Frame*. Cambridge: Cambridge University Press, 2000: 172–173.

Kraus, Jody S. *The Limits of Hobbesian Contractarianism*. Cambridge: Cambridge University Press, 1993.

Lewis, David. *Convention*. Cambridge, MA: Harvard University Press, 1969.

Lewis, David. "Prisoner's Dilemma Is a Newcomb Problem." In Richmond Campbell and Lanning Sowden, eds., *Paradoxes of Rationality and Cooperation: Prisoner's Dilemma and Newcomb's Problem*. Vancouver, BC: University of British Columbia Press, 1985: ch. 14.

List, Christian, and Philip Pettit. "Aggregating Sets of Judgments: An Impossibility Result." *Economics and Philosophy*, vol. 18 (2002): 89–110.

Luce, R. Duncan, and Howard Raiffa. *Games and Decisions*. New York: John Wiley & Sons, 1957.

Lyons, David. *The Forms and Limits of Utilitarianism*. Oxford: Oxford University Press, 1966.

Mackie, Gerry. *Democracy Defended*. Cambridge: Cambridge University Press, 2003.

Madison, James, Alexander Hamilton, and John Jay. *The Federalist Papers*, edited by Clinton Rossiter. New York: New American Library, 1961.

Mansfield, Jane J., ed. *Beyond Self-Interest*. Chicago: University of Chicago Press, 1990.

May, K. O. "A Set of Independent, Necessary and Sufficient Conditions for Simple Majority Rule." *Econometrica*, vol. 20 (October, 1952): 680–684.

McClennen, Edward F. *Rationality and Dynamic Choice*. Cambridge: Cambridge University Press, 1990.

McMahon, Christopher. *Collective Rationality and Collective Reasoning*. Cambridge: Cambridge University Press, 2001.

Menger, Carl. *Principles of Economics*, translated by James Dingwall and Bert F. Hoselitz. Grove City, PA: Libertarian Press, 1994.

Mill, John Stuart. "On Liberty." In John Gray, ed., *On Liberty and Other Essays*. New York: Oxford University Press, 1991.

Morrow, James D. *Game Theory for Political Scientists*. Princeton: Princeton University Press, 1994.

Mortimore, G. W. "Rational Action." In S. I. Benn and G. W. Mortimore, eds., *Rationality and the Social Sciences*. London: Routledge and Kegan Paul, 1976: 93–110.

Mueller, Dennis. *Public Choice III*. Cambridge: Cambridge University Press, 2003.

Nisbett, Richard E., and Lee Ross. *Human Inference: Strategies and Shortcomings of Social Judgments*. Englewood Cliffs, NJ: Prentice-Hall, 1980.

Nozick, Robert. *The Nature of Rationality*. Princeton: Princeton University Press, 1993.

Nozick, Robert. "Newcomb's Problem and Two Principles of Choice." In Paul K. Moser, ed., *Rationality in Action*. Cambridge: Cambridge University Press, 1990: 207–234.

Okun, Arthur M. *Equality and Efficiency: The Big Tradeoff*. Washington DC: The Brookings Institution, 1975.

Padover, Saul K., ed. *Thomas Jefferson on Democracy*. New York: Appleton-Century-Crofts, 1939.

Pettit, Philip. "The Prisoner's Dilemma Is an Unexploitable Newcomb Problem." *Synthese*, vol. 76 (July 1988): 123–134.

Pettit, Philip. *A Theory of Freedom*. Blackwell: Polity Press, 2001.

Pinker, Steven. *How the Mind Works*. New York: Norton, 1997.

Plato, "The Republic" in *The Dialogues of Plato*, B. Jowett, trans., 3rd edition. Oxford University Press, 1892: vol. III.

Pollock, John. *Thinking About Acting*. Oxford: Oxford University Press, 2006.

Poundstone, William. *Prisoner's Dilemma*. New York: Anchor Books, 1992.

Rabin, Matthew. "Psychology and Economics." *Journal of Economic Literature*, vol. 36 (March 1998): 11–46.

Rawls, John. *Political Liberalism*. New York: Columbia University Press, 1996.

Rawls, John. *A Theory of Justice*. Cambridge, MA: Harvard University Press, 1971.

Riker, William. *The Art of Political Manipulation*. New Haven: Yale University Press, 1986.

Riker, William. *Liberalism Against Populism*. Prospect Heights, IL: Waveland Press, 1988.

Rosenberg, Alexander. *Philosophy of Social Science*, 2nd edition. Boulder, CO: Westview, 1995.

Rousseau, Jean Jacques. *Discourse on the Origin of Inequality*. In *The Social Contract and Discourses*, translated by G. D. H. Cole. London: J.M. Dent and Sons, 1913.

Samuelson, Paul. "Consumption Theory in Terms of Revealed Preference." *Economica*, vol. 15 (1948): 243–253.

Samuelson, Paul. "A Note of the Pure Theory of Consumer Behavior." *Economica*, vol. 5 (1938): 61–71.

Sandler, Todd. *Economic Concepts for the Social Sciences*. Cambridge: Cambridge University Press, 2001.

Schmidtz, David. *The Limits of Government: An Essay on the Public Goods Argument*. Boulder, CO: Westview Press, 1991.

Schmidtz, David. *Rational Choice and Moral Agency*. Princeton: Princeton University Press, 1995.

Sen, Amartya. "Choice, Orderings and Morality." In Stephen Körner, ed., *On Practical Reason*. New Haven: Yale University Press, 1974: 54–67.

Sen, Amartya. *Collective Choice and Social Welfare*. San Francisco: Holden-Day, 1970.

Sen, Amartya. "The Impossibility of a Paretian Liberal." *The Journal of Political Economy*, vol. 78 (Jan.–Feb. 1970): 152–157.

Sen, Amartya. "Liberty, Unanimity, and Rights." *Economica*, New Series, vol. 43 (Aug. 1976): 217–245.

Sen, Amartya. "Maximization and the Act of Choice." In his *Rationality and Freedom*. Cambridge, MA: Harvard University Press, 2002: 159–205.

Senior, Nassau William. *An Outline of the Science of Political Economy*, 5th edition. Edinburgh: Charles Black, 1864.

Simon, Herbert. "Theories of Decision Making in Economics and Behavioral Science." *American Economic Review*, vol. 49 (1959): 258–283.

Skyrms, Brian. *Evolution of the Social Contract*. Cambridge: Cambridge University Press, 1996.

Skyrms, Brian. *The Stag Hunt and Evolution of Social Structure*. Cambridge: Cambridge University Press, 2005.

Slote, Michael. "Two Views of Satisficing." In Michael Byron, ed., *Satisficing and Maximizing*. Cambridge: Cambridge University Press, 2004: 14–29.

Smith, John Maynard. "The Evolution of Behavior." *Scientific American*, vol. 239 (1978): 176–192.

Smithies, Arthur. "Optimum Location in Spatial Competition." *Journal of Political Economy*, vol. 49 (1941): 423–439.

Sobel, Jorden Howard. "Not Every Prisoner's Dilemma Is a Newcomb Problem." In Richmond Campbell and Lanning Sowden, eds., *Paradoxes of Rationality and Cooperation: Prisoner's Dilemma and Newcomb's Problem*. Vancouver, BC: University of British Columbia Press, 1985: ch. 16.

Stigler, George J. *The Economist as Preacher*. Chicago: University of Chicago Press, 1982.

Sunstein, Cass. *Free Markets and Social Justice*. Oxford: Oxford University Press, 1997.

Tversky, Amos, and Daniel Kahneman. "Belief in the Law of Small Numbers." In Daniel Kahneman, Paul Slovic, and Amos Tversky, eds., *Judgments Under Uncertainty: Heuristics and Biases*. Cambridge: Cambridge University Press, 1983: 23–31.

Tversky, Amos, and Daniel Kahneman. "Rational Choice and the Framing of Decisions." In Daniel Kahneman and Amos Tversky, eds., *Choices, Values and Frame*. Cambridge: Cambridge University Press, 2000: 209–223.

Vanderschraaf, Peter. *Learning and Coordination: Inductive Deliberation, Equilibrium and Convention*. London: Routledge, 2001.

Vanderschraaf, Peter. "War or Peace?: A Dynamical Analysis of Anarchy." *Economics and Philosophy*, vol. 22 (2006): 243–279.

van Praag, Bernard, and Ada Ferrer-I-Carbonell. *Happiness Quantified: A Satisfaction Calculus Approach*. Oxford: Oxford University Press, 2004.

von Mises, Ludwig. *Human Action: A Treatise on Economics*, 3rd edition. Chicago: Contemporary Books, nd 1966.

von Neumann, John, and Oskar Morgenstern. *Theory of Games and Economic Behavior*. Princeton: Princeton University Press, 1944.

Waldron, Jeremy. *Law and Disagreement*. Oxford: Oxford University Press, 1999.

Walzer, Michael. "Political Action: The Problem of Dirty Hands." *Philosophy & Public Affairs*, vol. 2 (1973): 160–180.

Wicksteed, Philip H. *The Common Sense of Political Economy*, 2 vols, edited by Lionel Robbins. London: Routledge & Sons, 1946.

Winfrey, John C. *Social Issues: The Ethics and Economics of Taxes and Public Programs*. Oxford: Oxford University, 1998.

Wolf, Charles Jr. *Markets or Governments: Choosing between Imperfect Alternatives*. Cambridge, MA: MIT Press, 1993.

Index

CPSIA information can be obtained
at www.ICGtesting.com
Printed in the USA
FFOW01n1755060518
46490980-48428FF